Popular Science

Do-it-yourself Supplement

Grolier Book Clubs Inc.
Danbury, Connecticut

COVER PHOTO BY SCOTT LANDIS

Copyright © 1989 by Popular Science Books

Published by:
    Popular Science Books
    Grolier Book Clubs Inc.
    Sherman Turnpike
    Danbury, CT 06816

Special thanks to:
    Porter Cable, Jackson, TN
    Ryobi America Corp., Bensenville, IL
    Shopsmith, Inc., Dayton, OH
    The Family Handyman
    The Woodworker's Journal magazine

Production staff:
    Producer/Executive Editor: Al Gutierrez
    Copy Editor: Dianne Talmage
    Copy Editor: Cheryl Clark
    Technical Consultant: Gary Branson
    Illustrator: Eugene Marino III
    Book Designer: Linda Watts, Bookworks, Inc.

Produced by Jonathan Press

ISSN: 1040–8002
ISBN: 1–55654–057–4

Manufactured in the United States of America

Preface

We are pleased to present this year's selection of woodworking projects and woodworking techniques. There is a project to suit every skill level and taste. Functional, but easy-to-construct projects such as the Microwave Cart, Folding TV Trays and Redwood Potting Bench are just a few examples of projects for the beginner. If you want a challenge and furniture that will grow into an heirloom, build the Contemporary Standing Cabinet or Vienna Regulator Clock. We think you will agree that there is no other book with this quantity and quality of projects.

Our techniques section features tips on selecting the right router bit and learning specialized skills, such as making tambour doors and tripod legs.

To guide you through project construction we have included detailed step-by-step photographs showing the most critical building steps. Detailed illustrations along with a bill of materials list provide you with all the information to replicate each project. Plus, the text is easy to understand and explains each step in detail.

No doubt you'll have difficulty deciding what project to build first. Don't let some woodworking joinery like finger joints (Old-Fashioned Coffee Mill) scare you away. There are different ways to join project parts, and there is a wide range of methods you can use. Of course, the type of joinery you decide upon should be based upon your skills and the tools you have available. Feel free to substitute the author's joinery for joinery methods with which you feel comfortable. When substituting joinery, remember to make appropriate diagram modifications to suit your technique.

We are very thankful to you, our readers, who make this annual supplement such a success. We appreciate your feedback about our projects as well as suggestions on how we can improve. It is our goal to make each supplement in some ways better than the last. Please continue with your input!

It takes many people a great deal of time and effort to produce this supplement. Our thanks to Shopsmith, Inc., which contributed tools for our shop construction and *The Woodworker's Journal* magazine, which contributed twelve of our stories.

We also commend the efforts of many of the finest woodworking contributors in the industry. Woodworkers' names often go unnoticed, but we thank them for the projects that reflect their personalities and interests. Like all professionals, they strive to make each new project worthy of your attention. Keep up the good work!

A special thank you goes to the loving family of Dennis Watson. Dennis, who died of leukemia in 1988, loved woodworking. Even when his time was at hand he was still designing new projects. Eight of his projects are featured here and serve as a testament to this man's talents as a craftsman and designer.

Also behind the scenes are the talented technical staff who helped produce this book. Thanks to artist Gene Marino III and the staff and the associates of Jonathan Press.

Al Gutierrez

Contributors

Graham Blackburn ♦ Graham learned woodworking in London, where his family had been in the trade for several generations. After completing his studies in New York, he moved to Woodstock, where he built his own house and settled down to found his own custom furniture making business. He now divides his time between New York and California and contributes articles to *Fine Woodworking*, *Popular Woodworking* and *Woodwork*. Graham has written almost a dozen books on wood and woodworking.

George Campbell ♦ George has been a professional writer for numerous woodworking and how-to magazines for over a decade. George's philosophy of design stresses functionality. He believes that a design that does its job will naturally be attractive. To a large degree he is influenced by Shaker and Scandinavian designs, which are the epitome of simplicity and beauty. His projects are designed for creation with modern power tools. He has also authored *The Backyard Builder's Book of Outdoor Building Projects* for Rodale Press. George resides in California.

Rosario Capotosto ♦ Ro has been designing, building, photographing and writing instructions for how-to articles for over 30 years. He is one of the most prolific writers in the how-to business. Residing in New York, he has crafted hundreds of projects and taken many thousands of step-by-step photos. Ro's specialty is woodwork, but he also tackles home improvement stories and tool testing. He has written three books and has a fourth in the works. In the past, Ro spent many years as a teacher of commercial photography while doing how-to articles in his spare time. He is now a full-time contributing editor for *Popular Mechanics*.

Doug Geller ♦ Doug has been a professional woodworker since 1972. Early in his career he studied joinery with Charles Caffall of the North Family Joiners, famed for their Shaker furniture. In 1975 he helped found the Woodsmith's Studio, which under his leadership became one of the largest schools for woodworkers in the United States. Since 1979 he has run Petersen/Geller Inc., his own firm, specializing in furniture making and architectural woodworking. He lives with his wife and two children in Hillsdale, New York.

Thomas H. Jones ♦ Tom is a full-time writer specializing in magazine articles and books on home improvement, furniture building and restoration, and the use of woodworking tools. His articles have appeared in *Popular Science*, *Home Mechanix*, *Workbench*, *Popular Mechanics*, *Homeowner* and *The Family Handyman*. Prior to his writing career which began in 1970, he was an aerospace engineer. His first book was an electronic components handbook. His hobbies include photography, building model ships, restoring antique clocks and playing the bagpipe. He lives in Pennsylvania.

Fergus Retrum ♦ With a broad range of interests, Fergus enjoys music, photography, printmaking, writing, drawing, oil and watercolor painting and sculpture, and is fascinated with tools. His editorial illustrations have appeared in *House Beautiful*, *Better Homes and Gardens*, *McCalls*, *Successful Farming*, *Country Gentleman*, *Popular Science* and other magazines and books. Invention and the creative aspects of woodworking are his special interests. Fergus resides in Minnesota. The current target of his wood chisel is a 24 in. family group relief.

David Wakefield ♦ David is a native of Australia and the son of Oliver Wakefield, a famous English comedian. His family traveled extensively, but David eventually came to rest in Athens, Ohio. He operates Howling Wolf Woodworks, manufacturing moving wooden toys. David is the author of *How to Make Animated Toys* by Popular Science Books and *Woodworker's Book of Dinosaurs* by Sterling Publishing.

Dennis Watson ♦ With a constant flow of suggestions and ideas from his wife, Missourian Dennis Watson found he enjoyed being a part-time woodworker and began designing pieces that were not only functional but also artistic. Right up to his death from leukemia in October of 1988, one of his greatest joys was working with his son and daughter on woodworking projects such as bug cages, hand carved dinosaurs, a variety of wood toys and his last project, a gun cabinet for his teenage son. Even though Dennis was a full-time aerospace engineer, he found time to be a member of St. Louis Woodworkers Guild and presented workshops and demonstrations in the St. Louis area. Dennis' work has been featured over the years in *Workbench*, *The Family Handyman*, *American Woodworker* and several woodworking books.

***The Woodworker's Journal* magazine** ♦ When woodworking enthusiast Jim McQuillan founded *The Woodworker's Journal* magazine in 1977, his first issue was mailed to 627 subscribers. Today, over 130,000 subscribers across the United States and in 56 foreign countries look forward to *The Journal* six times a year. Jim started *The Journal* because he saw the need for a magazine exclusively for woodworkers. Still published in New Milford, Connecticut, *The Journal* today includes a variety of special features, articles, shop tips and techniques, in addition to over 50 complete project plans each year. As projects reprinted in this yearbook attest, *The Woodworker's Journal* is noted for plans with clear illustrations, accurate bills of materials and thorough instructions.

Contents

Projects

Techniques

PROJECTS

Designed and built by Thomas H. Jones and courtesy of *The Family Handyman*

Oak Chest of Drawers

Clean lines combined with dramatically accented oak graining give this chest the distinctive character to stand on its own as an attractive piece of furniture, even outside the bedroom.

Building a respectable chest of drawers is no piece of cake. However, we've simplified the procedure by using oak veneer plywood for all the exterior panels and applying ⅛ in. thick strips of oak to the exposed plywood edges. Besides simplicity, plywood has the advantage of stability — there will be little seasonal dimensional change that can cause drawers to stick.

You'll need just one 4 by 8 ft. sheet of ¾ in. oak plywood. Buy A-grade sliced veneer (rather than rotary cut), and select a sheet with an even grain pattern and consistent coloration. Paying an extra $15 or $20 for a first rate sheet of plywood will more than pay off in the appearance of the finished piece.

We used pine to make the six interior drawer frames. While there is more work involved in building this kind of internal framework, the result is a lighter, more professionally built piece of furniture with more precise drawer fit.

The mouldings under the top and above the base are routed from solid oak. However, you might want to buy milled oak moulding to simplify the building process a bit more.

Drawers are made with glued and nailed joints. Sides and back are ½ in. thick pine. The plywood drawer fronts are rabbeted at the ends to receive the sides. For smooth operation, the drawer's weight is supported on low friction plastic guides at both sides and center.

Construction

Begin by cutting the drawer frame parts as shown in the illustration. Note that only the first and second frames from the top have center drawer supports (K). Notch the rails (H), and drill and countersink pilot holes for screws. Assemble frames with glue and use a carpenter's square to make sure they are clamped perfectly square. Then drive in the screws. For all frame and carcass assembly, we used No. 6 drywall screws.

After all frames are glued up, stack them to see that they are all square and the same size. Saw slots for the plastic

	BILL OF MATERIALS — Chest of Drawers		
	Finished Dimensions in Inches		
A	Side	¾ x 15⅞ x 34½ oak plywood	2
B	Top	¾ x 16⅝ x 26¾ oak plywood	1
C	Drawer Front	¾ x 3⅞ x 11½ oak plywood	2
D	Drawer Front	¾ x 4⅞ x 23⅞ oak plywood	1
E	Drawer Front	¾ x 6⅜ x 23⅞ oak plywood	3
F	Base Front	¾ x 3¾ x 27 oak plywood	1
G	Base Side	¾ x 3¾ x 16¾ oak plywood	2
H	Drawer Rail	¾ x 1⅝ x 24½ pine	12
J	Drawer Support	¾ x 1⅝ x 13¼ pine	12
K	Drawer Center Support	¾ x 2¾ x 13¼ pine	2
L	Drawer Stile	¾ x 3 x 4 pine	1
M	Front/Back Filler	¾ x 1¼ x 24 pine	4
N	Side Filler	¾ x 1½ x 13½ pine	4
P	Drawer Side	½ x 3¹³⁄₁₆ x 14¾ pine	4
Q	Drawer Side	½ x 4¹³⁄₁₆ x 14¾ pine	2
R	Drawer Side	½ x 6⁵⁄₁₆ x 14¾ pine	6
S	Drawer Back	½ x 2¹⁵⁄₁₆ x 10⅝ pine	2
T	Drawer Back	½ x 3¹⁵⁄₁₆ x 23 pine	1
U	Drawer Back	½ x 5⁷⁄₁₆ x 23 pine	3
V	Drawer Bottom	¼ x 10⅝ x 14½ plywood	2
W	Drawer Bottom	¼ x 23 x 14½ plywood	4
X	Cabinet Back	¼ x 24¾ x 34½ plywood	1
Y	Base Back	¾ x 3¾ x 26½ pine	1
Z	Base Cleat	¾ x 2 x 15¼ pine	2
AA	Base Cleat	¾ x 1¼ x 21½ pine	2
BB	Corner Brace	¾ x 2½ x 3¼ pine	4

drawer guides on a table saw or radial arm saw. Use a ³⁄₃₂ in. thick blade. Temporarily remove the screws before you saw the slots.

Notch the ends of the center drawer tracks so they will seat ⅝ in. high on the rails. Drill and countersink screw pilot holes in the top two frames for installing the drawer stile (L). Glue and screw the drawer stile to the second frame.

Cut all the oak veneer plywood parts to size. Clamp the carcass sides to the workbench, front edge to front edge, and mark locations for the frame dadoes at the front edges. Accuracy is important here. If the dadoes are not precisely located, spacing between the drawers will be inconsistent. Cut the dadoes with a router. Rabbet the carcass sides to receive the back.

Begin assembling the carcass by gluing the frames to one side. Be careful to keep them aligned with the carcass edges. Use the second side as a jig, placing it on the frames without glue. Square the assembly and clamp with bar clamps. After the first side has dried, glue, square and clamp the second side. Complete the carcass assembly by adding the fillers (M, N) at the top and bottom.

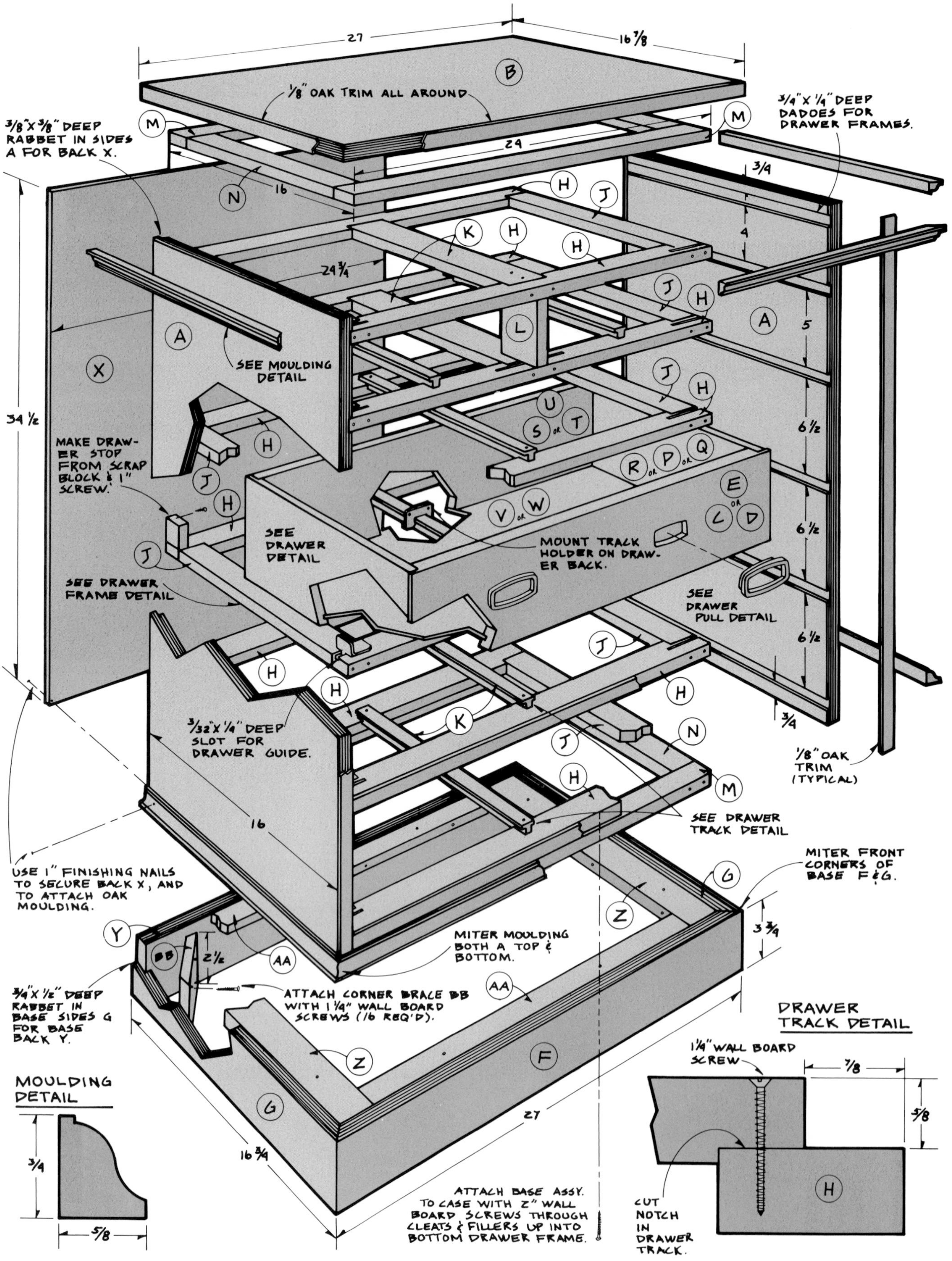
27
16 7/8
B
1/8" OAK TRIM ALL AROUND
3/8" X 3/8" DEEP RABBET IN SIDES A FOR BACK X.
M
24
M
3/4" X 1/4" DEEP DADOES FOR DRAWER FRAMES.
3/4
N
16
H
J
K
H
H
24 3/4
4
J
H
A
L
A
5
X
SEE MOULDING DETAIL
J
H
U
S OR T
34 1/2
6 1/2
MAKE DRAWER STOP FROM SCRAP BLOCK & 1" SCREW.
H
J
H
R OR P OR Q
E OR C D
V OR W
SEE DRAWER DETAIL
MOUNT TRACK HOLDER ON DRAWER BACK.
6 1/2
J
SEE DRAWER FRAME DETAIL
SEE DRAWER PULL DETAIL
6 1/2
J
H
H
H
K
3/32" X 1/4" DEEP SLOT FOR DRAWER GUIDE.
J
N
3/4
1/8" OAK TRIM (TYPICAL)
H
M
16
SEE DRAWER TRACK DETAIL
USE 1" FINISHING NAILS TO SECURE BACK X, AND TO ATTACH OAK MOULDING.
MITER FRONT CORNERS OF BASE F & G.
G
Z
3 3/4
Y
BB
2 1/2
AA
MITER MOULDING BOTH A TOP & BOTTOM.
AA
3/4" X 1/2" DEEP RABBET IN BASE SIDES G FOR BASE BACK Y.
ATTACH CORNER BRACE BB WITH 1 1/4" WALL BOARD SCREWS (16 REQ'D).
Z
F
G
27
16 3/4
ATTACH BASE ASSY. TO CASE WITH 2" WALL BOARD SCREWS THROUGH CLEATS & FILLERS UP INTO BOTTOM DRAWER FRAME.
MOULDING DETAIL
3/4
5/8
DRAWER TRACK DETAIL
1 1/4" WALL BOARD SCREW
7/8
5/8
H
CUT NOTCH IN DRAWER TRACK.

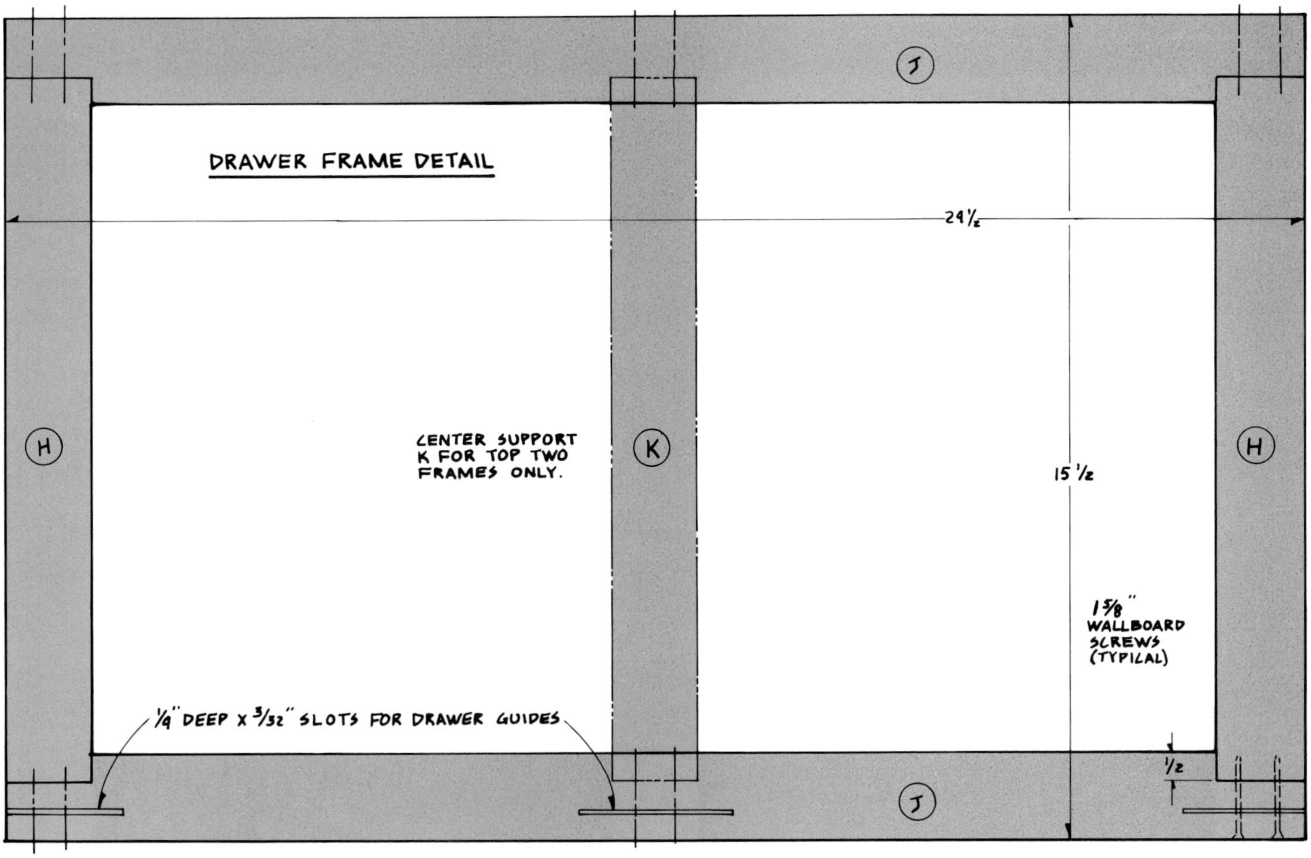
DRAWER FRAME DETAIL
J
H
K
H
J
24 1/2
15 1/2
CENTER SUPPORT
K FOR TOP TWO
FRAMES ONLY.
1 5/8"
WALLBOARD
SCREWS
(TYPICAL)
1/4" DEEP x 3/32" SLOTS FOR DRAWER GUIDES
1/2

DRAWER DETAILS

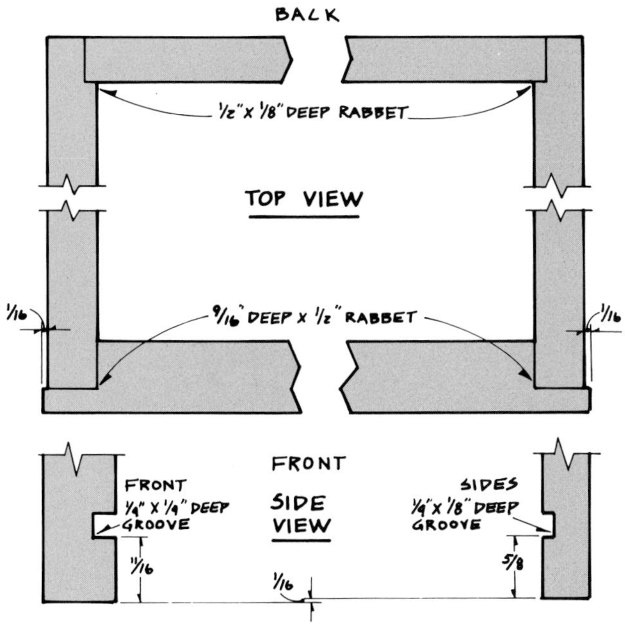
BACK
1/2" x 1/8" DEEP RABBET
TOP VIEW
9/16" DEEP x 1/2" RABBET
1/16
1/16
FRONT
FRONT
1/4" x 1/4" DEEP
GROOVE
SIDE
VIEW
SIDES
1/4" x 1/8" DEEP
GROOVE
11/16
5/8
1/16

DRAWER PULL DETAIL

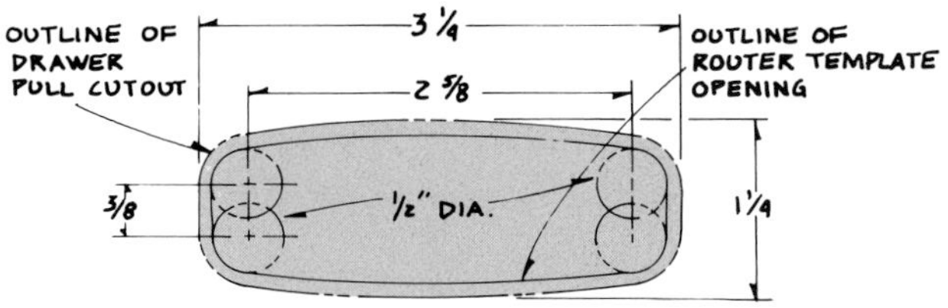
OUTLINE OF
DRAWER
PULL CUTOUT
3 1/4
2 5/8
OUTLINE OF
ROUTER TEMPLATE
OPENING
3/8
1/2" DIA.
1 1/4

FRONT VIEW

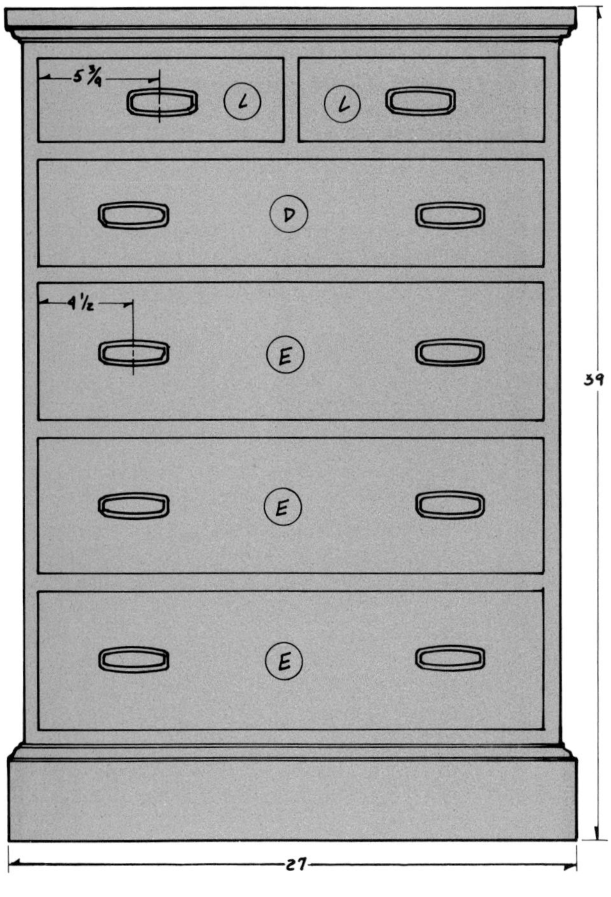
5 3/4
L
L
D
4 1/2
E
E
E
39
27

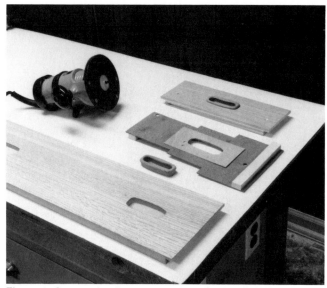

Figure 1. Cut wood pull recesses using a 3/16 in. straight bit and guide bushing. Make a jig to center and mill the recess as shown.

Figure 2. Carefully align and clamp the two sides to all drawer frames. Use carpenter's glue for assembly.

Trim the plywood edges of the carcass with 1/8 in. oak strips. Cut the trim slightly wider than 3/4 inches. Glue and clamp it in place, or tape it with masking tape until the glue dries. Then sand the edges flush.

Miter and rabbet the base parts (F, G, Y) and assemble. Add cleats (Z, AA) and reinforce the corners (BB) with diagonal glue blocks.

Assemble the base to the carcass with 2 in. screws through the base cleats and filler pieces and into the bottom drawer frame. Mount the top also with screws from inside the carcass.

Miter the top and bottom moulding; glue and tack it in place with 1 in. finishing nails. Drill pilot holes for the nails.

Drawers

Cut rabbets and grooves in the oak veneer plywood drawer fronts and the pine sides as shown in the illustration details. Make a template for routing the pull recesses. The template dimensions given are for a 3/16 in. bit and a 5/16 in. router bushing guide. Check your jig on scrap first.

The drawer sides are for a 1/16 in. bit and a 5/16 in. router bushing guide. Check your jig on scrap first.

The drawer sides are 1/16 in. narrower than the fronts. Drawer sides, fronts and backs should all end up flush on the top edges, so assemble each drawer upside down on a flat surface. First put the parts together without glue to make sure the grooves in drawer sides align with the bottom edge of the back so you can slide the drawer bottom in. We used two frame clamps for drawer assembly. After gluing, install the pulls (be sure to get them right-side up).

Install the plastic drawer guides in the slots, and center each drawer in the carcass. Then attach the track holders to the back of each drawer with No. 5 by 1/2 in. pan head screws. When closed, the drawers should fit 1/16 in. back from the carcass front edge for the best appearance. Locate drawer stops on the carcass sides to catch the back edges of the drawer sides, with an extra stop on the second frame for the two top drawers (refer to the illustration).

Figure 3. Glue the oak trim strips to the front rails using a scrap strip and numerous C-clamps, as shown. The small blocks attached to the scrap strip prevent the strips from slipping sideways during clamping.

Finishing

For a light-colored, dramatically figured finish, start with a sealer coat of thinned polyurethane varnish. When dry, wipe on a coat of ZAR No. 111 walnut satin stain. The stain will fill the pores, but the sealer coat will keep it from coloring the rest of the wood. After 24 hours, sand with 180 grit paper to remove all trace of stain except in the pores. Complete finishing with two coats of ZAR satin polyurethane, sanding lightly between coats.

Give exposed plywood edges of the drawer fronts an opaque paint finish before varnishing. Match the overall oak color of the wood. Japan color is best, but any thinned-down flat interior paint may be used. □

Designed and built by Dennis Watson

Computer Desk with Printer Stand

Here is enough storage space for your computer, printer, diskettes, files, software and more!

This contemporary oak desk provides space and beauty, making it the ideal location for typing letters, keeping track of your finances and just having a good time. The optional printer stand rolls under the desk and out of the way when it is not in use.

Desk Construction

The desk is supported by a U-shaped frame made from 1¾ in. oak. Begin by ripping the stock for the upper arm (A) and lower arm (C) 4 in. wide. Crosscut the upper arm to 26 in. and the lower arm to 24 in. Rip the leg (B) 5 in. wide and crosscut to 27½ in. long.

To join the arms to the legs, cut half lap joints. This is a strong joint and is easily made using a radial arm saw or table saw and a dado blade. Before assembling, cut the taper required for the upper and lower arms on the band saw or table saw, and round over the edges using a ¼ in. rounding over cutter and router. Glue and clamp the half lap joints together, making sure they pull up tight and that they are square.

Cut the rear upper rail (D), the lower rail (E) and the front upper rail (F) from ¾ in. oak. Next, cut the center divider (K) to size and dowel to the front and rear rails using two ⅜ in. diameter by 2 in. dowels in each end of K. Glue together. After the glue has dried, round over the wood edges with a ¼ in. rounding over cutter. To complete the desk frame, join the rails to the side frame (A, B, C) using two ⅜ in. diameter by 2 in. dowels in each end. Make sure the assembly pulls up tight; check for squareness.

Cut the ¾ in. by ¾ in. ledger strips (G, H, J) to length and screw to the base as shown in the diagram with 1½ in. flathead screws.

The desk top is made from ¾ in. oak plywood (L) with hardwood edging (M). Cut these pieces to size. Glue the edging in place using bar clamps to keep the mating edges tight. When dry, round over the desk's front edges and the top side of the back edge with a ¼ in. rounding over cutter.

Shelf Unit Construction

The shelf unit is made from solid wood with a ¼ in. oak plywood back.

Rip the sides (N), top shelf (P), upper rail (Q) and the lower rail (R) to their proper lengths and widths. Round over the edges where indicated in the diagram.

When you are through with this next step, the top shelf will be doweled to the sides with seven ⅜ in. diameter by 1½ in. dowels and the lower rail joined with two ¼ in. diameter by 1½ in. dowels in each end. The top back rail is simply butt joined to the top shelf and sides. Begin by running a ¼ in. by ½ in. deep rabbet in the bottom edge of the top shelf (P), the upper edge of the lower back rail (R) and the inside edge of the sides (N) for the back. Dry-fit the unit together. Glue and clamp the assembly only when you are satisfied with the joints. Make sure the unit is square.

Cut the vertical divider (T) and shelves (S) to size. Then attach the vertical divider to the upper and lower shelves (P, S) and in turn attach this subassembly to the sides (N). Glue and dowel this section all at one time, making sure everything is square.

Cut the back (U) from ¼ in. thick oak plywood and drill 1 in. holes for any power cord that runs through the back. Before drilling the holes, determine where your equipment is going and where the holes should be placed. Extra holes can be covered with a hole cover (V, W). Begin by cutting a plywood plug (V) to fit tightly in the 1 in. holes. Cut the plug cover (W) from hardwood and chamfer the edge; glue to the plywood back. Tack the back in place using small brads.

Next, drill ¼ in. holes in the sides and vertical divider for accepting the adjustable shelf supports.

Drawer Unit Construction

The three-drawer unit is the next order of business. Make the sides (X) from ¾ in. oak plywood. To help keep the cost low, make the top and bottom (Y) from ¾ in. fir plywood.

Cut a rabbet-dado joint into the cabinet top and bottom (Y) and sides (X) as shown in the diagram. Make these cuts on a table saw or radial arm saw using a ¼ in. dado blade.

Now run a ¼ in. by ½ in. deep rabbet in the back edge of the top, bottom and sides for accepting the ¼ in. fir plywood back (Z). Glue and clamp the carcass (less the back) together and allow it to set overnight to dry.

Next, glue the hardwood edging (AA, BB) in place using bar clamps to insure a tight joint. Round over the edging with a ¼ in. rounding over cutter.

The drawers are three simple boxes made from ½ in. oak with ¾ in. oak false fronts and supported inside the cabinet with ball bearing guides.

Cut each drawer front and back (FF, GG, HH) and sides (CC, DD, EE) to size.

Cut rabbet-dado joints for assembling the drawers. Now run a ¼ in. groove in the drawers for accommodating the bottom (JJ). Glue and clamp each drawer, making sure each is square.

Attach the ball bearing guides to the drawer's outside and to the inside of the carcass sides. Cut the false fronts (KK, LL, MM) from ¾ in. solid oak. Rout the recess for the handles using a template and guide (see photo).

Screw the false fronts to the drawer fronts using four 1¼ in. flathead screws in each drawer. Glue the handles in place.

Cut and fasten the ledger (NN) to the desk's lower arm (C). Then nail the drawer unit's plywood back in place with small brads. Attach the drawer unit to the desk top, the arm (C) and the ledger with 1½ in. flathead screws.

Printer Stand

The printer unit is a scaled-down version of the desk. Cut all the parts as specified in the bill of materials.

Make the side frames (A, B, C) in a manner similar to the way you constructed the desk. Join the side frames to the upper and lower rails (D, E).

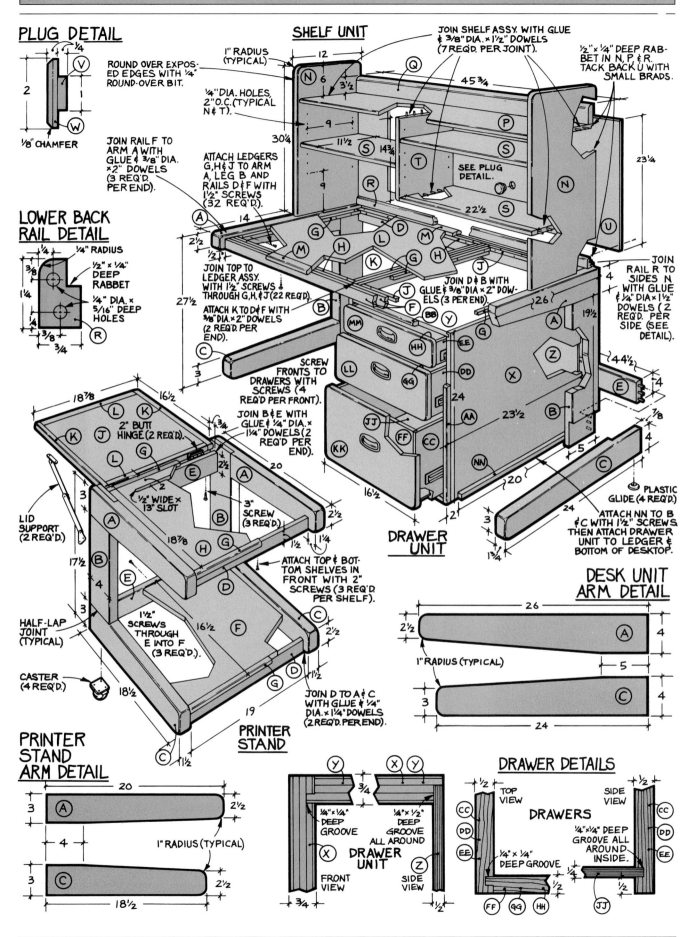

PLUG DETAIL

2

¼

V

1

W

⅛" CHAMFER

ROUND OVER EXPOSED EDGES WITH ¼" ROUND-OVER BIT.

LOWER BACK RAIL DETAIL

¼" RADIUS

½" × ¼" DEEP RABBET

¼" DIA. × 5/16" DEEP HOLES

R

SHELF UNIT

JOIN SHELF ASSY. WITH GLUE & ⅜" DIA. × 1½" DOWELS (7 REQ'D. PER JOINT).

½" × ¼" DEEP RABBET IN N, P & R. TACK BACK U WITH SMALL BRADS.

1" RADIUS (TYPICAL)

12

N 6 3½

¼" DIA. HOLES, 2" O.C. (TYPICAL N & T).

30¼

9

11½

9

R

Q

45¾

P

S 14¾

T

SEE PLUG DETAIL.

22½

S

23¼

N

U

JOIN RAIL F TO ARM A WITH GLUE & ⅜" DIA. × 2" DOWELS (3 REQ'D. PER END).

ATTACH LEDGERS G, H & J TO ARM A, LEG B AND RAILS D & F WITH 1½" SCREWS (32 REQ'D.).

A 14

2½

½

27½

JOIN TOP TO LEDGER ASSY. WITH 1½" SCREWS THROUGH G, H & J (22 REQ'D).

ATTACH K TO D & F WITH ⅜" DIA. × 2" DOWELS (2 REQ'D. PER END).

B

C

3

G M L D M H K G H J

J F

BB Y

MM

HH

LL

GG

JOIN D & B WITH GLUE & ⅜" DIA. × 2" DOWELS (3 PER END).

26

EE

DD

AA

24

JJ

FF

KK

G

Z

X

23½

A 19½

B

CC

NN

20

16½

2

3

1¾

JOIN RAIL R TO SIDES N WITH GLUE & ¼" DIA. × 1½" DOWELS (2 REQ'D. PER SIDE (SEE DETAIL).

4 4½

E 4

⅞

4

C

5

24

PLASTIC GLIDE (4 REQ'D.).

ATTACH NN TO B & C WITH 1½" SCREWS THEN ATTACH DRAWER UNIT TO LEDGER & BOTTOM OF DESKTOP.

DRAWER UNIT

18⅞

16½

L K J K

2" BUTT HINGE (2 REQ'D.).

K L G

E

A

½" WIDE × 13" SLOT

18⅞

A

H G

B

2

3" SCREW (3 REQ'D.)

20

2½

2½

1½ 1¼

JOIN B & E WITH GLUE & ¼" DIA. × 1¼" DOWELS (2 REQ'D. PER END).

LID SUPPORT (2 REQ'D.)

17½

B

4

3

E

D

C

HALF-LAP JOINT (TYPICAL)

1½" SCREWS THROUGH E INTO F (3 REQ'D.).

16½

F

2½

ATTACH TOP & BOTTOM SHELVES IN FRONT WITH 2" SCREWS (3 REQ'D. PER SHELF).

CASTER (4 REQ'D.)

18½

19

PRINTER STAND

G D

1½

JOIN D TO A & C WITH GLUE & ¼" DIA. × 1¼" DOWELS (2 REQ'D. PER END).

C

1½

SCREW FRONTS TO DRAWERS WITH SCREWS (4 REQ'D. PER FRONT).

DESK UNIT ARM DETAIL

26

2½

A 4

1" RADIUS (TYPICAL)

5

3

C 4

24

PRINTER STAND ARM DETAIL

20

3

A 2½

4

1" RADIUS (TYPICAL)

3

C 2½

18½

DRAWER DETAILS

Y X Y

¾

¼" × ¼" DEEP GROOVE

¼" × ½" DEEP GROOVE ALL AROUND

X

DRAWER UNIT

FRONT VIEW

¾

Z

SIDE VIEW

½

½

TOP VIEW

CC

DD

EE

¼" × ¼" DEEP GROOVE

DRAWERS

SIDE VIEW

CC

DD

EE

¼" × ¼" DEEP GROOVE ALL AROUND INSIDE.

¼

½

FF GG HH

JJ

½

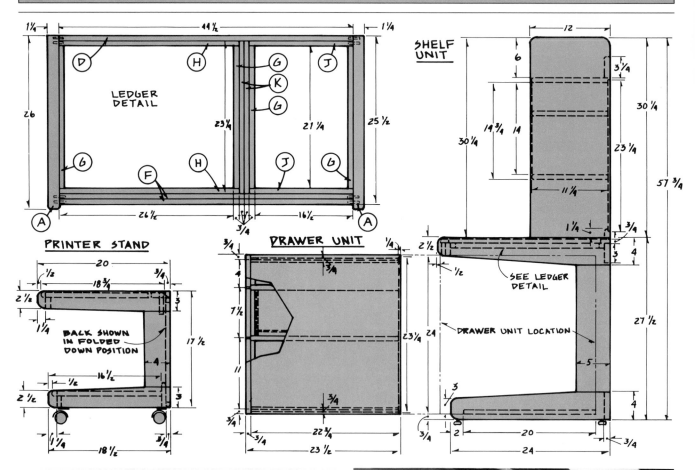

LEDGER DETAIL

SHELF UNIT

PRINTER STAND

BACK SHOWN IN FOLDED DOWN POSITION

DRAWER UNIT

SEE LEDGER DETAIL

DRAWER UNIT LOCATION

Figure 1. Cut the drawer pull recess with a router using a guide bushing to follow the inside pattern of a homemade template.

Figure 2. An abrasive stationary sander does an excellent job of finishing rounded corners. Rotate the workpiece quickly and maintain light belt contact.

Make the top (H) and bottom (F) by gluing ¾ in. square oak edging (G) to the edges of oak plywood (see diagram). Round over the oak's edges where indicated with a ¼ in. rounding over cutter. Then use a saber saw to cut a 1 in. slot in the top panel (for the paper to feed through). Secure the top and bottom panels in place.

Edge-glue oak edging to all four sides of the back panel (J). Now attach the back to the rear rail with two 1½ in. by 2 in. brass butt hinges. The back also lifts up to hold the paper that is run through the printer. Thus, two lid support brackets are screwed to the back panel and the side frames.

Finishing Touches

Sand the desk, shelf unit, drawer unit and printer stand with 150 grit paper followed by 220 grit. The desk, shelf and drawer units were finished with two coats of Watco Natural Danish Oil. Because the desk top and printer stand top receive hard use, give them two coats of satin polyurethane varnish after the oil is thoroughly dry.

Most computer components require electrical power which can add up to quite a few amps, so it is a good idea to plug them into a power strip rated for 15 amp, preferably one with its own circuit breaker.

Install the casters and desk levelers and you are ready to start computing. ☐

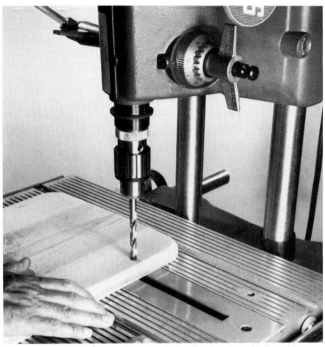

Figure 3. Drill the ⅜ in. diameter holes for the dowel joint with a stationary or portable drill guide. Set the depth of cut carefully.

BILL OF MATERIALS — Computer Desk with Printer Stand

Finished Dimensions in Inches

Desk

A	Upper Arm	1¾ x 4 x 26 oak	2
B	Leg	1¾ x 5 x 27½ oak	2
C	Lower Arm	1¾ x 4 x 24 oak	2
D	Rear Upper Rail	¾ x 3 x 44½ oak	1
E	Lower Rail	¾ x 4 x 44½ oak	1
F	Front Upper Rail	¾ x 2 x 44½ oak	2
G	Ledger	¾ x ¾ x 21¾ oak	4
H	Ledger	¾ x ¾ x 26½ oak	2
J	Ledger	¾ x ¾ x 16½ oak	2
K	Divider	¾ x 2 x 23¼ oak	2
L	Top	¾ x 23¼ x 44½ oak plywood	1
M	Edging	¾ x 1¼ x 44½ oak	2
N	Sides	¾ x 12 x 30¼ oak	2
P	Top Shelf	¾ x 11¾ x 45¾ oak	1
Q	Top Back Rail	¾ x 3¼ x 45¾ oak	1
R	Lower Back Rail	¾ x 1¼ x 45¾ oak	1
S	Shelf	¾ x 11½ x 22½ oak	3
T	Divider	¾ x 11½ x 14¾ oak	1
U	Back	¼ x 23¼ x 46¾ oak	1
V	Cover Back	¼ x 1 oak plywood	
W	Plug Cover	¼ x 2 oak	4
X	Sides	¾ x 22¾ x 24 oak plywood	2
Y	Top and Bottom	¾ x 17 x 22¾ fir plywood	2
Z	Back	¼ x 17½ x 23½ fir plywood	1

AA	Side Facing	¾ x ¾ x 24 oak	2
BB	Top & Bottom Edging	¾ x ¾ x 16½ oak	2
CC	Drawer Sides	½ x 10½ x 22 oak	2
DD	Drawer Sides	½ x 7 x 22 oak	2
EE	Drawer Sides	½ x 3½ x 22 oak	2
FF	Drawer Front & Back	½ x 10½ x 15 oak	2
GG	Drawer Front & Back	½ x 7 x 15 oak	2
HH	Drawer Front & Back	½ x 3½ x 15 oak	2
JJ	Drawer Bottom	¼ x 15 x 21½ fir plywood	3
KK	False Fronts	¾ x 11 x 16½ oak	1
LL	False Fronts	¾ x 7½ x 16½ oak	1
MM	False Fronts	¾ x 4 x 16½ oak	1
NN	Ledger	¾ x ¾ x 20 oak	1

Printer Stand

A	Upper Arm	1½ x 3 x 20 oak	2
B	Leg	1½ x 4 x 17½ oak	2
C	Lower Arm	1½ x 3 x 18½ oak	2
D	Rail	¾ x 1½ x 19 oak	2
E	Rail	¾ x 2½ x 19 oak	2
F	Bottom Shelf	¾ x 15¾ x 19 oak plywood	1
G	Edging	¾ x ¾ x 19 oak	3
H	Top	¾ x 17¼ x 19 oak plywood	1
J	Back	¾ x 15 x 17⅜ oak plywood	1
K	Edging	¾ x ¾ x 16½ oak	2
L	Edging	¾ x ¾ x 17⅜ oak	2

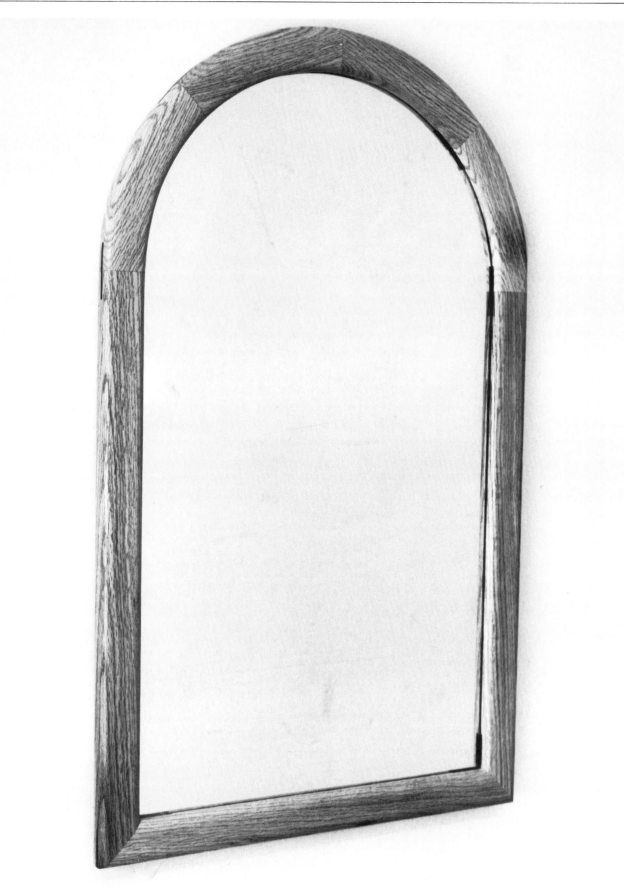

Designed and built by Dennis Watson

Curved-Top Wall Mirror

Whether over a dresser or on an entry wall, this oak framed mirror is bound to attract attention.

BILL OF MATERIALS — Curved-Top Wall Mirror			
Finished Dimensions in Inches			
A	Side	3/4 x 1 3/4 x 24	2
B	Bottom	3/4 x 1 3/4 x 24	1
C	Top	3/4 x 3 3/4 x 10 7/16	4
D	Mirror Glass	1/8 x 21 1/4 x 33 1/4	1
E	Plywood Back	1/4 x 22 x 34	1

The curved top is glued from four separate pieces joined with 22 1/2 degree miters. The miters are reinforced with walnut splines which contrast nicely with the oak.

You may be tempted to order the glass for the mirror before you've built the frame. Instead of trying to build a frame to match a pre-cut mirror, it's better to order the mirror after you've cut the mirror rabbet in the back of the frame. Make a cardboard template that fits the opening, and let the glass company cut a mirror to match your opening.

Begin construction by cutting the parts from 3/4 in. stock. Rip the sides, bottom, and top pieces to the widths shown in the bill of materials, but leave them at least 1/2 in. longer than the given length so that you don't have to cut miters on the very end of the board.

The next step is to cut the 22 1/2 degree miters that join the four top pieces. The best way to get the precise setting on a saw is by trial and measure. The measurement scales on most machines are notoriously bad — trust them to get you close, then cut a test joint on two scrap pieces of wood. Hold the boards together to form a trial 45 degree joint, and check it against your 45 degree square. If the joint isn't perfect,

adjust the saw slightly and try again. When the sample joint is perfect, miter the four top pieces. Putting a stop on the miter gauge insures that each piece is exactly the same length.

Even a well-cut miter isn't very strong, because most of the glue surface is end-grain, making for a weak joint. Strengthen each joint by inserting an exposed walnut spline. To do this, cut a 1/4 in. by 1 in. groove for the spline on the table saw or with a 1/4 in. slot cutter on a router table. If you saw the spline groove on the table saw, don't try to make the cuts freehand. Clamp the frame parts in a tenoning jig to keep your fingers safely away from the blade.

Make the miter splines from walnut. Start by ripping a 2 in. wide strip from a 3/4 in. walnut board. Resaw the strip on the table saw or band saw into two 5/16 in. thick strips and either hand plane the strips to final thickness or run them through the planer. Check the fit as you go or you're likely to end up with splines that are too thin for the groove. Once the thickness is right, cut the strip into 1 in. wide splines.

Before gluing, dry-fit the top pieces together to make sure the joints pull up tight. Miters tend to slip under pressure from clamps, so glue clamping blocks to the frame as shown. Glue both surfaces as you normally would but put a piece of heavy paper between the blocks and the frame. Let the glue dry before you clamp up the miters. When the time comes, you

Figure 1. Cut splines into adjoining workpieces with a table saw. Guide the workpiece in a jig to securely position the workpiece at a 45 degree angle. Be careful of your finger positioning.

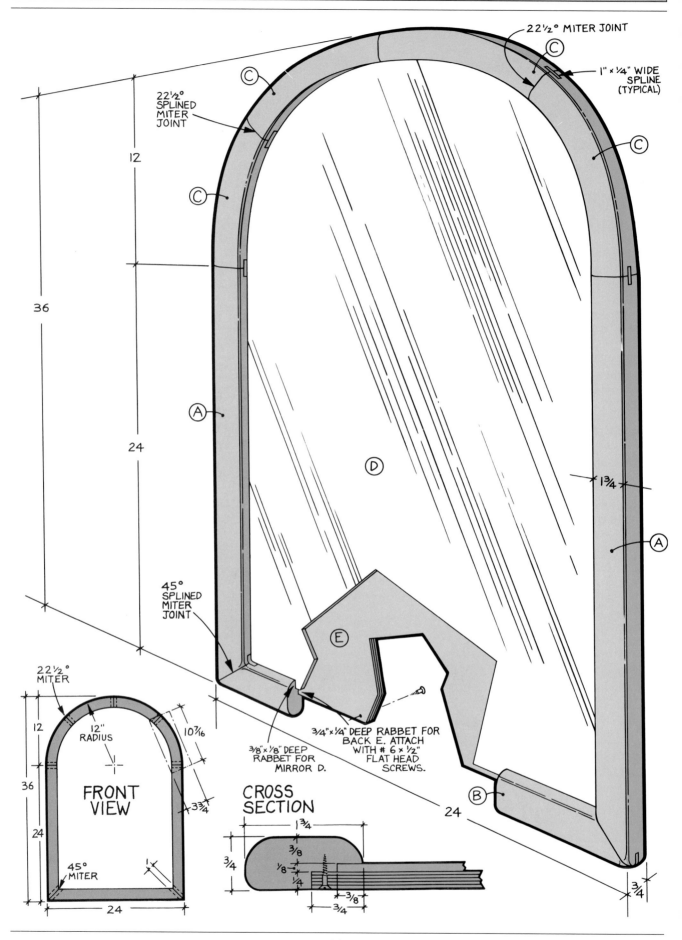

22½° MITER JOINT

C

1" × ¼" WIDE
SPLINE
(TYPICAL)

C

22½°
SPLINED
MITER
JOINT

C

C

12

C

36

A

24

1¾

A

D

E

45°
SPLINED
MITER
JOINT

3¾" × ¼" DEEP RABBET FOR
BACK E. ATTACH
WITH # 6 × ½"
FLAT HEAD
SCREWS.

3/8" × 1/8" DEEP
RABBET FOR
MIRROR D.

B

24

22½°
MITER

12

12"
RADIUS

10 7/16

36

FRONT
VIEW

3¾

24

45°
MITER

1

24

CROSS
SECTION

1¾

3/8

3/4

1/8

1/4

3/8

3/4

3/4

Figure 2. Trace the mirror's radius with a bar compass and cut out the silhouette with a band saw.

can remove the blocks by tapping sharply with a hammer. A scraper will remove the paper and glue.

Glue the top of the frame in two sections. First glue up two pieces to form one half of the curve, and then glue up the other two pieces to make the other half. Clamp across the face of the joint to keep the frame tight against the spline. When both sections are dry, glue the pair together to form the entire arch.

Now miter the joints for the bottom. Set up the 45 degree miter with the technique you used earlier, but check the sample joint against a 90 degree square. Cut the top ends of the mirror sides at 90 degrees.

Before you glue the top to the sides, lay out the curve with trammel points, and band saw the inside curve of the top. Once the frame is assembled, you can't get inside with a band saw to make the cut. After sawing, smooth the inside of the curve with a drum sander in a power drill.

Glue the assembled top, the sides and the bottom together. Clamp across the lower miters, using clamping blocks as explained above. After the glue has dried, band saw the outer curve of the top and clean up the curve with a spokeshave.

Round over the front edges of the frame with a router and a ½ in. round over bit with a ball bearing guide as illustrated in the drawing. Ball bearing guides are much better than stationary bearings, which tend to burn the wood. Round over the outer edge on the back of the frame with a ¼ in. rounding over bit.

The mirror glass and the plywood back are housed in separate rabbets cut in the back of the frame as shown in the illustration. Cut the rabbet for the mirror glass with a router and rabbeting bit. Unfortunately, you can't cut the rabbet for the back with a rabbeting bit — there isn't any place for the pilot bearing to ride. Rout the rabbet for the back by outfitting your router with a guide bushing and guiding the bushing against a hardboard template.

If you haven't done this type of pattern routing before, it isn't hard. The template guide, which looks like a little top hat through which the bit projects, screws to the base of your router. The outside edge of the guide bushing rides against a hardboard template to guide the cut as shown in the drawing.

Make the template as shown, out of ¼ in. hardboard. The opening should be the shape of the back, but larger in all

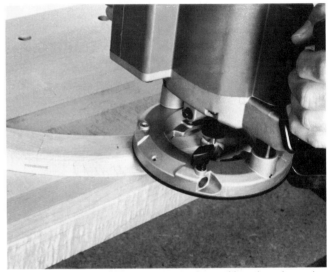

Figure 3. Clamp the frame securely to the workbench and round over the mirror's edges with a router. Make sure to use a bearing guide. Wear a face shield.

directions by the difference between the outer diameter of the guide and the diameter of the bit.

Saw the curve in the template with a saber saw, and smooth it with a half-round file. Cut the straight edges with a router and fence. Tack the template in place on the back of the mirror (make sure it's centered) and set the router for a ¼ in. deep cut. Make the cut, keeping the guide bushing snug against the template. When the rabbet is finished, square up the bottom corners with a chisel and cut the plywood back to fit.

To hang the mirror, cut two keyhole slots in each side of the frame with a special keyhole bit (available from specialty hardware stores and mail order sources). Or, attach screw eyes to each side and hang the mirror on picture wire.

Finish the frame as desired. We applied two coats of Watco Natural Danish Oil. Wet sand the second coat with 600 grit wet-dry paper and then gave the frame a good coat of paste wax.

Clean the mirror glass with any glass cleaner and put it in place. Install the plywood back with No. 6 by ½ in. brass flathead screws to complete the project. □

Project courtesy of Jonathan Press

Covered Gate

Designed in 1927 for a house on the California coast, this gate has withstood the test of time.

Build it for your own yard, and it will be welcoming guests into your home for years to come. Choose all-heart redwood lumber for the gate for weather resistance, and fasten all joints with brass or stainless steel screws.

Begin construction by cutting the 4 x 4 posts to their finished 106 in. length. On the top of each post, form a 1½ in. by 3½ in. notch for the spreaders. Cut the notches with multiple passes of a circular saw. Space the cuts ¼ in. apart, then clean out the waste with a chisel.

Next, locate the post positions and dig post holes, 12 in. in diameter and 36 in. deep. Drop the posts into the holes and fill with concrete. Before the concrete sets, use a level to help you make the posts vertical. Check on two adjacent sides of each post.

While the concrete is setting up, build the gate. Start with the diamond-shaped insert. Cut 1 x 4 stock, 24 in. long, with 45 degree miters. Use a doweling jig to bore ⅜ in. diameter matching dowel pin holes, 1⅝ in. deep. Assemble the diamond with dowel pins and resorcinol glue. Clamp the insert with pipe or bar clamps and set aside to dry.

The stiles and rails are made by sandwiching together three layers of ¾ in. material. Cut the stiles and rails, paying careful attention to their various widths and lengths. Also, cut

BILL OF MATERIALS — Covered Gate			
Finished Dimensions in Inches			
A	Post	3½ x 3½ x 114 treated pine	2
B	Brace	1½ x 3½ x 25 pine	4
C	Brace	1½ x 3½ x 11½ pine	2
D	Spreader	1½ x 3½ x 12 pine	2
E	Slat	¾ x 1½ x 21 pine	23
F	Outside Stile	¾ x 3½ x 45⅞ pine	4
G	Inside Stile	¾ x 2 x 45⅞ pine	2
H	Outside Top Rail	¾ x 3½ x 31 pine	2
I	Outside Bottom Rail	¾ x 5½ x 31 pine	2
J	Inside Top Rail	¾ x 3½ x 34 pine	1
K	Inside Bottom Rail	¾ x 5½ x 34 pine	1
L	Decorative Brace	¾ x 3½ x 24 pine	4
M	Fence Slats	¾ x 1½ x 31 pine	10

the angles on the tops of the stiles. Now, lay out the four pieces forming the middle sandwich. Place the diamond-shaped insert on top, and mark the top and bottom rails for cutting. Then cut these marked areas with a saber saw.

Now assemble the sandwiched gate along with the diamond insert, using No. 10 by 2 in. brass flathead wood screws and glue. Countersink the screw heads flush with the surface of the wood.

Rip 2 in. wide strips from 1 x 6 stock to form the slats for the gate. Cut these 31 in. long, then attach them to the diamond-shaped insert with 4d galvanized finishing nails. Space the strips 1 in. apart.

Next, build the rafters for the gate's cover. Cut 45 degree bevels on each end of the outer sections, and a 75 degree miter on the inner end. The middle section has two 75 degree miters. Fasten the components together with long dowel pins and waterproof resorcinol glue.

Figure 1. Notch the 4 x 4 post for the spreaders with several passes of a circular saw. Work from the end inwards. Remove the waste with a hammer and smooth with a wide wood chisel.

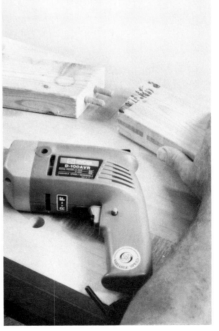

Figure 2. Assemble the rafter with dowel pins and resorcinol glue. Use a doweling jig to bore dowel pin holes 1⅝ in. deep into mating edges.

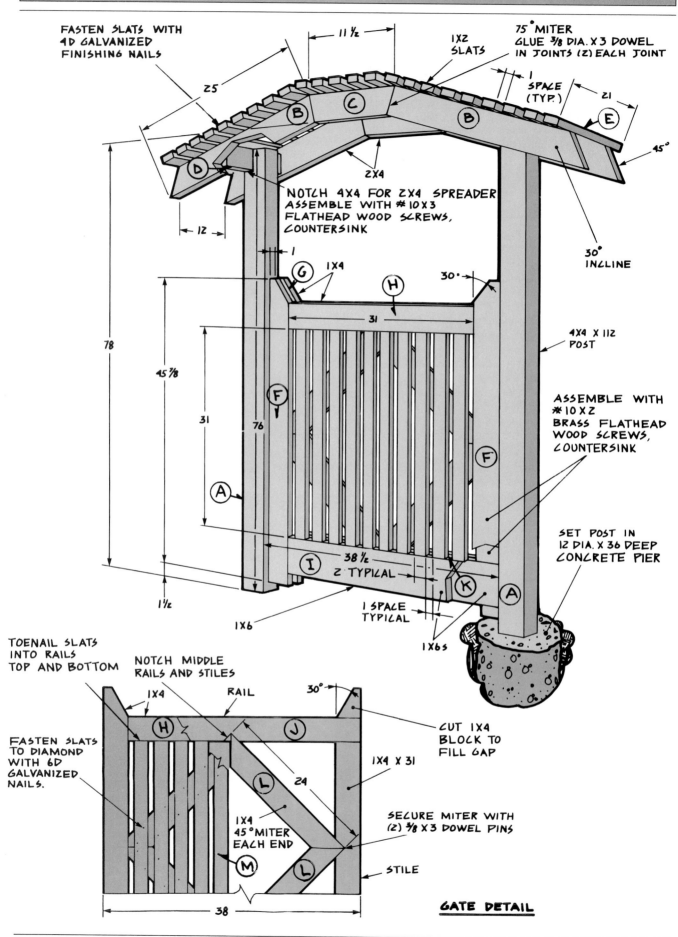

FASTEN SLATS WITH
4D GALVANIZED
FINISHING NAILS

11 1/2

1X2
SLATS

75° MITER
GLUE 3/8 DIA. X 3 DOWEL
IN JOINTS (2) EACH JOINT

25

1
SPACE
(TYP.)

21

B   C   B   E

D

2X4

45°

NOTCH 4X4 FOR 2X4 SPREADER
ASSEMBLE WITH #10X3
FLATHEAD WOOD SCREWS,
COUNTERSINK

12

30°
INCLINE

1

G   1X4   H   30°

31

4X4 X 112
POST

78

45 7/8

F

31   76

ASSEMBLE WITH
#10X2
BRASS FLATHEAD
WOOD SCREWS,
COUNTERSINK

F

A

SET POST IN
12 DIA. X 36 DEEP
CONCRETE PIER

1 1/2

I   38 1/2
2 TYPICAL

K   A

1X6

1 SPACE
TYPICAL

1X6s

TOENAIL SLATS
INTO RAILS
TOP AND BOTTOM

NOTCH MIDDLE
RAILS AND STILES

1X4   RAIL   30°

H   J

CUT 1X4
BLOCK TO
FILL GAP

FASTEN SLATS
TO DIAMOND
WITH 6D
GALVANIZED
NAILS.

L   24

1X4 X 31

1X4
45° MITER
EACH END

M   L

SECURE MITER WITH
(2) 3/8 X 3 DOWEL PINS

STILE

38

GATE DETAIL

Figure 3. Use a post hole digger to make the post hole. Then mix and pour concrete. Support the post with wood braces while the concrete cures.

Cut two 2 x 4 spreaders, 12 in. long, and fasten them to the posts with No. 10 by 3 in. flathead wood screws and glue. Attach the rafter assemblies to these spreaders, making certain that they are centered and even with each other.

Next, cut 23 strips of 1 x 2 stock, 21 in. long, for the slatted roof. Nail these to the top of the rafters with 4d galvanized finishing nails, spacing the slats evenly, about 1 in. apart. Adjust the spacing if necessary.

Hang the gate between the posts with decorative T-hinges. Position the gate flush with the posts on the hinge side and 1½ in. above the surface of the ground. Add a matching gate latch to the opposite side of the opening, and the project is complete.

You can leave the gate unfinished to weather naturally or apply clear wood sealer and preservative. Another option is to paint the gate to match your home or the color of your fence. If you paint it, use high-quality exterior latex enamel for a long life. □

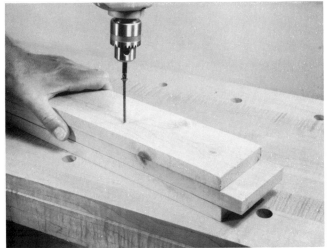

Figure 4. The gate's stiles and rails are each comprised of three separate workpieces. The upper rail is shown here.

Project courtesy of Jonathan Press

Shaded Swing

It fits perfectly on any deck or patio, and is ideal for homes without a porch. Designed to last for years, the swing will seat two comfortably.

Sitting in an outdoor swing is a wonderful way to pass a warm summer afternoon or evening. This freestanding swing, with its shaded sides and top, is ideal for those lazy days.

Take care in selecting the materials for the swing. All lumber should be straight and knot-free, especially the 2 x 4 material used for the legs and the 2 x 8 for the beam. Hand-select these parts, if possible, at your lumberyard or home center. You can use any type of lumber you choose, but for long life in harsh weather conditions, select redwood.

Start construction by cutting the lower ends of the legs to the 66 degree angle shown in the diagram. Set the arm of your radial arm saw to the correct angle, then cut one end of each of the 2 x 4 legs.

You can also cut these angles with a portable circular saw. Use an adjustable protractor guide and use a straight piece of 1 x 4 clamped to the workpiece to guide the circular saw. It is important that all four legs be identical.

Now measure the legs and mark the 76½ in. dimension on each leg. Use a protractor to lay out the 24 degree bevel at the tops of the legs. Cut these angles with your portable saw. For the greatest accuracy, clamp a straight board to the legs to help guide your saw. Stack the legs to check their lengths. Trim the legs where necessary to make them identical.

Lay out the notches in the legs to hold the swing support beam. Each notch should be ¾ in. by 5½ inches. The sides of the notches should parallel the 24 degree bevel you already cut. Take your time with this layout to make the beam fit tightly.

Cut the notches with a saber saw. Use a blade designed to cut 1½ in. thick material, and work slowly to make the notches perfectly square. Avoid side pressure as you cut to keep the blade vertical in the wood. Once the notches are cut, place each pair of legs together and check the fit with a scrap of 2 x 6.

Set the legs aside for the time being, and begin construction of the lattice panels. Set your radial arm saw to cut the 75 degree angles on the lower crosspieces and one end of each side of the side frames. Cut both lower crosspieces to length and cut one end of the vertical side pieces.

To save time and to help make the parts identical, make all of the cuts at one angle before changing your setup. These parts can also be cut with a portable saw. As you did before, use a guide to keep the cuts straight and at the correct angle.

Now reset the saw to cut the 60 degree angles on the remaining parts forming the side of the frames. Cut each part to the length shown in the diagram. Take care to make the parts identical. Check them by stacking matching parts and trimming as needed.

Cut the parts for the top frame in the same way, this time making all of the angles square. Observe the length of the front and rear frame members carefully to make the final project assembly correct.

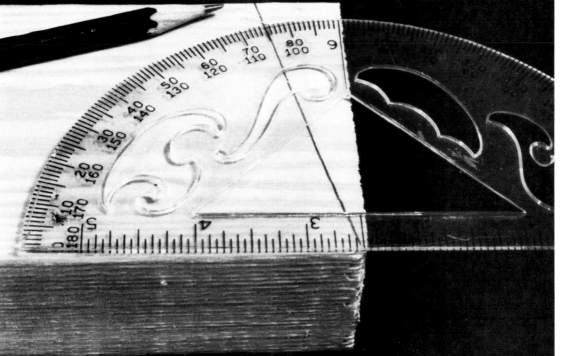

Figure 1. This project has many angles which must be laid out on individual workpieces. Ideally, use a protractor and adjustable bevel to make precise layouts.

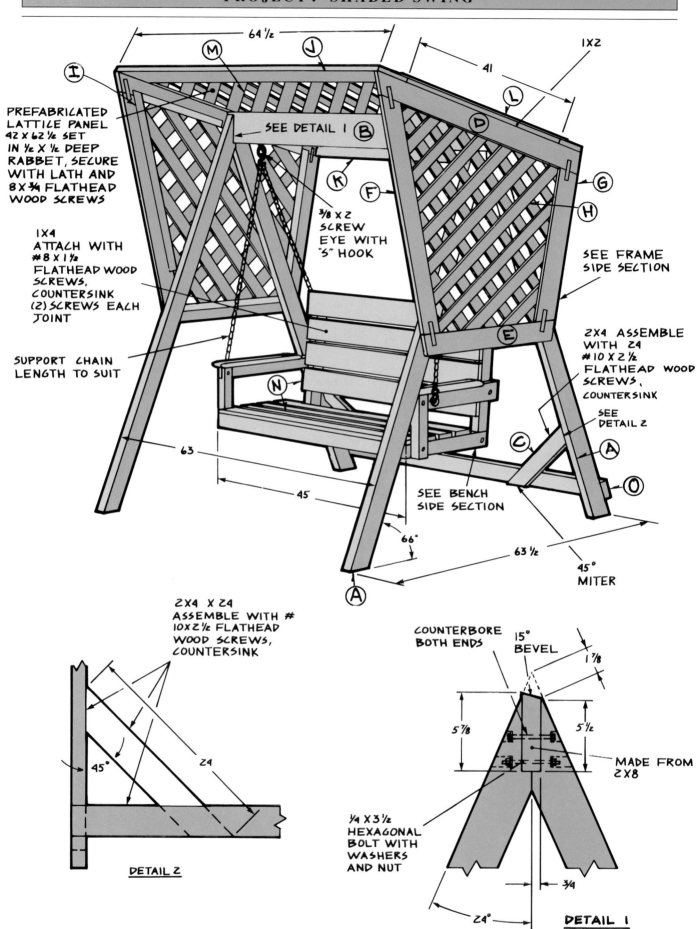

PREFABRICATED LATTICE PANEL 42 X 62½ SET IN ½ X ½ DEEP RABBET, SECURE WITH LATH AND 8 X ¾ FLATHEAD WOOD SCREWS

1X4 ATTACH WITH #8 X 1½ FLATHEAD WOOD SCREWS, COUNTERSINK (2) SCREWS EACH JOINT

SUPPORT CHAIN LENGTH TO SUIT

64½

1X2

41

SEE DETAIL 1

⅜ X 2 SCREW EYE WITH "S" HOOK

SEE FRAME SIDE SECTION

2X4 ASSEMBLE WITH 24 #10 X 2½ FLATHEAD WOOD SCREWS, COUNTERSINK

SEE DETAIL 2

63

45

SEE BENCH SIDE SECTION

66°

63½

45° MITER

2X4 X 24 ASSEMBLE WITH # 10 X 2½ FLATHEAD WOOD SCREWS, COUNTERSINK

45°

24

DETAIL 2

COUNTERBORE BOTH ENDS

15° BEVEL

1⅞

5⅞

5½

MADE FROM 2X8

¼ X 3½ HEXAGONAL BOLT WITH WASHERS AND NUT

24°

¾

DETAIL 1

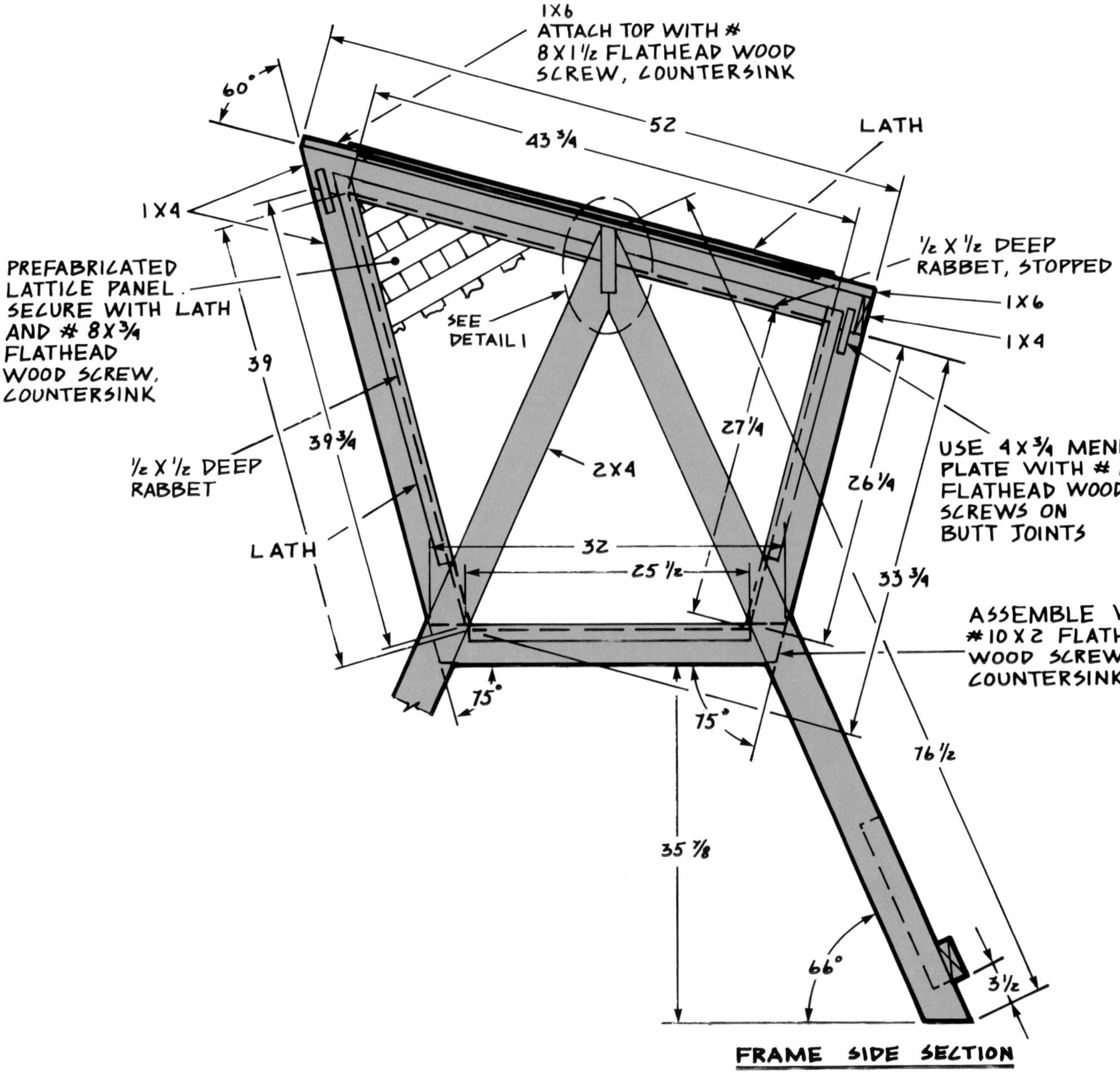
1X6
ATTACH TOP WITH # 8X1½ FLATHEAD WOOD SCREW, COUNTERSINK
60°
52
43¾
LATH
1X4
PREFABRICATED LATTICE PANEL. SECURE WITH LATH AND # 8X¾ FLATHEAD WOOD SCREW, COUNTERSINK
½X½ DEEP RABBET, STOPPED
1X6
1X4
SEE DETAIL 1
39
39¾
27¼
2X4
½X½ DEEP RABBET
USE 4X¾ MENDING PLATE WITH # 10X⅝ FLATHEAD WOOD SCREWS ON BUTT JOINTS
26¼
LATH
32
25½
33¾
ASSEMBLE WITH # 10X2 FLATHEAD WOOD SCREWS, COUNTERSINK
75°
75°
76½
35⅞
66°
3½
FRAME SIDE SECTION

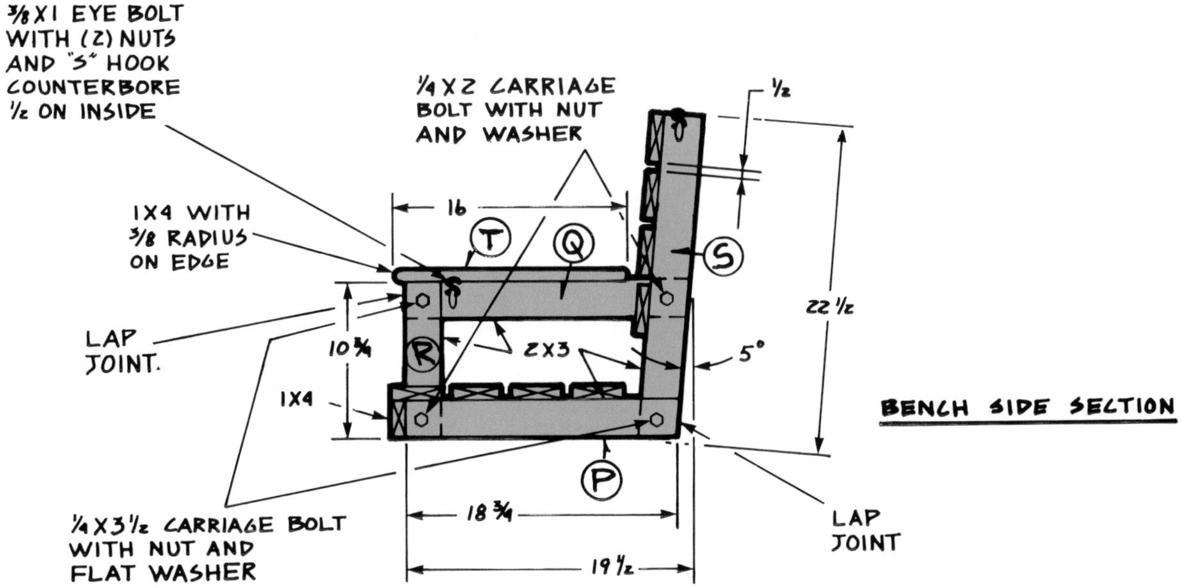
⅜X1 EYE BOLT WITH (2) NUTS AND "S" HOOK COUNTERBORE ½ ON INSIDE
¼X2 CARRIAGE BOLT WITH NUT AND WASHER
½
16
1X4 WITH ⅜ RADIUS ON EDGE
T
Q
S
LAP JOINT.
10¾
R
2X3
5°
22½
1X4
P
BENCH SIDE SECTION
¼X3½ CARRIAGE BOLT WITH NUT AND FLAT WASHER
18¾
19½
LAP JOINT

Assemble the frames, securing the joints with ¾ in. by 4 in. mending plates and No. 10 by ⅝ in. flathead wood screws. The top mending plates on the side frames will be left in place, while the lower plates will be removed later. Install the plates on the top frame so they will be located on the upper side of the frame after it is fastened to the swing.

Assemble one side frame, then build the second frame on top of the first to keep the two identical. Check the top frame as you build it to make sure it stays square. Check each corner with a framing square.

Next, cut the ½ in. by ½ in. rabbets in the frames. Use a ½ in. rabbeting bit, with a built-in pilot, in your router. Make the first cut ¼ in. deep, then finish the rabbets with a second cut that's ½ in. deep.

Make the cuts at a feed rate that cuts easily and smoothly. If the rate of feed is too slow, the pilot will burn the wood and cause an uneven rabbet. Feed the router into the wood so the bit rotates into the stock. If you move the router in the other direction, the wood is likely to splinter.

Finish the corners of the rabbet with a sharp wood chisel. Observe the angles of the sides carefully to make the rabbet's corners parallel with the sides. Push the edge of the chisel into the wood at each side of the rabbet, then cut the chip out to finish the corner. Repeat this process until the corner is the same depth as the rest of the rabbet.

Cut pre-fab lattice panels to fit inside the rabbets on each frame. Expand the lattice until the intersections are at a 90 degree angle. Orient the panels to place the lattice strips at a 45 degree angle.

Lay out the lattice panels carefully for a good fit. Place one of the frames on the lattice, then draw around the inside of the opening. Draw the cut lines ½ in. outside the first set of lines. Use a plywood blade on your saw to reduce splintering. Use your circular saw with a clamp-on guide to help keep the cuts straight.

Lay one pair of legs on a flat surface, positioning them as they will be in their final form. Use a long 2 x 4 at the base of the legs to help you establish the correct angle. Lay one of the side frames on the legs, positioning it carefully. The outside corners of the lower frame joints should be flush with

BILL OF MATERIALS — Shaded Swing

Finished Dimensions in Inches

A	Leg	1½ x 3½ x 76½ pine	4
B	Beam	1½ x 5⅞ x 63 pine	1
C	Leg Support	1½ x 3½ x 24 pine	2
D	Side Frame	¾ x 3½ x 52 pine	2
E	Side Frame	¾ x 3½ x 32 pine	2
F	Side Frame	¾ x 3½ x 39¾ pine	2
G	Side Frame	¾ x 3½ x 26¼ pine	2
H	Side Frame Lattice	½ x 34¾ x 44¾	2
I	Lath	¼ x 1½ x length to suit	12
J	Top Frame	¾ x 3½ x 64½ pine	2
K	Top Frame Brace	¾ x 3½ x 64½ pine	1
L	Top Frame	¾ x 3½ x 41 pine	2
M	Top Frame Lattice	½ x 42 x 58½	1
N	Seat Slats	¾ x 3½ x 45 pine	9
O	Brace	1½ x 3½ x 63 pine	1
P	Chair Frame	1½ x 3½ x 19¼ pine	2
Q	Chair Frame	1½ x 3½ x 19½ pine	2
R	Chair Frame	1½ x 3½ x 10¾ pine	2
S	Chair Frame	1½ x 3½ x 22½ pine	2
T	Chair Arm	¾ x 3½ x 16 pine	2

the outside of the legs. Measure from the 2 x 4 to make the bottom of the frame parallel with the base of the legs.

Mark the frame with light pencil lines where it crosses the legs. Remove the frame, then cut the lath strips that secure the lattice. Cut the side and bottom lath strips to fit inside the lines you just drew. You can cut the strips with square ends, as shown in the diagram, or cut them to match the angles of the frame and legs for a neater appearance.

Secure the lattice panels in the rabbets by screwing the lath strips to the frames with No. 8 by ¾ in. flathead wood screws. Drill countersunk pilot holes for the screws with a combination pilot bit and countersink. Space the screws 4 in. apart. Center the strips over the inside edge of the rabbet.

Lay one completed side panel on the pair of legs you already aligned. Remove the lower mending plates before

Figure 2. If you do not have a dado blade to mill the half lap joints, then make repetitive cuts with a circular saw or table saw in the workpiece's waste area. Make the saw passes as close as possible. Then break the waste with a hammer and chisel the joint smooth.

positioning the panel. Align the panel carefully, then attach it to the legs with No. 10 by 2 in. flathead wood screws. Use two screws through each frame part for maximum strength. Countersink the screw heads flush as you did before.

To make both sides of the swing's frame identical, assemble the second leg and panel on top of the first. Align the parts accurately, then attach the panel as you did before.

To form the beam at the top of the swing frame, rip a 15 degree bevel on one edge of a length of 2 x 8 lumber. Set up your saw to cut the part to the 5⅞ in. maximum width shown in the diagram. Use a combination planer-type blade for a smooth finish. Rip the beam from stock that is longer than the final dimension to minimize any damage at the end of the cut. Use a roller support to hold the beam as it leaves the saw.

Cut the beam to its finished 63 in. length, then cut the lower cross brace to match. Insert the beam in the notches at the top of the legs, then bore ¼ in. diameter holes through the legs and the beams. Locate the holes in the relative positions shown in the diagram.

Counterbore both ends of the holes with a ¾ in. bit, then insert ¼ in. by 4½ in. bolts through the holes. Notice that the lower counterbores are deeper. Add the nuts and washers and tighten securely. Check the assembly with a framing square as you work.

Add the lower cross brace, attaching it with No. 10 by 2½ in. flathead screws, countersunk flush. Finish the frame by cutting the two angled braces. Cut the ends of these braces at 45 degree angles. Attach them to the legs and brace with the same size screws. Fasten the joint between the two braces first, then attach the brace to the leg. Again, check the structure for squareness as you work.

Install the 1 x 4 rear brace at the rear of the side panels. Finally, add the top lattice panel, securing it with No. 8 by 1½ in. flathead wood screws. Drive the screws into the side frames and the rear brace.

Build the seat next. Cut the side frame components to the dimensions shown in the diagram. Cut the 5 degree angles for the backrest and seat supports with a table saw.

Now lay out the lap joint notches. Lay the parts together and mark the notch positions on all the parts. Be sure to observe the correct angles.

Cut the notches with a dado blade on your saw. Make the notches exactly half the thickness of the wood. Cut the 90 degree notches first, then reset the angle of cut to form the angled notches. Form each notch with multiple passes of your dado blade, increasing the depth of cut to reach the final depth.

Assemble the frames with ¼ in. by 2 in. carriage bolts. Drill through the joints, then insert the bolts with the heads inside the frame. Add nuts and washers and tighten securely.

Cut eight 1 x 4 seat and back slats 45 in. long. Attach these to the sides with No. 8 by 1½ in. flathead wood screws, countersinking the screw heads. Use two screws at each joint, spacing them 2½ in. apart. Space the slats ½ in. apart. Use a framing square to help keep the seat square as you install the slats.

Add the front brace to the seat, then form a ⅜ in. radius on the edges of the armrests with your router and a rounding over bit. Install the arms with screws, as you did the slats.

Complete the seat by installing the eyebolts in the locations shown in the diagram. Use nuts and washers on both sides of the wood to position the eyes outside the armrests.

Sand the completed frame and seat thoroughly, starting with 80 grit abrasive paper. Work to 220 grit for a smooth finish. Round off any exposed sharp edges slightly as you sand. Pay special attention to the end grain of the wood.

To protect the swing from weather damage, apply two coats of clear wood sealer or exterior latex enamel in the color of your choice. If you paint the swing, use an airless sprayer to help apply a smooth finish.

Let the paint dry. Install two ⅜ in. by 2 in. screw eyes in the beam. Drill 9/32 in. diameter pilot holes, 1½ in. deep, for the eyes. Hang the seat with S-hooks and 200 lb. test chain. Adjust the length of the chains to hang the seat at an angle that feels comfortable. Finally, close the S-hooks with large pliers. ☐

Figure 3. Rabbet the inside edge of the side panels with a rabbeting bit with bearing in your router. Work clockwise and wear eye protection.

Figure 4. Attach the side panels to the legs while stacking the assemblies to make them identical.

Project designed and built by Graham Blackburn

Contemporary Standing Cabinet

Stylistically this has a contemporary feeling, consisting solely of massed volumes, unadorned with any moulding, carving or surface decoration. The relationship of various parts, both in terms of respective shapes and wood colors, lends added interest.

Designed specifically as a silver cabinet — the drawers are intended to hold cutlery and the cupboard below to hold plates — it could serve a number of other purposes equally well. It can, for example, be adapted to use as a wood-carving cabinet — the drawers being fitted out to hold chisels and gouges, and the cupboard for storing mallets and clamps. Alternatively, use it as a collector's cabinet to hold any number of treasured items, from butterflies to coins.

An advantage of its design lies in its construction as several discrete units, thereby making its removal and transportation easy. While there are no real structural reasons why the overall dimensions cannot be changed nor why the relative sizes and spacings of the individual parts (such as the drawers or the panels of the doors) cannot be changed, care should be taken if such changes are contemplated to insure that the overall proportions of the cabinet remain harmonious and pleasing. This is, of course, largely a personal and very subjective matter, but it should be remembered that it is precisely the appropriate accommodation of the shape of any piece to its required function and purpose that makes it a pleasing and successful design.

The design calls for a working knowledge of a variety of joints, including mortise and tenons, several types of dovetails, splined miters, and splined and mitered clamp joints. If these types of joints are intimidating, use those with which you are comfortable, such as rabbet joints.

Choice of Material

Although, as previously stated, it is partly the use of differently colored woods that constitutes this particular cabinet's appeal, the same design can be constructed using other species — or even a single species if it were thought appropriate. We used Brazilian rosewood to make the drawer fronts and the door frame; amaranth (also known as purpleheart), which complemented the color of the rosewood very nicely; black walnut for the carcass; and maple for the drawer sides.

Wood that is not normally seen in a piece (such as bottoms and back, and various interior parts) is referred to as *secondary* wood and is usually not as fancy or expensive as the *primary* species. However, structural considerations — such as the necessity of a hard-wearing species for moving or rubbing parts such as drawers and runners — must always be borne in mind; hence the choice of maple for the interior parts of this cabinet.

The Carcass

The heart of this piece consists of two nearly equal *boxes* (dovetailed), the upper one housing the drawers and the lower one constituting the cupboard. Join the top, bottom and sides of these boxes with walnut, edge-jointed together to provide the requisite width. After joining, cut the lengths so as to provide the four sides for each box.

Then make frame-and-panel backs for both units. The panels, which comprise the bulk of the back and which are therefore the parts most likely to change dimension under different humidity conditions, are free to move within the frames. The frames, being of much narrower dimension, constitute little threat since any change in their width is likely to be very small.

It would be possible to fix the frame-and-paneled backs directly onto the backs of the two boxes, or cases, but by setting them into a rabbet the sides remain unspoiled by the possibly ill-matched side grain of the edges of the backs. Furthermore, setting the back panel within the sides provides a stronger method of insuring that the cases remain square.

Nothing need be done to accommodate the drawers or cupboard doors at this stage, but before beginning work on the dovetails that join the pieces of the cases together, cut the rabbet for the paneled back as a guarantee against laying out the dovetails in the wrong place.

Cut the rabbet on a table saw, jointer or router, or by hand with a rabbet plane. However you cut it, make sure that before you start you have all four pieces of each case carefully marked so there is no confusion about which is the front or back edge and which is the outside or inside; cut the rabbet on the back inside corner of each piece.

Special Dovetails

With all sides cut exactly square and to the proper width and length, and with the rabbets formed in the back edges, lay out the dovetails with mitered front corners. Normal through-dovetails are used, and they are arranged so that the tails are cut in the tops and bottoms. This leaves the square ends of the tails visible at the sides. While this may not be as impressive to your friends as the fan-shaped dovetails, it is

better since it provides the sides with the maximum strength. At the front of the cabinet cut a miter, which presents a neater appearance than butted edges. At the rear is the rabbet you cut for the back.

Both of these joining methods create slight difficulties that must be resolved. If a normal dovetail were cut at the rear, a gap caused by the rabbet would appear. To avoid this, you may set the dovetail further in from the edge than usual and then make a square cut on the tail, level with the rabbet, and cut the tail short. Or you can make the square cut on the tail as before, but leave it full length, and remove a corresponding amount (level with the rabbet) from the pin.

At the front, cut the mitered dovetail similar to the rabbeted dovetail. The end tail is cut with a square side and its whole end is then mitered. When cutting the corresponding miter in the pin, do not cut the miter deeper than the width of the tail. If you do the end of the first pin to fit between the end two tails this will show a gap. The most important thing to remember is to cut on the waste side of the miter line, or the joint will not be tight and the whole effect will be spoiled. It is better to leave a bit too much wood, assemble the joint and then saw through the resultant bulging miter with your thinnest dovetail saw. The wood removed by the saw's kerf should be sufficient to allow the joint to close nicely.

Frame and Paneling

The backs and cupboard door are made to a similar pattern, their respective overall sizes being measured from the assembled cases. But do not glue the cases together when taking these measurements; wait until the backs are ready to install, since by gluing and clamping everything at once, the backs will help insure that the cases are kept square.

Cut the pieces for the frames to length and width first, and then carefully mark them so that there is no confusion regarding inside and outside faces and edges. Now cut the grooves to hold the panels along all inside edges. Once again, there are several methods by which this may be done, including the table saw, router or plough planes. But it will help if the grooves, however they may be cut, are made the same thickness as the mortises and are cut in the same plane. Mortises are usually made about a third as thick as the stock in which they are cut and are usually centered for maximum strength.

Whether you cut the mortises first and then the tenons or vice-versa depends on your own preference and the method used for cutting these joints. Try all the joints for fit, and check the frame for flatness before preparing the panels. Although the grooves for these panels are best located in the center of the frames' edges, the panels can be cut to fit into the grooves so that they may present a recessed surface (as in the backs) or a flush surface (as in the doors).

Assemble the panels with glue, taking care to keep any glue from entering the panel grooves since the panels must remain completely free. Then finish-plane the two backs, and use these to keep the cases square during assembly. Fit the cupboard door to the opening so that there is slightly less than a ⅛ in. gap all around. Bevel its opening edge 15 degrees to allow it to open and close easily. Do not hang it until both cases are fixed together and the interior is finished.

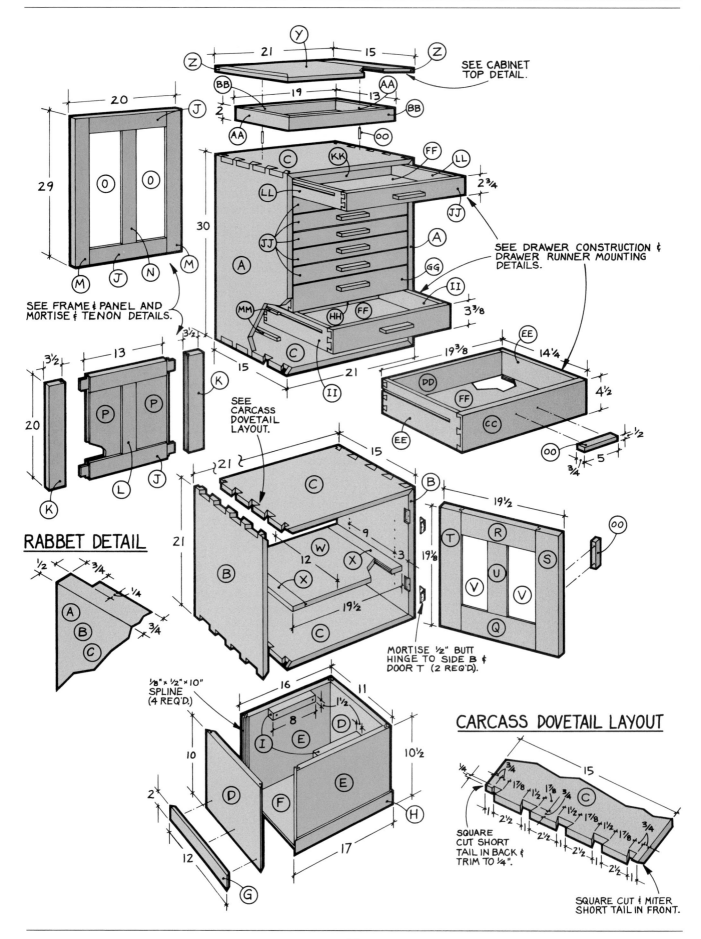

SEE CABINET
TOP DETAIL.

SEE FRAME & PANEL AND
MORTISE & TENON DETAILS.

SEE DRAWER CONSTRUCTION &
DRAWER RUNNER MOUNTING
DETAILS.

SEE
CARCASS
DOVETAIL
LAYOUT.

RABBET DETAIL

MORTISE ½" BUTT
HINGE TO SIDE B &
DOOR T (2 REQ'D).

⅛" x ½" x 10"
SPLINE
(4 REQ'D.)

CARCASS DOVETAIL LAYOUT

SQUARE
CUT SHORT
TAIL IN BACK &
TRIM TO ¼".

SQUARE CUT & MITER
SHORT TAIL IN FRONT.

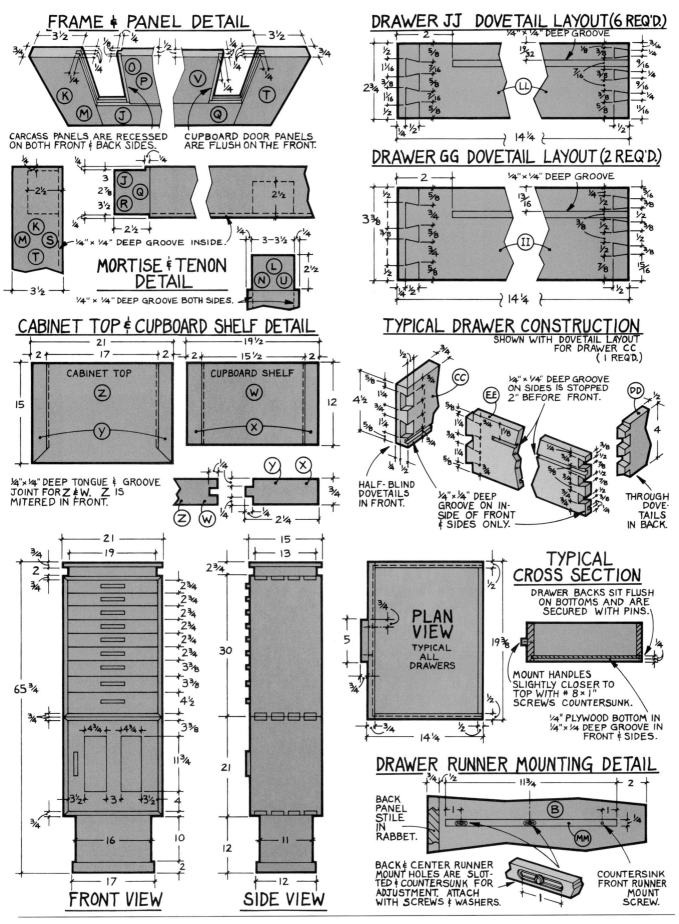

FRAME & PANEL DETAIL

CARCASS PANELS ARE RECESSED ON BOTH FRONT & BACK SIDES.

CUPBOARD DOOR PANELS ARE FLUSH ON THE FRONT.

¼" × ¼" DEEP GROOVE INSIDE.

MORTISE & TENON DETAIL

¼" × ¼" DEEP GROOVE BOTH SIDES.

CABINET TOP & CUPBOARD SHELF DETAIL

CABINET TOP

CUPBOARD SHELF

¼"× ¼" DEEP TONGUE & GROOVE JOINT FOR Z & W. Z IS MITERED IN FRONT.

DRAWER JJ DOVETAIL LAYOUT (6 REQ'D.)

¼" × ¼" DEEP GROOVE

DRAWER GG DOVETAIL LAYOUT (2 REQ'D.)

¼" × ¼" DEEP GROOVE

TYPICAL DRAWER CONSTRUCTION

SHOWN WITH DOVETAIL LAYOUT FOR DRAWER CC
(1 REQ'D.)

¼" × ¼" DEEP GROOVE ON SIDES IS STOPPED 2" BEFORE FRONT.

HALF-BLIND DOVETAILS IN FRONT.

¼"× ¼" DEEP GROOVE ON INSIDE OF FRONT & SIDES ONLY.

THROUGH DOVE-TAILS IN BACK.

TYPICAL CROSS SECTION

DRAWER BACKS SIT FLUSH ON BOTTOMS AND ARE SECURED WITH PINS.

PLAN VIEW
TYPICAL ALL DRAWERS

MOUNT HANDLES SLIGHTLY CLOSER TO TOP WITH # 8 × 1" SCREWS COUNTERSUNK.

¼" PLYWOOD BOTTOM IN ¼" × ¼" DEEP GROOVE IN FRONT & SIDES.

DRAWER RUNNER MOUNTING DETAIL

BACK PANEL STILE IN RABBET.

BACK & CENTER RUNNER MOUNT HOLES ARE SLOTTED & COUNTERSUNK FOR ADJUSTMENT. ATTACH WITH SCREWS & WASHERS.

COUNTERSINK FRONT RUNNER MOUNT SCREW.

FRONT VIEW

SIDE VIEW

BILL OF MATERIALS — Contemporary Standing Cabinet

Finished Dimensions in Inches

A	Drawer Carcass Side	¾ x 15 x 30	2	T	Cupboard Door Right Side Stile	¾ x 3½ x 19⅛		1
B	Cupboard Carcass Side	¾ x 15 x 21	2	U	Cupboard Door Center Stile	¾ x 3 x 16¾		2
C	Carcase Top & Bottom	¾ x 15 x 21	4	V	Cupboard Door Panel	½ x 5¼ x 12¼		2
D	Base Side	¾ x 11 x 12	2	W	Cupboard Shelf	¾ x 15½ x 12		1
E	Base Front & Back	¾ x 16 x 12	2	X	Cupboard Shelf Cleat	¾ x 2¼ x 12		2
F	Base Bottom	½ x 11 x 16	1	Y	Cabinet Top	¾ x 21 x 15		1
G	Base Side Moulding	½ x 2 x 12	2	Z	Cabinet Top Cleat	¾ x 2¼ x 15		2
H	Base Front & Back Moulding	½ x 2 x 17	2	AA	Top Frame Side	¾ x 2 x 19		2
I	Base Cleat	1½ x 1½ x 8	2	BB	Top Frame Front & Back	¾ x 2 x 13		2
J	Back Panel Rail	¾ x 3½ x 18	4	CC	Large Drawer Front	¾ x 4½ x 19⅜		1
K	Cupboard Back Panel End Stile	¾ x 3½ x 20	2	DD	Large Drawer Back	½ x 4 x 19⅜		1
L	Cupboard Back Panel Center Stile	¾ x 3½ x 18	1	EE	Large Drawer Side	½ x 4½ x 14¼		2
M	Drawercase Back Panel End Stile	¾ x 3½ x 29	2	FF	Drawer Bottom	¼ ply x 13¾ x 18⅞		9
N	Drawercase Back Panel Center Stile	¾ x 3½ x 27	1	GG	Medium Drawer Front	¾ x 3⅜ x 19⅜		2
O	Drawercase Back Panel	½ x 5¼ x 22½	2	HH	Medium Drawer Back	½ x 2⅞ x 19⅜		2
P	Cupboard Back Panel	½ x 5¼ x 13½	2	II	Medium Drawer Side	½ x 3⅜ x 14¼		4
Q	Cupboard Door Bottom Rail	¾ x 4 x 17½	1	JJ	Small Drawer Front	¾ x 2¾ x 19⅜		6
R	Cupboard Door Top Rail	¾ x 3⅜ x 17½	1	KK	Small Drawer Back	½ x 2¼ x 19⅜		6
S	Cupboard Door Left Side Stile	¾ x 3½ x 19⅛	1	LL	Small Drawer Side	½ x 2¾ x 14¼		12
				MM	Drawer Runner	¼ x ¼ x 11¾		18
				NN	Drawer/Cupboard Handle	½ x ¾ x 5		10
				OO	Dowel	¼ dia. x 2½		2

Drawers

The drawers fit inside the upper case, flush with its front edge. There is thus no overhang or lipping to hide any gaps, and consequently the fronts of the drawers must be measured and cut very exactly if a neat and precise appearance is to be obtained. For this reason, it is best to prepare the drawer fronts first, leaving a very even but narrow (1/16 in.) gap between each drawer and its neighbor and the sides of the case.

As well as preparing your stock carefully to fit, pay attention to the effects created by arranging the drawer fronts in different orders. Not only should the color and grain of adjacent drawers look well together, but the relative sizes should be considered. By placing the largest at the bottom, a comfortable feeling is obtained, but the rate at which each succeeding drawer diminishes in height also affects the balance of the piece.

Having prepared the fronts (and marked them carefully to show front, top and order), the next step is to make the sides and backs. The sides need not be as thick as the fronts, which have to accommodate lapped dovetails, but they should still have enough thickness to securely accommodate the ¼ in. groove cut in them to fit over the drawer runners. The backs may be even thinner — although it makes cutting the through-dovetails, which join the backs and sides, easier if both pieces are the same thickness. Cut the sides to be exactly the same height as the fronts to which they will be joined and short enough to allow the drawer front to be pushed in flush with the sides of the cabinet. It is safest to allow a little extra room

here since the alignment of the fronts is managed by careful positioning of the runners in the grooves.

Cut the stopped grooves before assembling the drawers. Take care to lay out the through-dovetails for the sides and backs in such a way that the groove does not hit a tail. Similarly, carefully lay out the lapped dovetails that join the sides to the fronts. Note that the groove for the drawer bottom runs through a tail — so that its end is covered by the drawer front.

Take note that the backs of the drawers, while being level with the tops of the sides and the fronts, are only as deep as the grooves cut in the sides for the bottoms.

After test-fitting the front, sides and back of each drawer within the case, cut the bottoms to fit. Then glue and clamp together with the bottoms. Slide the bottoms into place, and secure with small pins driven into the bottom edge of the backs.

After all the drawers are assembled, attach the handles, first locating the screw holes which hold them from the inside. The handles are no more than simple oblongs of amaranth, but by subtly decreasing their size with the decreasing height of the drawers and by placing the larger ones slightly closer to the top of the fronts than those of the smaller drawers (whose handles are more nearly centered), an elegance is attained that is more pleasing than the mere mechanical centering of each handle on its respective drawer front.

To hang the drawers in the case, prepare twice as many runners (made from strips of maple) as there are drawers so

Figure 1. Use a stop on your table saw to set the length of the shoulder cut. Use a dado blade and flip the workpiece over to cut the remaining shoulder. Finish with a wood chisel.

that the runners fit snugly in the grooves cut in the sides of the drawers. Make sure that these runners are very straight and smooth. In order for the drawers to open and close well, there should be very little play, but no binding either. To allow for accurate adjustment of the runners so that the drawers close perfectly flush with the front of the case and also to allow for dimensional changes in the case's sides, slot the runners for screws. This simply means making elongated holes for the screws in the runners (including, of course, an elongated countersink on which the head of the screw rides below the level of the runner's surface).

Accurate placement is achieved by working from the bottom drawer up, using a piece of thin card as a spacer between drawers and measuring carefully.

The Cupboard

The lower case, fitted with a cupboard door, also contains an adjustable shelf. This shelf is made from a walnut board (or boards joined to form the requisite width) fitted with cleats in breadboard fashion to keep it flat. There are several ways of doing this: the board may have tongues formed on the ends, over which a grooved cleat is fitted (fixed only at the center to allow the board to swell and shrink without being restrained by the cleat); the board itself can be grooved and the cleat formed with a matching tongue; or both board and cleat can be grooved, both being held together by a separate spline. A really elegant method is to cut a long, sliding dovetail in the cleat, but should the shelf be required to support much weight, a simple square tongue-and-groove is probably stronger.

The adjustable shelf is supported by removable shelf supports inserted in holes bored in the inside of the cabinet. Locate and drill these holes to suit your requirements. Use a boring template, pre-bored to match the position of the re-quired shelf support holes. To prevent the misfortune of boring right through the case, use a depth stop or guide on the drill bit, having first made a test boring to check that the hole will be deep enough to accommodate the shelf support but not so deep as to penetrate the case's sides.

Hang the cupboard door within the case so that, like the drawers, it is flush with the front edges of the case. For a neat appearance, use knife hinges at top and bottom. If you use regular cabinet butts, take care to position them so that they relate equally to the top and bottom rails of the door; the bottom hinge being set further from the bottom than the top hinge is set from the top of the door. This small detail further balances the look of the cabinet. The handle is simply a vertical version of those used on the drawers. Affix it with glue and a screw driven from inside the door. Last, install a bullet catch at the bottom edge of the door. It is the neatest way to insure an aligned closure and provides a measure of anti-sag support to the heavy frame and panels.

The Base

Construct the base. The base is a simple, four-sided box joined with a splined miter joint and finished with a square moulding of amaranth — also mitered at the corners — at the bottom. If the stock used to make the sides of the base is thinner than 1 in., it is helpful to screw a thicker cleat around the inside top edge through which the screws that connect the base to the case above it may be inserted.

The Top

Make the top in two parts: a simple walnut cover, cleated similarly to the cupboard shelf to keep it flat but with mitered ends at the front so that no end grain is visible, and a supporting frame of amaranth that matches the moulding around the bottom of the base. Bore a hole vertically through the center of each side of the amaranth frame, and then use the frame as a boring template to bore matching holes in the top of the upper case and the underside of the cover. Tightly fit dowels into the holes in the frame so that they project $\frac{1}{4}$ in. on both sides — just enough to engage the matching holes in the case and cover. Thus, a shallow secret compartment is created.

Assembly

Screw the base to the bottom case through the cleat provided around the inside of the top of the base; affix the upper case to the lower by screwing up through the top of the lower case; and drop the cover onto the protruding dowels of the top frame, which, in turn, is dropped into the matching holes bored in the top of the upper case.

Finishing

Rosewood and amaranth are both such dense woods in that little more than paste wax is necessary to bring out their rich color and beauty. Give the walnut carcass a well rubbed coat or two of oil, plain boiled linseed oil, or a faster drying proprietary finishing oil, if preferred. When thoroughly dry, give it a coat of paste wax as well. Whatever you do, do it all over and, most importantly, do to all surfaces so that any change is equalized and you do not encourage cupping or warping. □

Project courtesy of *The Woodworker's Journal* magazine

Oak Barrister's Bookcase

The recent popularity of an old favorite, the barrister's bookcase, makes this a very current project.

Although these handsome cases once only served to hold books, they can also be used as display cases. The fact that they are enclosed keeps dust off treasures displayed inside. Oak is the traditional favorite for this piece.

The cases are basically a simple frame and panel construction. We incorporated a handy guide pin system that permits the glass doors to slide up into the case when they are

opened. For the door system to work and for the various component parts of the bookcase to fit easily together, we suggest taking extra care with all measurements and cuts to insure accuracy.

The three cabinet carcasses are identical. They are simply bolted together with the top and base then added to complete the bookcase.

Build the base first. Begin by ripping ¾ in. stock to size for parts A and B. Using a ¼ in. core box bit, rout the half-round cove detail. Then, with the band or saber saw, cut the 1 in. radius reveal in part A. Miter the base corners, cut the spline dadoes and splines, and assemble the base. As noted in the base detail, stop the spline groove ¾ in. from the top of the base.

Next, cut stock for the bottom and side panels (parts C, D, E, F, I, J, K and L), the remaining carcass parts (G, H, M, P and Q), the doors (R and S) and the top (W). The bottom panel parts and the top are 1 in. thick, while all the remaining panel and carcass parts are ¾ in. thick. Unless you have access to extra wide stock, it is necessary to glue up stock to form the panels and top.

Note that the front post (H) and the front stile of the side frames (I) are initially cut 1⅝ in. wide, as shown in Fig. A. The purpose of this is to allow sufficient stock to accurately miter these parts.

As shown in the illustration, the side frames and panels and the doors consist of mortise and tenon construction, while the bottom frames and panels feature a splined miter. Although the panel dadoes in both frames can be cut with the dado head, we suggest using a ¼ in. bearing guided wing cutter, with the frames temporarily dry-assembled. This results in a truer panel groove and an overall better fit for the panels.

When constructing the bottom frames and panels, note that in laying out the miters where part E meets part D the miter on part D must be started ¼ in. from the edge (Fig. C). This allows for the decorative moulding around the perimeter of the frame. Mill the decorative moulding with the router using a ¼ in. round over bit and a ½ in. V-groove bit. First mould one side with the round over, then flip the panel and mould the other side. Finally, cut the V-groove in the center.

The raised panels are sized to allow for expansion and contraction within the frames. A total of ½ in. (¼ in. on either side) across the panel's width and ⅛ in. (¹⁄₁₆ in. on either end) along the panel's length should accommodate any changes in humidity. When laying out the panel's raised profile (note in Fig. C and the corner detail), the distance from the raised profile to the edge is ¾ in. on the sides and ¹⁵⁄₁₆ in. on the ends.

Cut the raised profile using a ¾ in. core box bit. Also note that the profile depth on the side panels is ½ in., while the profile depth on the bottom panels (both sides raised) is ⅜ inch. After the frames and panels are assembled, center the panels with ¹⁄₁₆ in. pins to equalize whatever dimensional changes that may occur. Before assembling the door frames, cut the ⅜ in. by ½ in. rabbet to accept the door glass. Use either ⅜ in. square rippings or ¼ in. quarter round moulding, tacked in place to hold the glass.

Size the door to allow a little space between the front posts. Shape the front stretcher along its bottom edge with a

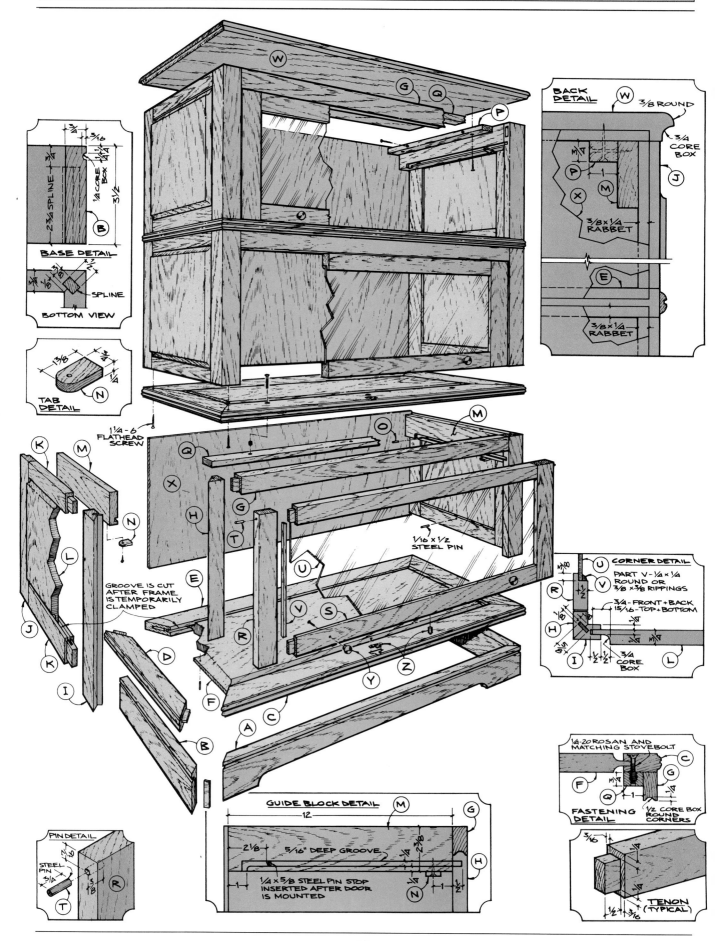

BACK DETAIL

W

3/8 ROUND

3/4 CORE BOX

3/4

P

M

X

J

3/8 × 1/4 RABBET

E

3/8 × 1/4 RABBET

3/4
3/16
3/4
1/4
1/2
2 3/4 SPLINE
1/4 CORE BOX
3 1/2
B

BASE DETAIL

3/4
1/8
3/16
SPLINE

BOTTOM VIEW

3/8
3/4
1/4
N

TAB DETAIL

W

G

Q

P

1 1/4 - 6 FLATHEAD SCREW

M

O

Q

X

H

G

T

U

1/16 × 1/2 STEEL PIN

K

M

N

L

E

GROOVE IS CUT AFTER FRAME IS TEMPORARILY CLAMPED

J

K

I

D

F

A

C

B

V

S

R

Y

Z

CORNER DETAIL

U

PART V - 1/4 × 1/4 ROUND OR 3/8 × 3/8 RIPPINGS

V

R

3/4 - FRONT + BACK 15/16 - TOP + BOTTOM

H

I

L

3/4 CORE BOX

PIN DETAIL

STEEL PIN 5/4

R

T

3/8

GUIDE BLOCK DETAIL

M

12

2 1/8

5/16" DEEP GROOVE

2 3/8

G

H

1

1/4 × 5/8 STEEL PIN STOP INSERTED AFTER DOOR IS MOUNTED

N

1/4 - 20 ROSAN AND MATCHING STOVEBOLT

C

G

F

Q

1/2 CORE BOX ROUND CORNERS

FASTENING DETAIL

3/16

TENON (TYPICAL)

1/2
3/16

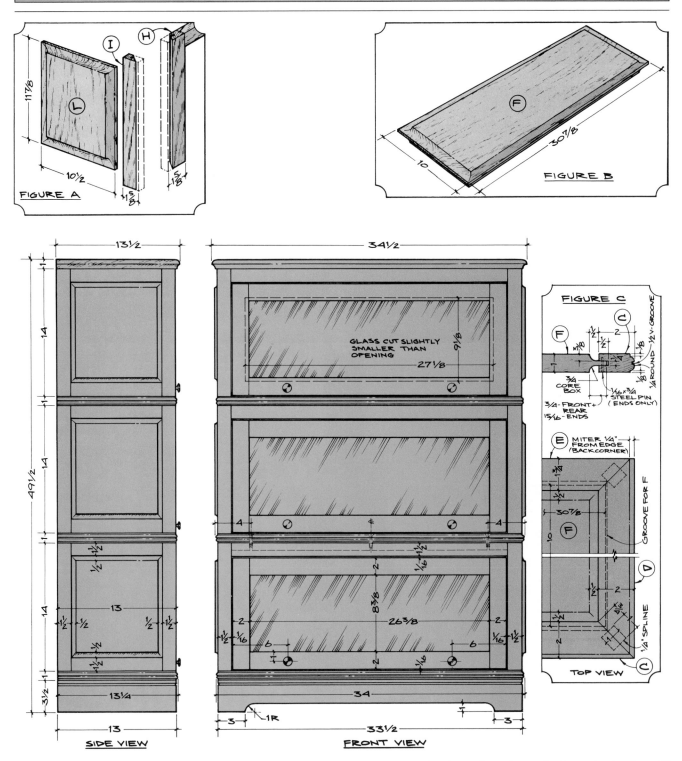

FIGURE A

FIGURE B

FIGURE C

GLASS CUT SLIGHTLY SMALLER THAN OPENING

SIDE VIEW

FRONT VIEW

TOP VIEW

½ in. core box bit to accommodate the action of the door. Drill for and insert the ¼ in. steel guide pins in the door as shown in the pin detail. The door works by tilting out at the bottom and then riding along the guide blocks up and into the cabinet. Rout the ¼ in. wide by ⁵⁄₁₆ in. deep groove into the guide blocks, and chisel the dog leg portion of the groove by hand, rounding the inside corner. Chisel the section of the groove that extends ½ in. into the front posts by hand *after* the guide block is glued to the carcass assembly. Drill the steel pin stop holes as shown in the guide block detail. Locate these

pins to stop the doors just short of where the knobs will contact the case front.

Build the bookcase in sections. First assemble the three carcasses. Each carcass consists of two sides, a bottom, posts and stretcher, guide blocks and inner stretcher. Join the side frame-and-panel and the front post-and-stretcher assembly with a full length splined miter. Glue all parts. Screw the bottom up into the front posts and side as shown in the illustration. It is important to countersink these screws. Fix the top onto the top section with screws through slotted holes

BILL OF MATERIALS — Oak Barrister's Bookcase

Finished Dimensions in Inches

A	Base Front	¾ x 3½ x 33½	1
B	Base Side	¾ x 3½ x 13	2
C	Bottom Panel Front	1 x 2 x 34	3
D	Bottom Panel Side	1 x 2 x 13¼	6
E	Bottom Panel Back	1 x 1¾ x 33½	3
F	Bottom Panel	1 x 10 x 30⅞	3
G	Front Stretcher	¾ x 1½ x 31½	3
H	Front Post	¾ x 1½ x 14*	6
I	Front Side Stile	¾ x 1½ x 14*	6
J	Back Side Stile	¾ x 1½ x 14	6
K	Side Rail	¾ x 1½ x 11	12
L	Side Panel	¾ x 10½ x 11⅞	6
M	Guide Block	¾ x 2⅜ x 12	6
N	Tab	¼ x ¾ x 1⅜	6
O	Dowel Stop	¼ x ⅝ steel rod	6
P	Cleat	¾ x 1 x 11	2
Q	Inner Stretcher	¾ x 1 x 30½	3
R	Door Stile	¾ x 2 x 12 ⅜	6
S	Door Rail	¾ x 2 x 27⅜	6
T	Guide Pin	¼ in. x ¾ in. steel rod	6
U	Glass	Cut to fit	3
V	Retainer	¼-¼ round or ⅜ in. sq. stock	as needed
W	Top	1 x 13½ x 34½	1
X	Back	¼ x 14¾ x 32¾ plywood	3
Y	Knob	1 in. diameter brass	6
Z	Bullet Catch	9/32 diameter	3

*H and I are rough cut 1⅝ in. wide (⅛ in. allowed for mitering).

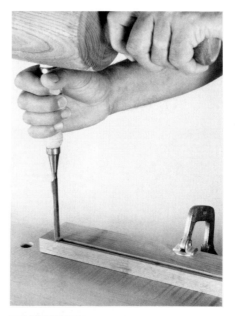

Figure 1. After routing the groove into the guide block (M), chisel the dog leg portion (shown) with a wood chisel. Round the inside corner. This allows the door to be inserted and removed.

in the cleats (P). Note that these cleats are only used with the top and are not used where the cabinet sections are joined. Make the decorative edge around the perimeter of the top using a ⅜ in. round over bit first to cut the radius and a ¾ in. core box bit to cut the cove.

Now assemble the sections. As shown in the fastening detail, join the sections with Rosan nuts and countersunk stove bolts. The advantage of this system is the ease of disassembly should you wish to add more sections in the future. Glue the base to the lower section.

Rabbet the section backs to accept the ¼ in. plywood back pieces (X) as shown in the back detail. These backs should be screwed but not glued in place (for ease of disassembly).

The tabs (N) are designed to hold the doors in place when the case is open. Mount the doors by tipping them into the cabinet, front side facing up. Fit the steel guide pins at the top end of the doors up into the grooves of the guide blocks. Lift the doors up past the tabs and then turn the tabs to lock the doors in place. Test the doors, and make adjustments if necessary so they operate smoothly. Add a bit of graphite on the pins and in the tracks to lubricate the guide system. Finally, insert the steel stop pins and mount the 1 in. brass knobs (Y).

Add the bullet catches (Z), to locate and fix the doors in place. Although the bullet part of the catch may be inserted in the doors when they are assembled, do not add the strike

Figure 2. Cut tenons on a table saw using a dado blade. Process workpieces having the same shoulder depth at one time. Smooth the tenon with a wood chisel.

until the doors are mounted and the exact strike position can be determined.

Finish the case with varnish, or for a more natural look simply rub in several coats of penetrating oil. □

Designed and built by Dennis Watson

Children's Circus Wagon

This is a great project for parent and child team building.

A simple, but functional project, this wagon is designed to hold wild, furry creatures. With a little help from a child the project can be a lot of fun to build.

Young children, of course, are just developing eye and hand coordination, and some tasks are difficult for them. One way to minimize frustration is to design and use jigs or fixtures which hold and align the parts or otherwise simplify the child's task. For example, when drilling the holes in the rails for the dowel bars, it would be difficult for a child to hold the rail in position, align the bit and drill the hole. However, a simple jig to hold the rail in place makes the job easy; he or she only needs to align the bit then drill the hole. Safety is of the utmost concern; the jig allows him or her to position the wood with the drill off, then with his or her hands, move safely away from the bit and drill the hole.

The construction of the circus wagon is pretty basic; the rail and stile construction of the side and end assemblies use a mortise and tenon joint. The side assembly is joined to the end assembly with a simple butt joint. Since the joint is mostly long grain to long grain, additional reinforcing with splines, dowels, etc., is not required.

We used red and white oak for the wagon, but most any hardwood or softwood will work just fine.

The first order of business is to rip the top rails 3 in. wide. Cut the side rails (A) 30 in. long and the end rails (B) 22½ in. long. Rip the bottom rails 4 in. wide and crosscut the side rails (C) and end rails (D) similar to the top rails. Rip the side stiles (E) 1½ in. wide and the end stiles (F) ¾ in. wide. Don't forget to allow 1½ in. extra length for the tenons.

It is best to cut the mortises first, then the tenons. There are numerous ways to cut the mortises, but use a router with a ¼ in. carbide straight cutter. A scrap piece of ¼ in. plywood clamped to the base serves as a guide. Feed the router so the cutter pulls the fence tightly against the workpiece; take several light cuts and the mortise will turn out perfect.

Tenons are easily cut on the table saw using the tenoning jig (see photo). Cut them just a hair oversize, then trim with a sharp chisel for a perfect fit. The tenons should be snug but not so tight you have to drive them in.

Up to now it has been pretty much an adult job, but now your child can start to help out. Clamp the four side rails together and lay out the location of the holes; center punch the holes. We used a brad point bit because it's easy to see the center of the bit and align the bit exactly over the center of the hole.

At what age should you allow your child to use the drill press? It depends, of course, on the maturity of the child. Some young children are mature enough to realize this is a potentially dangerous machine that must be treated with the utmost care; on the other hand, some teenagers are not mature enough. Allow your children to use some power tools but only under close supervision and obeying all the safety rules. There are, of course, some power tools such as the radial arm saw, table saw, jointer, etc. that children should never be allowed to use.

After drilling all the holes, chamfer each hole slightly to ease the dowels in place during assembly.

Expand the design for the top rail to full size then band saw to shape. Stay just to the outside of the line, finish up to

BILL OF MATERIALS — Children's Circus Wagon

Finished Dimensions in Inches

A	Top Side Rail	¾ x 3 x 30	2
B	Top End Rail	¾ x 3 x 22½	2
C	Bottom Side Rail	¾ x 4 x 30	2
D	Bottom End Rail	¾ x 4 x 22½	2
E	Side Stile	¾ x 1½ x 18½	4
F	End Stile	¾ x ¾ x 18½	4
G	Dowel Bar	⅜ x 18	28
H	Plywood Bottom	½ x 23¼ x 29¼	1
I	Dowel Axle	½ x 26½	2
J	Wheel	¾ x 8 x 8	4
K	Hub	¾ x 1¼ x 1¼	4
L	Handle Extension	¾ x 1½ x 21	1
M	Handle	¾ x 2 x 12	1
N	Bracket	¾ x 1½ x 7	1

the line and remove the saw marks with a round bottom spokeshave. A drum sander mounted in a hand drill or drill press finishes the job.

If you are going to paint the wagon as we did, it's a good idea to paint the bars (G) and the inside edges of the rails before assembly. Dry-assemble the sides and ends to make sure the joints pull up tight and all the dowels fit properly. Add glue, check for squareness and allow to dry overnight.

Run a ½ in. by ⅜ in. groove for the bottom (H). The groove runs the full length of the end assembly but should stop about ⅜ in. short on the side assembly.

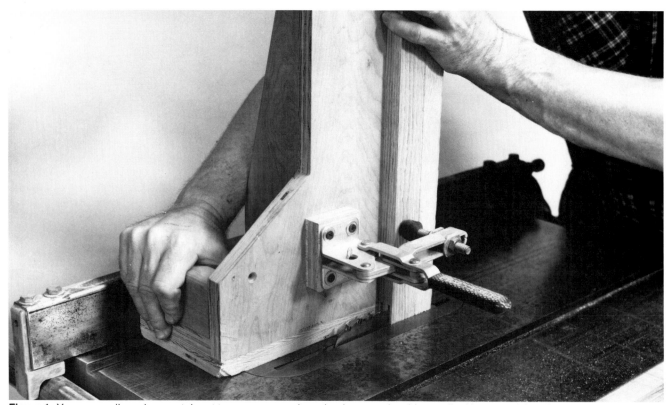

Figure 1. You can easily and accurately cut tenons on a purchased or homemade table saw jig. Here, a quick acting, over center clamp has been added which holds the work securely and speeds up the tenon-cutting process.

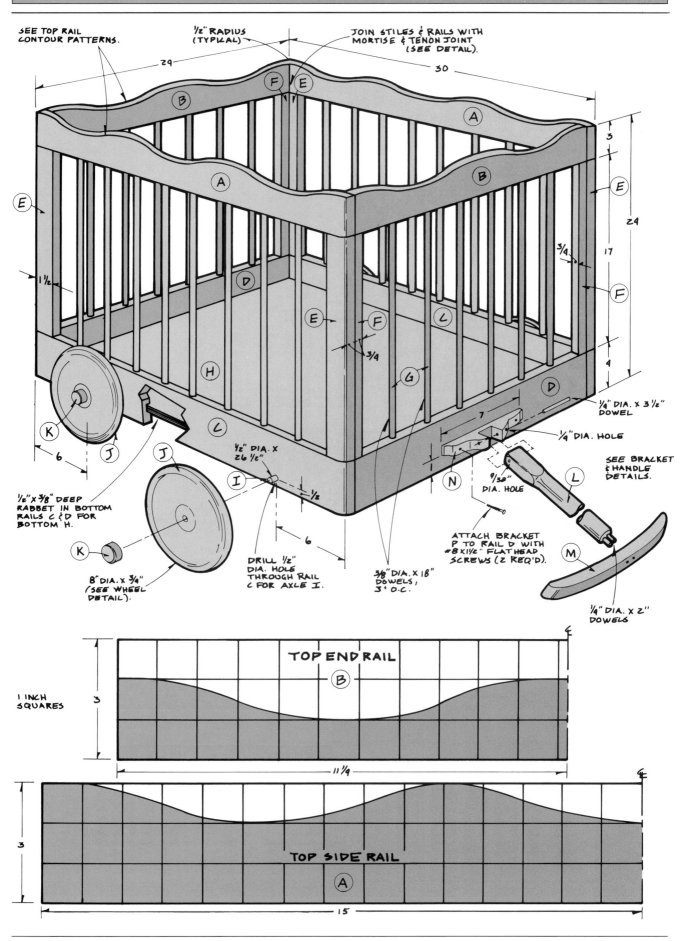

SEE TOP RAIL CONTOUR PATTERNS.

½" RADIUS (TYPICAL)

JOIN STILES & RAILS WITH MORTISE & TENON JOINT (SEE DETAIL).

29

30

3

24

17

¾

1½

¼" DIA. X 3½" DOWEL

¼" DIA. HOLE

7

SEE BRACKET & HANDLE DETAILS.

9/32" DIA. HOLE

½" DIA. X 26½"

DRILL ½" DIA. HOLE THROUGH RAIL C FOR AXLE I.

½" X ⅜" DEEP RABBET IN BOTTOM RAILS C & D FOR BOTTOM H.

8" DIA. X ¾" (SEE WHEEL DETAIL).

6

½

⅜" DIA. X 18" DOWELS, 3" O.C.

ATTACH BRACKET P TO RAIL D WITH #8 X 1½" FLATHEAD SCREWS (2 REQ'D).

¼" DIA. X 2" DOWELS

TOP END RAIL

B

1 INCH SQUARES

3

11¼

TOP SIDE RAIL

A

3

15

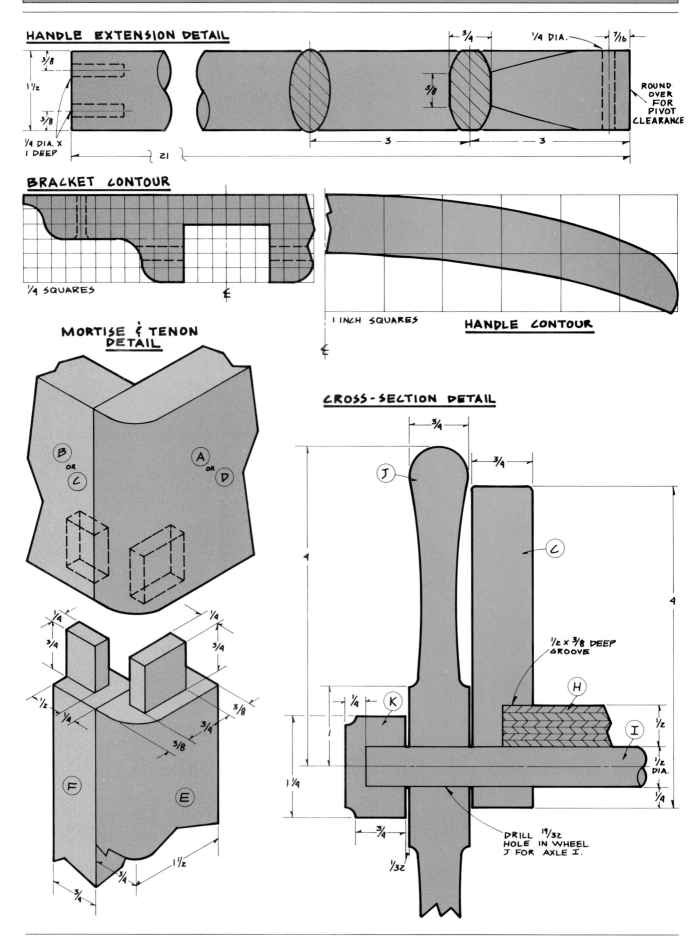

HANDLE EXTENSION DETAIL

3/8

1 1/2

3/8

1/4 DIA. X 1 DEEP

21

3/4

5/8

1/4 DIA.

7/16

ROUND OVER FOR PIVOT CLEARANCE

3

3

BRACKET CONTOUR

1/4 SQUARES

1 INCH SQUARES

HANDLE CONTOUR

MORTISE & TENON DETAIL

B or C

A or D

CROSS-SECTION DETAIL

3/4

3/4

J

L

4

4

1/2 X 3/8 DEEP GROOVE

H

1/4

K

I

1/2

1

1/2 DIA.

1 1/4

1/4

3/4

1/32

DRILL 19/32 HOLE IN WHEEL J FOR AXLE I.

1/4

3/4

1/4

3/4

1/2

1/4

3/8

3/8

3/4

F

E

1/2

3/4

1 1/2

3/4

Round over the top rails with a ¼ in. round over cutter with a pilot guide. On the inside of the sides, stop about 1 in. from the ends; finish rounding over the edge after assembly with a chisel and file.

Cut the plywood bottom to size and paint if desired. Dry-fit the wagon together to make sure all the joints pull up tight and the wagon is square. Add glue and allow to dry overnight.

We wanted to add a little decoration to the wheels (J) so we turned them on the lathe. Scoop out the front and back face of the wheel, leaving rounded edges on the outside and a small hub at the center. If you don't have a lathe, cut the wheel to shape on the band saw or with a saber saw, then round over the edges with a ⅜ in. round over cutter and pilot guide. Drill a ¹⁹/₃₂ in. hole for the ½ in. dowel axle (I). Again, we turned the hubs (K) on the lathe, but you could also band saw to size and run a cove around the outer edge with a router.

Lay out the location of the axle, then drill a ½ in. hole. Give the wagon a thorough sanding, check all pieces for splinters and round any sharp edges with sandpaper. Finish the wagon to suit your tastes, or more exactly, your child's taste. If you didn't turn the wheels, scooping out the front and back face, you'll want to add a washer between the wheel and the side of the wagon to prevent rubbing. Glue the hub to the axle. A piece of wax paper between the hub and wheel will prevent the wheels from becoming glued to the axle.

Expand the squared drawing for the handle bracket (N), then band saw to shape staying just to the outside of the line; finish up with a file or drum sander chucked in a drill.

Cut the handle extension (L) 1½ in. wide and 21 in. long. The extension is rectangular where it attaches to the bracket and transitions to an elliptical cross section at the handle. Roughly shape the extension with a drawknife or spokeshave, then finish up with a wood rasp or file.

Expand the squared drawing for the handle (M), then cut to shape. Attach the handle to the extension by drilling two ¼ in. holes through the handle into the extension, add glue

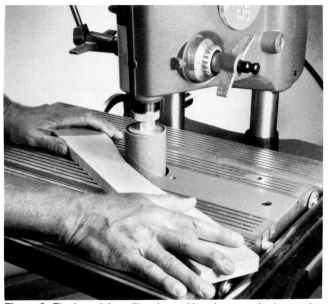

and drive two ¼ in. by 2 in. dowels in place. Trim the dowels then round over the edges with a ¼ in. round over cutter.

Paint the bracket, extension and handle, then drill a ¼ in. hole through the bracket and the extension. Redrill the extension with a ⁹/₃₂ in. bit to allow the handle to turn easily. Drive the dowel pin home (a little glue may be required on one end), then screw the handle assembly to the wagon using two No. 8 by 1½ in. flathead brass screws. Fill with stuffed animals and you are ready for the ringmaster. □

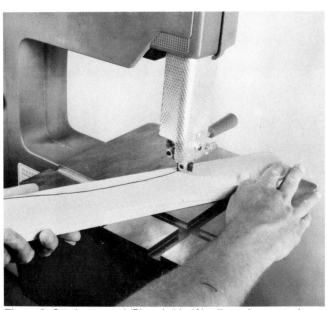

Figure 2. Cut the top end (B) and side (A) rails to shape, staying just to the outside of the line. Remove the saw marks and finish up to the line with a spokeshave or rasp.

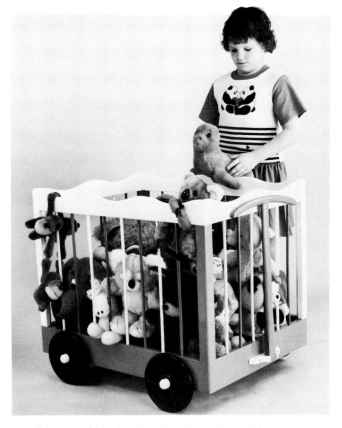

Figure 3. Final sand the rail's edges with a drum sander inserted in a drill press or drill guide. Move the wood from right to left past the sander.

Project designed and built by George Campbell

Contemporary Quilt Rack

Built entirely without metal fasteners and finished with hand-rubbed tung oil, the rack is an ideal weekend project.

Whether you use this oak quilt rack to store an heirloom quilt or just to hang up extra bedding, its simple lines complement any bedroom decor.

The quilt rack utilizes wood pins and half-lap joints for the majority of its construction. Start by ripping quality oak stock to a width of 2 inches. You need 13 ft. of this material.

Next, cut the oak to length. You get the most out of the wood by cutting the 45 degree miters for two pieces at once.

Lay out the 1 in. radius curves on the ends of parts A and C; cut these with a saber saw. Clamp these components together, and use a sanding disk to smooth the rounded ends.

Locate and drill the 1 in. diameter holes in the upper arms (C). Use a back-up board to prevent splintering the wood.

Now place the components of each side together as they will be after assembly, and mark pencil lines where the parts intersect.

Use a dado blade in your table or radial arm saw to form the rabbets for the half-lap joints. Measure your stock's thickness accurately, and make the rabbets exactly half that deep. Test the accuracy of your setup with scrap before working on the actual components.

While the dado blade is still in place, mill the notches in the uprights (B) for the brace (D).

Assemble the two side frames using yellow carpenter's glue. Clamp the assemblies well, and allow the frames to dry. After the glue dries, lay out and drill ¼ in. holes through the

BILL OF MATERIALS — Contemporary Quilt Rack

Finished Dimensions in Inches

A	Base	¾ x 2 x 14 oak	2
B	Upright	¾ x 2 x 24 oak	2
C	Upper Arm	¾ x 2 x 20 oak	2
D	Brace	¾ x 2 x 30 oak	1
E	Quilt Bars	1 in. dia. x 30 oak dowel	3
F	Pins	¼ in. dia. x ⅞ birch dowel	16
G	Pins	¼ in. dia. x 1¾ birch dowel	10

Figure 1. Use a stationary disk sander to smooth the rounded, mating ends (cut with a saber saw) of parts A and C. Rotate the workpiece clockwise. Work to the cutting line. Make sure to wear eye protection, and avoid wearing loose fitting clothes or items that can get easily caught.

Figure 2. Secure the long dowels to the quilt rack's frame with glue and inserted dowel pins. Tap the pins in and sand flush.

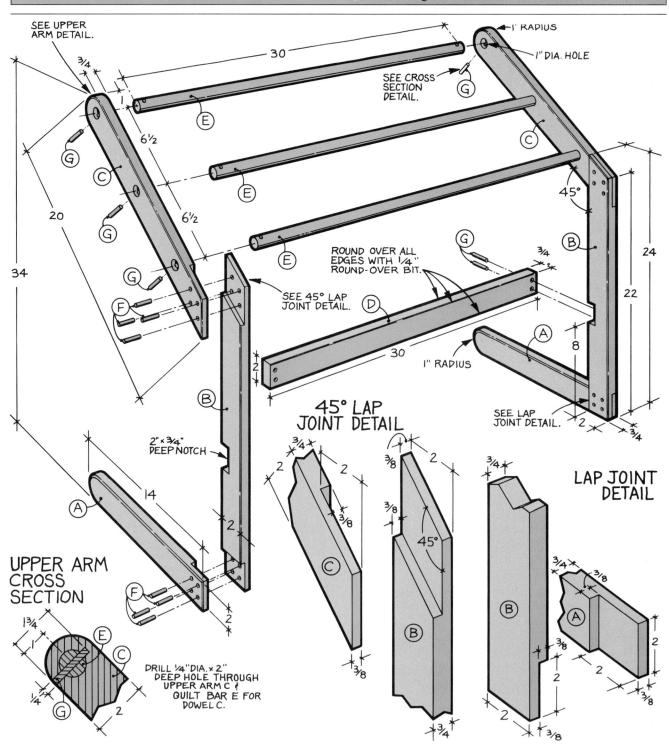

SEE UPPER
ARM DETAIL.

¾

30

1" RADIUS

1" DIA. HOLE

SEE CROSS
SECTION
DETAIL.

G

E

6½

C

G

C

6½

20

G

E

45°

B

24

G

34

E

¾

22

ROUND OVER ALL
EDGES WITH ¼"
ROUND-OVER BIT.

G

G

D

2

SEE 45° LAP
JOINT DETAIL.

F

B

A

30

8

2" × ¾"
DEEP NOTCH

B

1" RADIUS

SEE LAP
JOINT DETAIL.

2

¾

45° LAP JOINT DETAIL

¾

2

2

3⁄8

2

3⁄8

3⁄8

3⁄8

45°

LAP JOINT DETAIL

¾

¾

3⁄8

14

A

2

C

B

B

A

2

UPPER ARM CROSS SECTION

1¾

1

E

C

¼

1¼

G

2

3⁄8

2

2

2

3⁄4

2

3⁄8

3⁄8

F

2

DRILL ¼"DIA.× 2"
DEEP HOLE THROUGH
UPPER ARM C &
QUILT BAR E FOR
DOWEL C.

joints for the strengthening dowel pins. Cut ⅞ in. long pins from a ¼ in. diameter birch dowel. Apply a thin film of glue to each dowel. Drive these through the pre-drilled holes. Leave the pins slightly proud of the surface on both sides.

Give the frames a preliminary sanding with a belt sander to level the dowel pins. Round over the edges of the frames with a ¼ in. ball bearing guided round over bit.

Install the brace (D) and the quilt bar (E), gluing them in place. Square up the assembly, and clamp the brace joint.

Once the glue has dried, drill ¼ in. diameter holes 1¾ in. deep for dowel pins as shown in the diagram. As you did

before, apply a thin layer of glue to each pin before driving it in place.

Round over the edges of the brace (D) with your router, finishing the corners with a rasp.

Give the entire assembly a thorough sanding, working down to 150 grit sandpaper; apply a coat of stain. We used ZAR Spanish Oak stain.

Once the stain has dried, apply two coats of Hope's 100% Tung Oil. Allow 24 hours between finish coats, and carefully rub the piece down with extra fine sandpaper before applying the second coat. □

Designed and built by Dennis Watson and courtesy of *The Family Handyman*

European-Style Workbench

Whatever your woodworking skill, you'll enjoy creating on a workbench with quality vises and conveniently organized tool storage.

The project looks rather formidable, but we've simplified construction by using a readily available laminated top which can be obtained locally at a kitchen or cutlery store. The vises are simply screwed to the top, requiring only a handle and a wood face.

The workbench is really two projects: the bench can be made first, followed by the tool cabinet, which fits on the lower rails of the bench. If you should ever need to move it, we've designed it so you can easily do so. The top is screwed to the base and the base itself is bolted together.

Workbench Construction

Select 1⅞ in. hard maple and rip the legs (A), upper arms and feet (B) and upper rails (C) 2¾ in. wide and lower rails (D) 2½ in. wide.

Cut a ½ in. wide mortise in the upper arms and feet for the legs, and cut the mortise about 1⅝ in. deep to allow room for excess glue. Now cut the matching tenon in the legs a little

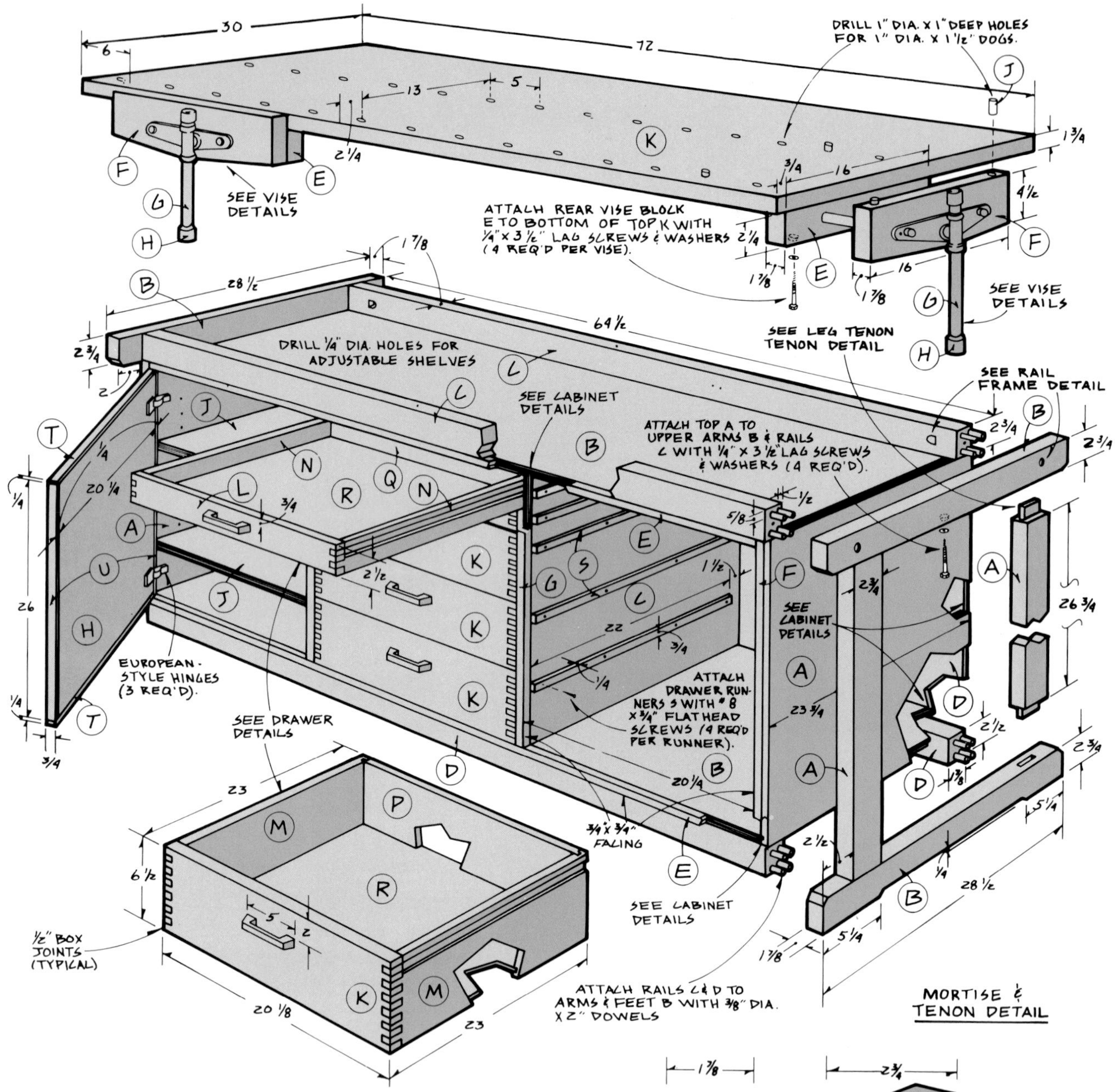

30
6
72
13
5
2 1/4
DRILL 1" DIA. X 1" DEEP HOLES FOR 1" DIA. X 1 1/2" DOGS.
1 3/4
3/4
16
4 1/2
SEE VISE DETAILS
ATTACH REAR VISE BLOCK E TO BOTTOM OF TOP K WITH 1/4" X 3 1/2" LAG SCREWS & WASHERS (4 REQ'D PER VISE).
2 1/4
1 7/8
16
SEE VISE DETAILS
1 7/8
28 1/2
64 1/2
2 3/4
2
DRILL 1/4" DIA. HOLES FOR ADJUSTABLE SHELVES
SEE LEG TENON TENON DETAIL
SEE RAIL FRAME DETAIL
SEE CABINET DETAILS
ATTACH TOP A TO UPPER ARMS B & RAILS C WITH 1/4" X 3 1/2" LAG SCREWS & WASHERS (4 REQ'D).
2 3/4
1/2
5/8
3/4
20 1/4
1/4
2 1/2
1 1/2
22
3/4
1/4
2 3/4
26 3/4
SEE CABINET DETAILS
26
EUROPEAN-STYLE HINGES (3 REQ'D).
ATTACH DRAWER RUNNERS S WITH #8 X 3/4" FLATHEAD SCREWS (4 REQ'D PER RUNNER).
23 3/4
2 1/2
2 3/4
1/4
3/4
SEE DRAWER DETAILS
20 1/4
3/4" X 3/4" FACING
1 7/8
5 1/4
2 1/2
1/4
28 1/2
23
6 1/2
5
2
1/2" BOX JOINTS (TYPICAL)
SEE CABINET DETAILS
1 7/8
5 1/4
ATTACH RAILS C & D TO ARMS & FEET B WITH 3/8" DIA. X 2" DOWELS
20 1/8
23
A B C D E F G H J K L M N P Q R S T U

MORTISE & TENON DETAIL

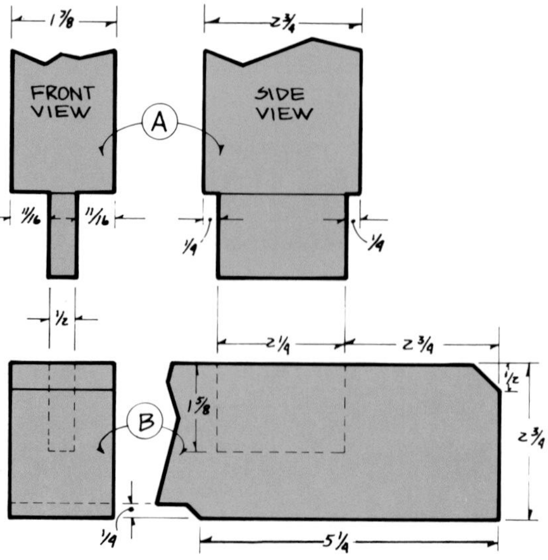

1 7/8
2 3/4
FRONT VIEW
SIDE VIEW
A
11/16
11/16
1/4
1/4
1/2
2 1/4
2 3/4
1/2
1 5/8
B
2 3/4
1/4
5 1/4

RAIL FRAME DETAIL

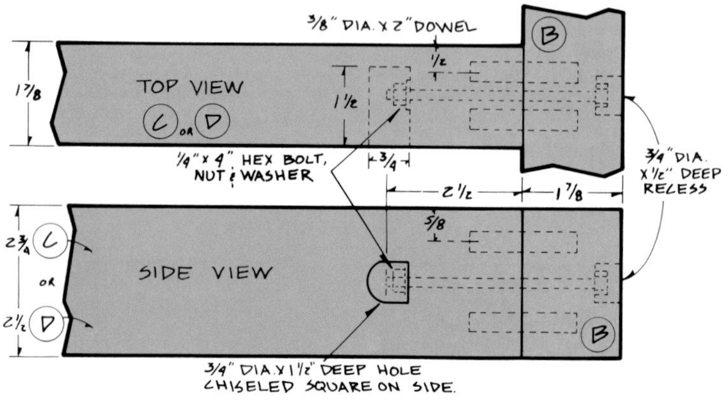

3/8" DIA. X 2" DOWEL
B
1/2
1 7/8
1 1/2
TOP VIEW
C OR D
1/4" X 4" HEX BOLT, NUT & WASHER
3/4
2 1/2
1 7/8
3/4" DIA. X 1/2" DEEP RECESS
5/8
2 3/4 C
OR
2 1/2 D
SIDE VIEW
B
3/4" DIA. X 1 1/2" DEEP HOLE CHISELED SQUARE ON SIDE.

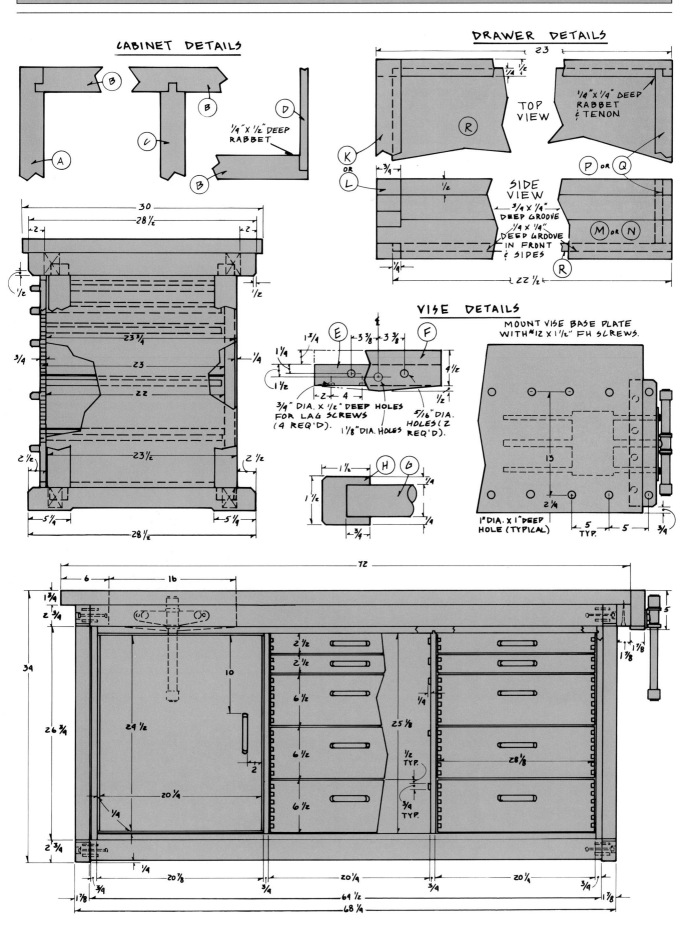

CABINET DETAILS

DRAWER DETAILS

TOP VIEW

SIDE VIEW

¼" X ½" DEEP RABBET

¼"X ¼" DEEP RABBET & TENON

¾ X ¼ DEEP GROOVE

¼ X ¼ DEEP GROOVE IN FRONT & SIDES

VISE DETAILS

MOUNT VISE BASE PLATE WITH #12 X 1½" FH SCREWS.

¾" DIA. X ½" DEEP HOLES FOR LAG SCREWS (4 REQ'D).

1⅛"DIA. HOLES.

5/16" DIA. HOLES (2 REQ'D).

1"DIA. X 1"DEEP HOLE (TYPICAL)

fat and trim to a snug fit with a sharp chisel. Dry-fit the legs, upper arm, and foot together, making sure the joint pulls up tight. Sand the inside parts of the frame, cut the relief in the foot and chamfer the upper arm and foot. Glue and clamp the frame together making sure it is square.

The rails (C, D) are doweled to the end frame using four ⅜ in. by 2 in. dowels in each end. The dowels are glued to the rails, but not to the end frame, which allows for disassembly. The dowel joint is pulled tightly against the frame using a ¼ in. by 4 in. hex bolt.

First drill a ¾ in. hole, ½ in. deep in the end frame. Then drill a 5/16 in. hole through the frame into the end rail. Next drill a ¾ in. hole into the inside of the rail, intersecting the

BILL OF MATERIALS — European-Style Workbench

Finished Dimensions in Inches

Cabinet

A	Side	¾ x 23¾ x 26⅝ birch plywood	2
B	Top and Bottom	¾ x 23¾ x 63⅜ fir plywood	2
C	Divider	¾ x 23½ x 25⅝ fir plywood	2
D	Back	¼ x 26⅛ x 63⅞ fir plywood	1
E	Top and Bottom Facing	¾ x ¾ x 62⅞ maple	2
F	Side Facing	¾ x ¾ x 26⅝ maple	2
G	Divider Facing	¾ x ¾ x 25⅛ maple	2
H	Door	¾ x 20¼ x 26 birch plywood	1
J	Shelf	¾ x 23½ x 20¾ fir plywood	2
K	Drawer Front	¾ x 6½ x 20⅛ maple	6
L	Drawer Side	¾ x 2½ x 20⅛ maple	4
M	Drawer Front	½ x 6½ x 23 maple	12
N	Drawer Side	½ x 2½ x 23 maple	8
P	Drawer Back	½ x 6 x 19⅝ maple	6
Q	Drawer Back	½ x 2 x 19⅝ maple	4
R	Drawer Bottom	¼ x 19⅝ x 22¼ fir plywood	10
S	Drawer Runner	¼ x ¾ x 22 maple	20
T	Door Border, Top & Bottom	¼ x ¾ x 20¾ maple	2
U	Door Border, Side	¼ x ¾ x 24⅝ maple	2

Workbench

A	Leg	1⅞ x 2¾ x 29¾ maple	4
B	Foot and Upper Arm	1⅞ x 2¾ x 28½ maple	4
C	Upper Rail	1⅞ x 2¾ x 64½ maple	4
D	Lower Rail	1⅞ x 2½ x 64½ maple	2
E	Rear Vise Block	1⅞ x 2¾ x 16 maple	2
F	Front Vise Block	1⅞ x 16 maple	2
F	Front Vise Block	1⅞ x 5 x 16 maple	2
G	Handle	1 x 12 hardwood dowel	2
H	End Cap	1½ dia. x 1½ walnut	4
J	Bench Dog	1 x 1½ hardwood dowel	4
K	Top	1¾ x 30 x 72 laminated maple	1

5/16 in hole. Square up the face to provide a surface for the nut and washer to pull up tight against.

You can glue the material for the top and plane to 1¾ in. thick, or you can take the easy way out as we did and purchase the top. The type we selected, a laminated butcher block table top, is quite popular. The top (K) is attached to the base with four ¼ in. by 3½ in. lag screws through the upper arm (B) and top rail (C).

The vises are the real heart of any bench. Recently, a shoulder vise has been developed with a quick-release, a vast improvement. You simply slide the vise up against the work, then tighten the screw.

To install the vise, turn the top over and screw the rear vise block (E) to the top with ¼ in. by 3½ in. lag screws. Drill two 15/16 in. holes for the guide bar and a 1⅛ in. hole for the rear vise block. Screw the vise base plate into the top with No. 12 by 1½ in. flathead screws. Now turn the top over, mark the location of the three holes in the upper arm and drill them ⅛ in. larger than the corresponding holes in the rear vise block.

Screw the top to the base, slide the vise in place and trace around the steel bushing plates. Rout a recess and screw the bushing in place with No. 12 by 1½ in. flathead screws. Drill the front vise block (F) and attach to the vise with No. 12 by 1½ in. flathead screws. A 1 in. hardwood dowel (G) with walnut end caps (H) turned on the lathe finishes the vise. An alternate vise can be similarly installed with a slight modification to the size and location of the holes.

The bench dogs (J) are made from a 1 in. hardwood dowel, 1½ in. long. Drill 1 in. dia. holes in the front vise block and also in the top on 5 in. centers.

Tool Cabinet Construction

Rip the sides (A) 23¾ in. wide from birch plywood and the top and bottom (B) from fir plywood. Rip the dividers (C) 23½ in. wide from fir plywood.

The sides are joined to the top and bottom using a dado-rabbet joint, which is easily cut on the table saw or radial arm saw with a ¼ in. dado blade. Run a ¼ in. by ¼ in. groove in the top and bottom for the dividers and a ½ in. by ¼ in. rabbet in the top, bottom and sides for the ¼ in. plywood back (D). Dry-assemble the carcass to insure all the joints pull up tight and the carcass is square. Add glue and nail together. Use the back to help keep the carcass square during assembly.

The raw plywood edges are covered with a ¾ in. by ¾ in. maple facing. Cut the side facing (F) to length and glue and nail in place, followed by the top and bottom facing (E), then the divider (G). Nail the back in place using nail brads.

The drawers use a box joint which is extremely strong, relatively easy to cut on the table saw with a ½ in. dado blade and attractive to boot. Rip the fronts (K, M) from ¾ in. maple and the sides (L, N) and backs (P, Q) from ½ in. maple, then cut to length. The key to a good fit on box joints is the jig, so take a little extra time in setting it up (see photos). Make a few sample cuts in scrap wood, and when you're satisfied, cut the drawer fronts and sides. The back is joined to the sides with a rabbet-dado joint, so run a ¼ in. by ¼ in. groove in the sides and a corresponding rabbet in the back. Run a ¼ in. by ¾ in. groove in the sides for the drawer runner; stop the groove ¾ in. from the front. After assembly, clear out the

Figure 1. Make a box joint jig from scrap plywood screwed to the miter gauge. Cut two slots, ½ in. wide, spaced ½ in. apart. Cut the guide pin to fit snugly inside the slot.

groove to provide a square face which acts as a drawer stop. Run a ¼ in. by ¼ in. groove for the ¼ in. plywood bottom (R) in the sides and front. Dry-fit the drawers, then add glue and clamp. Use the bottom to keep the drawer square.

Screw the drawer runners (S) to the sides and divider with No. 8 by ¾ in. flathead screws. If the drawers do not run smoothly, you can plane a little off the runner or shim it out with cardboard as required.

The door (H) is cut from ¾ in. birch plywood with a ¼ in. by ¾ in. maple border (T, U) glued on. Trim the door to fit the opening, then install the hinges. We used three fully

concealed European-style hinges made by the Blum Corporation. With the hinges installed, trim the door to allow about a ¹⁄₁₆ in. clearance all around.

Cut the adjustable shelves (J) from fir plywood and drill ¼ in. holes for the supports.

Give the project a thorough sanding. Install a catch for the door and the pulls.

The European-style workbench was finished with two coats of Watco Natural Danish Oil. An oil finish was used because it is easily repaired. A few coats of paste wax on the top will help prevent glue or paint from sticking. □

Figure 2. Make the first cut by sliding the workpiece against the guide pin. For additional cuts, place the workpiece's slot over the guide pin for spacing. Follow this same technique for cutting all finger joints.

Project courtesy of *The Woodworker's Journal* magazine

Pine Hutch/Cupboard

This hutch/cupboard has a Colonial flavor as well as elements of the Pennsylvania Dutch and Chippendale styles.

Ornamentation is kept to a minimum and the clean lines result in an appearance that looks good in just about any dining room, from Colonial to contemporary. For versatility, this piece is designed so you have the option of making only the base, which stands alone well as a handsome cupboard. Our cabinet is built in pine but can be built from cherry or a figured maple.

As you will note from the bill of materials, almost the entire cabinet (except the drawers) is crafted from ¾ in. thick material. If you want to avoid the edge-gluing required to obtain the stock width necessary for the wider parts, consider buying glued-up ¾ in. pine. Sold in 24 in. widths, it is available at many building supply retailers.

Construct the Base Unit

Cut the sides (A), then use the dado head to make the ⅜ in. deep by ¾ in. wide grooves that accept the bottom (B) and the shelves (L). Square the stopped end of the shelf groove with a wood chisel, and use the dado head to cut the ⅜ in. by ¾ in. rabbet across the top end and the ¼ in. by ½ in. rabbet along the back edge of the sides. Notch the sides as shown in the side view to provide a reveal for the base moulding, and cut the ⅜ in. by ¾ in. by 1½ in. notches for the lower

stretchers (G and H). Make the bottom, notching it to accept the spacers (I). Use the dado head to cut the ¼ in. by ¾ in. groove that accepts the divider (C), squaring the stopped end of the groove with a wood chisel.

Make the divider using the dado head to cut the ¼ in. by ¾ in. grooves for the shelves. Next, cut the ½ in. deep by 7¾ in. long notch in the front edge of the divider as shown in Fig. 1. Cut a ¾ in. deep notch along the back edge to accept the correspondingly notched back lower stretcher (H), and make a ¾ in. by 1½ in. notch at the top back edge to accommodate part E.

Cut the back upper stretcher (E) to length and width; it is not notched. Notch the front upper stretcher (D) and front lower stretcher (G) in the same manner as one another to accept the divider (C) and the face piece (K). These notches in parts D and G are actually mirror images of each other. Cut a ¾ in. by ¾ in. notch into the back lower stretcher (H) to mate with the identically notched divider. Fig. 1 should help you visualize the joinery for all these parts and for the face piece (K), which is made next. Also notch G as shown in the exploded view to accept part I.

Now make the spacers (I), which serve to separate the cupboard doors. Note that the ends of parts I have ⅜ in. by ¾ in. notches to fit the similarly notched bottom (B) and front lower stretcher (G). Cut a ¾ in. by ¾ in. notch at the center point of parts I to accept the shelves (L), which can also be cut to length and width. Also make the short cleats (F) and long cleats (J).

Now fashion the front and side base mouldings (M and N). You need about 8 feet of ¾ in. by 4½ in. wide stock. First, use either the moulding head cutter in the table saw or a bearing guided ½ in. cove cutter in the router to make the ½ in. cove as shown in the moulding detail. Next, after rough cutting to length, miter the front ends of parts N and both ends of part M. Finally, lay out the grids (see side and front view) on parts M and N, band saw or jigsaw the illustrated profiles and sand smooth.

Cut the base top (O) to 19⅝ in. by 49¼ in., and use either the table saw moulding head cutter or router to apply the ¼ in. Roman ogee (see moulding detail) to the front and side edges. Form the back (P) from a 30½ in. by 47½ in. section of ¼ in. plywood. Make the drawer guides (Q) when you make the drawers.

Now assemble the base unit carcass using glue and/or screws throughout. Counterbore all visible exterior screws. Do not glue the side base moulding, but mount with screws inserted through slotted holes in the sides (as illustrated in the exploded view). This allows the sides to expand and contract in relation to the side base moulding. Secure the top in place with screws driven up through parts D and E and through the short cleats (F), which are screwed into the sides. Take special care with the joinery of parts D, G, I and K because these parts must be mated accurately to achieve the flush look across the front. Allow any glue squeeze-out to dry before scraping off. Make a dry test-fitting of all parts before final assembly.

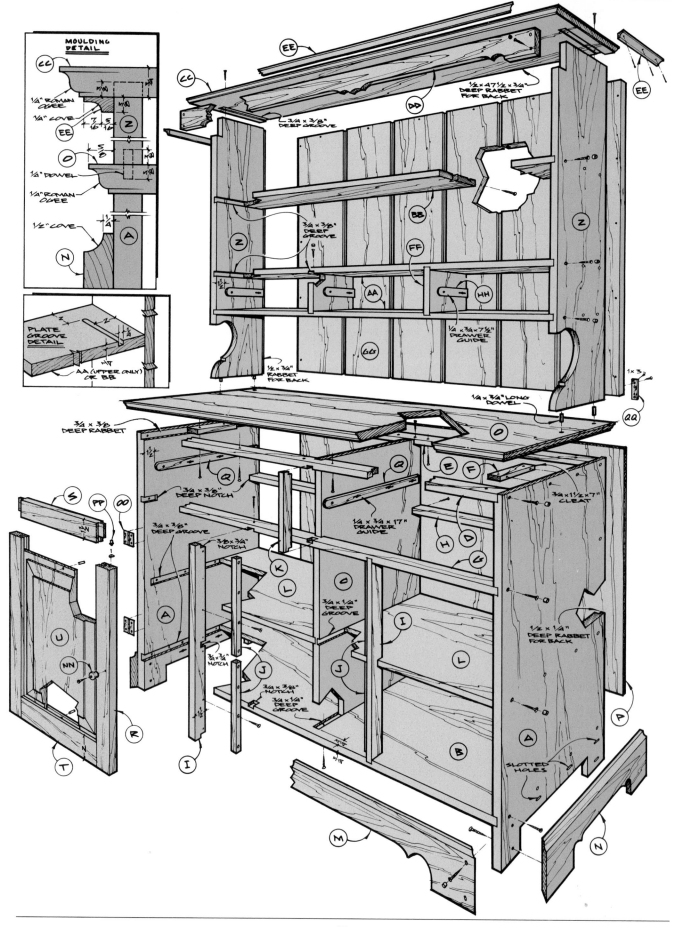

MOULDING DETAIL

1/4" ROMAN OGEE

1/4" COVE

EE

O

1/8" DOWEL

1/4" ROMAN OGEE

1/2" COVE

A

N

PLATE GROOVE DETAIL

AA (UPPER ONLY) OR BB

CC

CC

EE

EE

1/2 x 47 1/2 x 3/4" DEEP RABBET FOR BACK

DD

3/4 x 3/8" DEEP GROOVE

Z

Z

BB

3/4 x 3/8" DEEP GROOVE

FF

1 1/2"

AA

HH

1/4 x 3/4 x 7 1/2" DRAWER GUIDE

GG

1/2 x 3/4" RABBET FOR BACK

1 x 3"

QQ

1/4 x 3/4" LONG DOWEL

3/4 x 3/8 DEEP RABBET

O

Q

Q

E

F

1 1/2"

3/4 x 3/8" DEEP NOTCH

3/8 x 3/4" NOTCH

1/4 x 3/4 x 17" DRAWER GUIDE

3/4 x 11/2 x 7" CLEAT

S

PP

OO

3/4 x 3/8" DEEP GROOVE

H

D

G

K

L

O

3/4 x 1/4" DEEP GROOVE

I

U

A

3/4 x 3/4" NOTCH

J

J

L

1/2 x 1/4" DEEP RABBET FOR BACK

P

NN

3/4 x 3/8" NOTCH

3/4 x 1/4" DEEP GROOVE

A

R

1 1/2"

I

1/4"

1/4"

B

SLOTTED HOLES

T

I

M

N

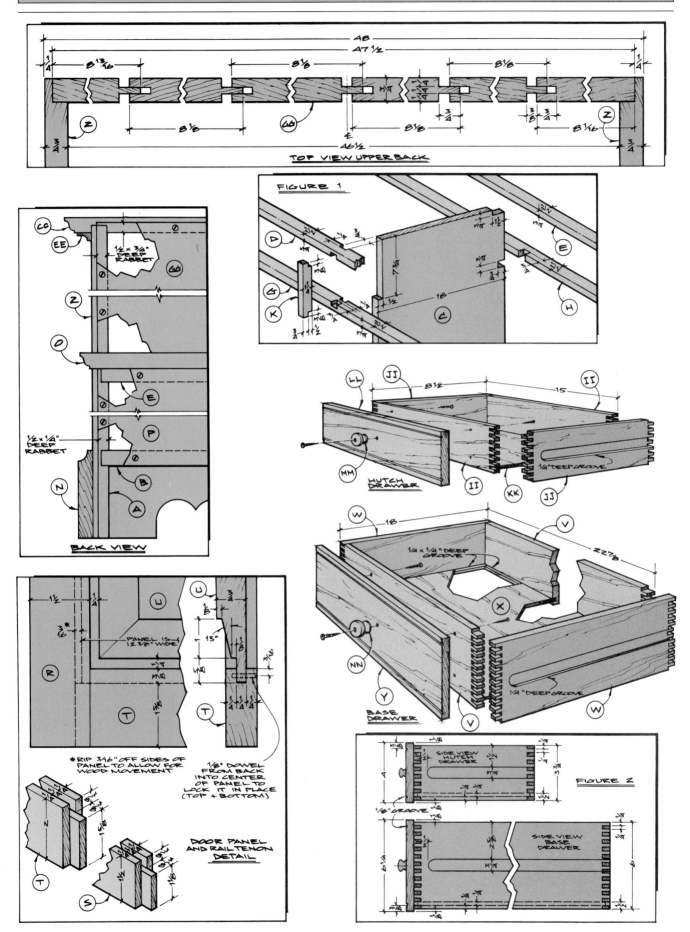

TOP VIEW UPPER BACK

FIGURE 1

BACK VIEW

HUTCH DRAWER

BASE DRAWER

½ x ¾" DEEP RABBET

½ x ¼" DEEP RABBET

*RIP 3/16" OFF SIDES OF PANEL TO ALLOW FOR WOOD MOVEMENT

PANEL IS 12 3/8" WIDE

1/8" DOWEL FROM BACK INTO CENTER OF PANEL TO LOCK IT IN PLACE (TOP + BOTTOM)

DOOR PANEL AND RAIL TENON DETAIL

SIDE VIEW HUTCH DRAWER

SIDE VIEW BASE DRAWER

FIGURE 2

¼ "DEEP GROOVE

¼ x ¼" DEEP GROOVE

1/8" GROOVE

Next, make the three doors. The two outside doors are working while the center door is fixed permanently. Tenon the rails (S and T) as shown in the door panel and rail tenon detail. Note that the top rail is 1½ in. wide, while the bottom rail is 2 in. wide. Use the dado head to cut the ¼ in. wide by ⅜ in. deep grooves that run the length of both the rails and the stiles (R). As shown in the exploded view, the ends of these grooves in the stiles serve as the mortises to accept the rail tenons.

Cut the raised panels (U) on a table saw, shaper or router using a panel raising bit. If you use the table saw, raise the blade to 1⅝ in., and set it at 13 degrees to establish the raised profile. Because the stock is passed through on edge, a fence extension is strongly recommended. Next, use the dado head to cut the ⅝ in. wide step at the edge. Clean the top of the raised edge to square it and remove any hair. Note from the door panel detail that the 12⅜ in. wide by 19⅛ in. long panels are sized to allow 3/16 in. on either side and 1/16 in. on either end for expansion. Fix the panels at the center point, both top and bottom, with ⅛ in. dowel pins to equalize panel movement. Do not glue the panels in place. Also, do not mount the doors yet.

Next, construct the base drawers, consisting of parts V, W, X and Y. Cut the box or finger joints (see Fig. 2 for finger joint layout). Then cut the ¼ in. by ¼ in. groove in the ½ in. thick front, back and sides to accept the ¼ in. thick plywood drawer bottom. Assemble the drawer carcass around the bottom using glue throughout. When dry, use the router and a straight bit to cut the ¼ in. deep by ¾ in. wide by 17 in. long grooves in the sides to accept the drawer guides (Q). Cut the drawer faces (Y) to length and width from ½ in. stock, and use the router equipped with a ⅛ in. veining bit to cut the ⅛ in. detail (Fig. 2).

Drill several oversize holes through the drawer front and temporarily screw the faces in place. As shown in Fig. 2, position the face so there is a ⅛ in. lip at both top and bottom. The oversized holes accommodate some adjustment of the drawer faces to fit the openings after mounting the drawers.

At this time make the drawer guides (Q). The guides must be positioned so that they both support the drawers (the drawers ride level and do not contact any of the stretchers) and act as stops (the drawers do not hit the plywood back (P)). We dimensioned the drawers to leave about ¼ in. space between the drawers and the plywood back. Position and mount the drawer guides, fixing their front ends first. The guides' slotted holes permit expansion in the center divider toward the back. This construction helps to keep the drawer faces flush with the front of the cabinet as the carcass

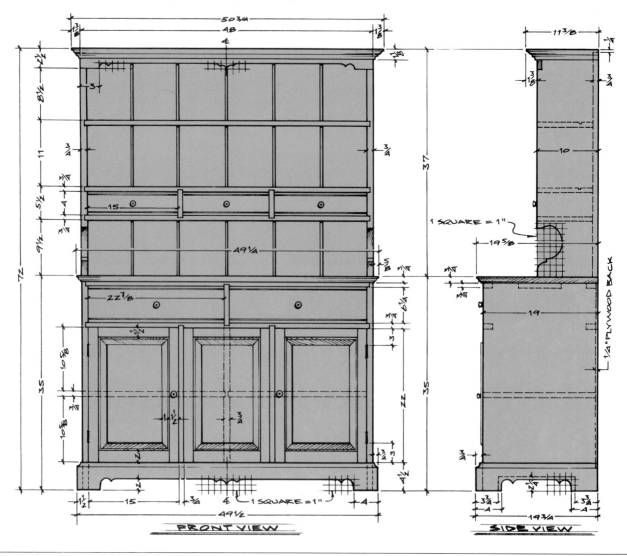

FRONT VIEW   SIDE VIEW

Figure 3. Make cove moulding (EE) by first cutting the cove on the edge of a wide board. Then rip the board to width on your table saw as shown. This method takes a bit longer to set up but eliminates dangerous kickback when thin strips bind between the blade and fence.

Figure 4. Here a panel raising bit is used to cut the door panels (U) on an overhead router. Notice that the steps that fit into the stiles and rails are already cut.

BILL OF MATERIALS — Pine Hutch/Cupboard

Finished Dimensions in Inches

Base Unit

A	Side	3/4 x 19 x 34 1/4	2
B	Bottom	3/4 x 18 3/4 x 47 1/4	1
C	Divider	3/4 x 18 x 30	1
D	Front Upper Stretcher	3/4 x 1 1/2 x 47 1/4	1
E	Back Upper Stretcher	3/4 x 1 1/2 x 47 1/4	1
F	Short Cleat	3/4 x 1 1/2 x 7	2
G	Front Lower Stretcher	3/4 x 1 1/2 x 47 1/4	1
H	Back Lower Stretcher	3/4 x 1 1/2 x 47 1/4	1
I	Spacer	3/4 x 1 1/2 x 22 3/4	2
J	Long Cleat	3/4 x 3/4 x 10 5/8	4
K	Face Piece	3/4 x 1 1/4 x 7	1
L	Shelf	3/4 x 18 x 23 1/2	2
M	Base Moulding, Front	3/4 x 4 1/2 x 49 1/2	1
N	Base Moulding, Side	3/4 x 4 1/2 x 19 3/4	2
O	Top	3/4 x 19 5/8 x 49 1/4	1
P	Back	1/4 x 47 1/2 x 30 1/2	1
Q	Drawer Guide	1/4 x 3/4 x 17	4

Doors

R	Stile	3/4 x 1 1/2 x 22	6
S	Top Rail	3/4 x 1 1/2 x 12 3/4*	3
T	Bottom Rail	3/4 x 2 x 12 3/4*	3
U	Panel	3/4 x 12 3/8 x 19 1/8	3

Base Drawers

V	Front & Back	1/2 x 6 x 22 7/8	4
W	Side	1/2 x 6 x 18	4
X	Bottom	1/4 x 17 1/2 x 22 3/8	2

Y	Face	1/2 x 6 1/4 x 22 7/8	2

Hutch Unit

Z	Side	3/4 x 10 x 36 5/8	2
AA	Lower Shelf	3/4 x 9 1/4 x 47 1/4	2
BB	Upper Shelf	3/4 x 9 1/4 x 47 1/4	1
CC	Top	3/4 x 11 3/8 x 50 3/4	1
DD	Fascia	3/4 x 1 3/4 x 48	1
EE	Moulding	3/8 x 3/4 (see moulding detail)	As Req'd.
FF	Divider	3/4 x 9 1/4 x 4 3/4	2
GG	Back	3/4 x 36 3/4 T&G	6
HH	Drawer Guide	1/4 x 3/4 x 7 1/2	6

Hutch Drawers

II	Front & Back	1/2 x 3 3/4 x 15	6
JJ	Side	1/2 x 3 3/4 x 8 1/2	6
KK	Bottom	1/4 x 8 x 14 1/2	3
LL	Face	1/2 x 4 x 15	3

Hardware

MM	Hutch Knob	3/4 in. dia. porcelain	3
NN	Base Knob	1 in. dia. porcelain	4
OO	Hinge	1/2 x 1 3/4 in. butt type	2 pair
PP	Bullet Catch	3/8 x 7/16**	2
QQ	Strap	1 x 3 in. steel	2

*Includes tenons.

**Available from: Constantine's, 2050 Eastchester Road, Bronx, NY 10461. Order part No. 75B11A; package of 10 costs $2.95.

Figure 5. Form the door tenons on rails S and T by first cutting the groove and then forming the shoulders with a dado blade as shown. Smooth the shoulders with a wood chisel.

responds to seasonal changes in humidity. Permanently mount the drawer faces after adjusting to suit the drawer openings.

Now mount the raised panel doors (left off earlier to facilitate mounting the drawers). Glue the fixed center door to parts J. If you prefer, hinge the center door to part I, in which case you may dispense with parts J. Mount the two outside doors with ½ in. by 1¾ in. butt hinges (OO). Don't forget to install the bullet catches (PP) and the 1 in. diameter porcelain knobs (NN), available at most hardware stores.

Build the Optional Hutch

If you've decided to make the hutch unit, start with the sides (Z). After cutting to length and width, cut the grooves for the shelves (AA and BB). Notch the top end ¾ in. by 2⅛ in. to accommodate the fascia (DD) and the top (CC). Cut the ½ in. by ¾ in. rabbets along the back edge to accept the back (GG). Transfer the side grid (see side elevation) cutout with the band saw or jigsaw and sand smooth. Cut the shelves to length and width; groove the two lower shelves as shown to accept the dividers (FF). Use the router with a ¼ in. straight bit to make the plate groove in shelf BB and the uppermost of shelves AA (see plate groove detail).

Lay out the grid pattern for the fascia (DD) as shown in the front elevation; then cut out and smooth the profile. Make the top (CC), cutting the ⅜ in. by ¾ in. by 9¼ in. grooves to accept the sides. Then cut the ½ in. by ¾ in. by 47½ in. long rabbet to accept the back. Finally, apply the same ¼ in. Roman ogee to the hutch top that you used on the base top.

The back (GG) is comprised of a series of tongue-and-groove ¾ in. boards. As shown in the back layout, size these boards so that each appears equal from the frontal view. Assemble the hutch carcass, consisting of parts Z, AA, BB, CC, DD, FF and GG. Use glue and/or counterbored and plugged screws as illustrated. Now cut about 6 ft. of the ¼ in. cove moulding (EE) shown in the moulding detail. Miter the ends, glue the fascia section of EE in place and apply the side sections with finishing nails, set and filled.

Make and assemble the hutch drawers (consisting of parts II, JJ, KK and LL) exactly as were the base unit drawers (see Fig. 2 for dimensions and box joint layout). Only the size is different. Follow the same mounting procedure, outlined earlier, for assembling the drawers and drawer guides (HH). Note that the hutch drawer knobs are ¾ in. diameter porcelain.

Mount the hutch unit to the base unit with four ¼ in. diameter by ¾ in. long dowels (see exploded view). The purpose of these dowels is to locate the hutch and keep it from sliding around. Do not glue the dowels. Thus, the hutch is easily disassembled for moving. We recommend two steel straps (QQ) screwed in place to prevent the hutch from tipping over.

After final sanding, stain the hutch/cupboard with Minwax Early American Wood Finish (No. 230), then finish it with a good satin finish polyurethane. Two coats (sprayed on) provide a nice soft satin sheen to this project.

Glue blocks with levelers can be added to the base, if necessary. □

Project designed and built by George Campbell

Folding TV Trays

These trays fold up for storage in their own handy rack.

These stylish solid birch folding trays are a way to fill the need for extra table space. When not in use, they store neatly in the matching rack.

Rip solid birch stock slightly wider than the dimensions shown in the bill of materials. Joint the edges to remove saw marks and to reach the correct dimensions.

Use a doweling guide to drill mating dowel holes in each top segment (A, B) after marking the face side of the parts for doweling. Alternate grain direction to minimize warping.

Glue up the tops with carpenter's glue and then clamp them securely using wooden cauls to prevent damage to the edges.

While the tops dry, cut the remaining tray components to be rounded (C, D, E, F) with a band saw. Clamp similar parts together, and smooth the curves with a belt sander.

Locate and drill the holes shown in the diagram in the legs and cleats (C, D, E, F). Use a Forstner-style bit for drilling the flat-bottomed holes which hold the Roto-Hinges.

Round over all edges of the legs (E, F, H) and the lower edges of the cleats (C, D) with a ¼ in. radius round over bit with ball bearing pilot. Sand the components thoroughly.

Drill mating dowel holes in parts F and H as shown in the diagram and then assemble the inner leg structures.

Next, glue the Roto-Hinges in the outer legs (E). Add the outer cleats (C) and attach the outer legs to the inner as-

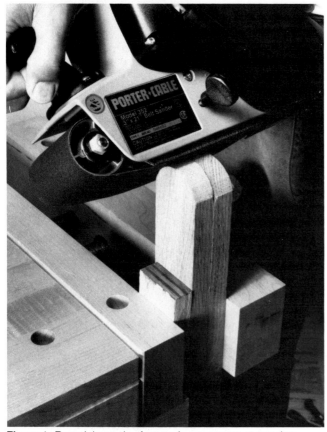

Figure 1. Round the ends of several components at one time using a belt sander. Clamp the components securely, and firmly grip the sander as shown. Smooth as much as you can of the semi-circle closest to you. Reposition the components, and sand the remaining semi-circular portion.

Figure 2. Use a drill press equipped with a Forstner bit to drill the Roto-Hinge holes. Make sure to securely clamp the workpiece and to wear eye protection. Carefully set the drill's depth stop to make sure you do not punch through the workpiece. Test on scrap material first and wear eye protection.

semblies. Cut the rounded corners of the tray tops and round over the edges. Drill the counterbored screw holes and give the tops a preliminary sanding.

On a flat surface, attach the tops to the leg assemblies. Add one of the inner cleats (D), then stand the tray on its legs before adding the other. This insures that the trays rest evenly on the floor.

Fold the trays and rest them on a bench top. Then insert the birch screw plugs. Level the tray tops with a belt sander. Finish sanding with a straight line power sander.

Now turn to the construction of the rack. Use a doweling guide to drill dowel holes in the ends of parts L, M, N and P. Transfer the locations of the holes to the other components with dowel center markers. Drill the mating holes with a drill press.

Assemble the end frames first with carpenter's glue. Once the glue has dried, use a radius round over bit to ease the edges and sand thoroughly.

Use a 1 in. Forstner bit to form the half holes in the lower braces (N).

Round over the edges of all three braces (N and P) before assembling the rack.

Finish the project by spraying the trays and rack with three coats of satin finish lacquer. We used Deft Clear Wood Finish. Sand between coats with 320 grit emery paper. □

BILL OF MATERIALS — Folding TV Trays

Finished Dimensions in Inches

A	Top Segment	½ x 6 x 24 birch	8
B	Top Segment	½ x 3 x 24 birch	8
C	Cleat	¾ x 2 x 14 birch	8
D	Cleat	¾ x 2 x 6 birch	8
E	Outer Leg	¾ x 2 x 32 birch	8
F	Inner Leg	¾ x 2 x 32 birch	8
G	Brace	⅝ dia. x 17 birch	4
H	Brace	¾ x 2 x 15½ birch	4
J	Locking pin	¼ x 2 birch dowel pins	8
K	Roto-Hinge*	¾ dia. Roto-Hinge	16
L	Upright	¾ dia. x 2 x 24 birch	4
M	Crosspiece	¾ x 2 x 16½ birch	4
N	Brace	¾ x 2 x 16 birch	2
P	Brace	¾ x 2 x 16 birch	1

*Roto-Hinges: Woodworker's Supply of New Mexico, 5604 Alameda Pl. NE, Albuquerque, NM 87113.

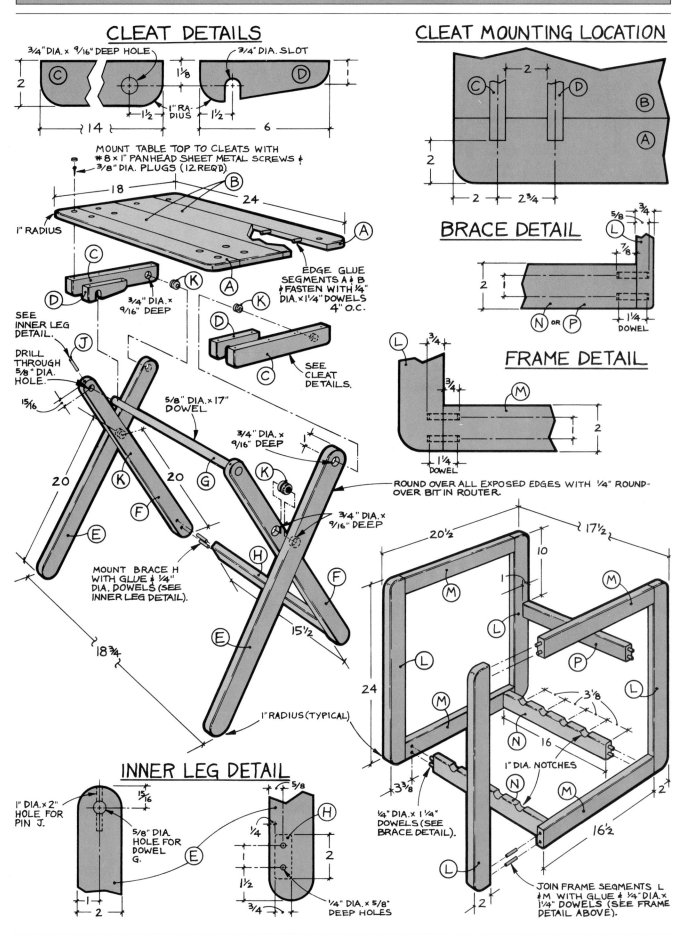

CLEAT DETAILS

3/4" DIA. × 9/16" DEEP HOLE
3/4" DIA. SLOT
C
2
1 1/8
D
1" RA-DIUS
14
1 1/2
1 1/2
6

CLEAT MOUNTING LOCATION

C
D
B
A
2
2
2 3/4
2

MOUNT TABLE TOP TO CLEATS WITH #8 × 1" PANHEAD SHEET METAL SCREWS & 3/8" DIA. PLUGS (12 REQ'D).

18
24
B
A

1" RADIUS
C
D
K
A
3/4" DIA. × 9/16" DEEP
K
D
C
SEE CLEAT DETAILS.

EDGE GLUE SEGMENTS A & B & FASTEN WITH 1/4" DIA. × 1 1/4" DOWELS 4" O.C.

BRACE DETAIL

5/8
3/4
L
7/8
2
1
N or P
1 1/4 DOWEL

FRAME DETAIL

L
3/4
3/4
M
2
1 1/4 DOWEL

SEE INNER LEG DETAIL.

DRILL THROUGH 5/8" DIA. HOLE.
J
15/16

5/8" DIA. × 17" DOWEL
3/4" DIA. × 9/16" DEEP
1
K

20
20
K
G
F
F
E

MOUNT BRACE H WITH GLUE & 1/4" DIA. DOWELS (SEE INNER LEG DETAIL).

H
3/4" DIA. × 9/16" DEEP

E
E
15 1/2
18 3/4

1" RADIUS (TYPICAL)

ROUND OVER ALL EXPOSED EDGES WITH 1/4" ROUND-OVER BIT IN ROUTER.

20 1/2
17 1/2
10
M
1
M
L
L
P
24
M
L
3 1/8
N
16
M
1" DIA. NOTCHES
3 3/8
N
M
1/4" DIA. × 1 1/4" DOWELS (SEE BRACE DETAIL).
L
16 1/2
2

JOIN FRAME SEGMENTS L & M WITH GLUE & 1/4" DIA. × 1 1/4" DOWELS (SEE FRAME DETAIL ABOVE).

INNER LEG DETAIL

1" DIA. × 2" HOLE FOR PIN J.
15/16
5/8
H
5/8" DIA. HOLE FOR DOWEL G.
E
1/4
2
1 1/2
3/4
1/4" DIA. × 5/8" DEEP HOLES
1
2

Project courtesy of *The Woodworker's Journal* magazine

Desk with Tambour Top

Open the tambour to reveal a spacious and well-organized writing desk.

Although full-size secretaries and traditional rolltop desks are impressive, their size and complexity place them in a class of projects that only the most ambitious woodworkers will usually attempt. Furthermore, because a full-size rolltop desk occupies a good deal of space, it is often difficult to find an ideal location for one in the average home.

By contrast, this modest-sized writing desk fits in practically anywhere. In the den, the study, or the living room, a practical writing desk is a most welcome addition. The ample writing surface is large enough for a typewriter and is great for letter writing, bill paying or reading. The tambour front opens to reveal various cubbyholes and drawers for storage of envelopes, correspondence, bills, stamps and writing implements. The single longer drawer below is large enough for full-size paper, manila envelopes, etc.

The tambour top, the dovetailed drawers and the general construction of the desk require careful attention to detail. Although there are no especially difficult operations involved (when considering the total project), this is a project that is best undertaken by an intermediate level to advanced woodworker.

Our desk is made of oak, selected because of its strength and stability. A wood with these qualities helps to insure that the tambour continues to operate properly long after the piece is completed. Although other hardwoods could also be used for the desk, exercise care and select only the best clear, straight-grained material, especially for the tambour section.

The desk is actually divided into two separate sections, the lower or *base* section and the upper or *top* section. Make, assemble and finish these two sections as separate units. Then join them upon project completion.

Start with the Base Section

Mill 1¾ in. square blanks for the four legs (A), allowing extra length as needed for lathe mounting. Locate and mortise the legs (for the stretchers and aprons). Then turn them to the dimensions indicated in the front view. You will have little difficulty keeping all four legs consistent if you lay out and mark the various turning points for each. Use sharp skews and gouges and work carefully — oak tears out rather easily. Final sand the legs on the lathe.

Next, mill stock for the aprons and stretchers. Make the front apron (B) by ripping a 5½ in. wide board, crosscutting the center section to create the drawer opening. Joint the edges to obtain the two ¾ in. square strips and the two 3½ in. wide sections on either side of the drawer opening. The additional ½ in. on the part B width dimension allows for saw kerfs and a light pass of each piece over the jointer.

Glue and clamp the front apron parts and, when dry, cut the tenons on the ends using the table saw dado head. Make the back and side aprons (C and D) and the back and side stretchers (E and F). Also cut the tenons on the ends of these parts with the dado head (see Fig. 1 for tenon dimensions). Final sand parts A through F, test-fit, glue and assemble.

Now cut and fit the liners (G), filler blocks (H), side cleats (I), drawer guides (J) and apron cleats (K). Note the slotted holes required in the various cleats to accept the top mounting screws.

Now machine and edge-glue sufficient stock for the writing surface (L). When dry, cut the glued-up writing sur-

face to overall length and width and use a ½ in. bearing guided beading bit to form the decorative edge on all four sides.

Make and fit the base drawer, consisting of parts M through Q. Final sand and finish all base and base drawer parts. Do not mount the writing surface and do not cut the slotted holes until after the tambour carcass is completed.

Construct the Top Section

Start by gluing up stock for the sides (S). Then, referring to Fig. 2, make the template used as a router guide for cutting the tambour groove. Note that our template is ⁵/₃₂ in. smaller all around than the groove inside and is used with a ⁵/₈ in. outside diameter guide bushing and ⁵/₁₆ in. straight cutter. Use the radii shown in Fig. 2 as an aid in laying out for the template and groove. To find the center point of the 3¹³/₁₆ in. radius top front curve, measure 8 in. from the back edge and 5¼ in. down from the top edge. To find the 6⁵/₁₆ in. radius lower front curve, measure 1½ in. up from the bottom edge and 7 in. back from the front edge. The intersection of a 14 in. radius arc from this point and an 11½ in. radius arc from the previously located point provides the center point for scribing the 7⅜ in.

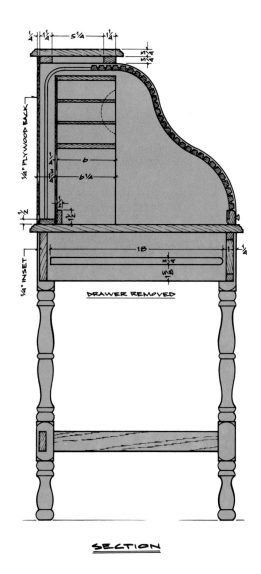

SECTION

61

radius reverse curve. Remember that the template must be sized somewhat smaller than the groove, with the exact dimension depending on the particular router and guide bushing you use. More about routing the groove is included in the story titled Making Tambour Doors.

After making the groove, saber saw or band saw the carcass sides to shape and cut the ¼ in. deep by ½ in. wide rabbet that accepts the back. Also cut the front and back cleats (T) and end cleats (U) that comprise a simple frame. Dimensions of the end cleat tenons are shown in Fig. 1. Glue and assemble this cleat frame and glue the carcass sides in place on either end. Make the top (V) and apply an edge treatment with the ½ in. beading bit. Mount the top as shown, fixed at the front edge with the slotted holes in the cleat frame, permitting movement toward the back. Cut and fit the plywood back (W), making certain that the sides are parallel. Also glue the tambour stop (X) in place as shown in the side view.

After making the top carcass, build the tambour front, consisting of the tambours (Y), the canvas (Z), the handle (AA) and the handle backing strip (BB). Again, refer to the

story Making Tambour Doors for a detailed description of machining the tambours and applying them to the canvas.

The canvas is 32¼ in. wide to provide clearance on either side so that it will not come near or bind in the grooves. The canvas should be at least 28 in. long. This provides overhang on the back end for tacking to the gluing fixture and an extra ⅞ in. on the front end for mounting the handle. After applying the canvas to the tambours, machine the handle and backing strip and mount by sandwiching the canvas as shown in Fig. 3. Also, drill for and glue in the location dowels in either end of the handle. When making the tambour front, remember that dimensions may vary slightly and the tambour must be sized to fit the tambour carcass.

Make the pigeonhole organizer (parts DD through LL) by milling ¼ in. and ½ in. stock as needed. Then cut to length and width, and rabbet and dado as required. Working from inner assemblies out, construct the organizer. Also make and fit the drawers (parts MM through QQ).

After oiling and prefinishing all subassemblies, slide the tambour front into the tambour track. Then screw the writing surface to the tambour carcass.

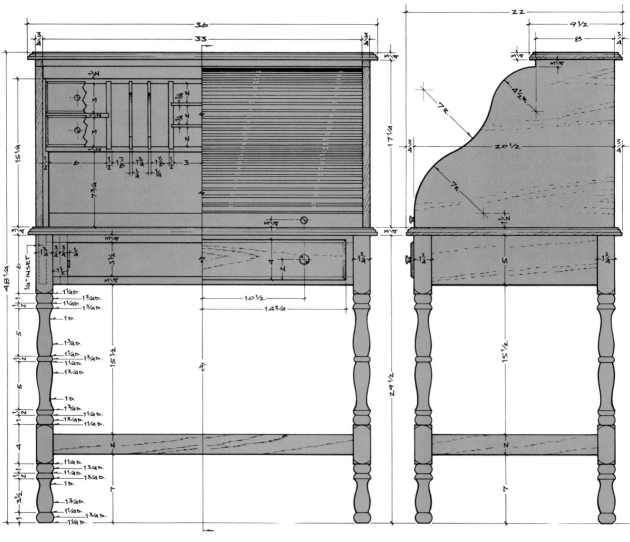

FRONT VIEW   SIDE VIEW

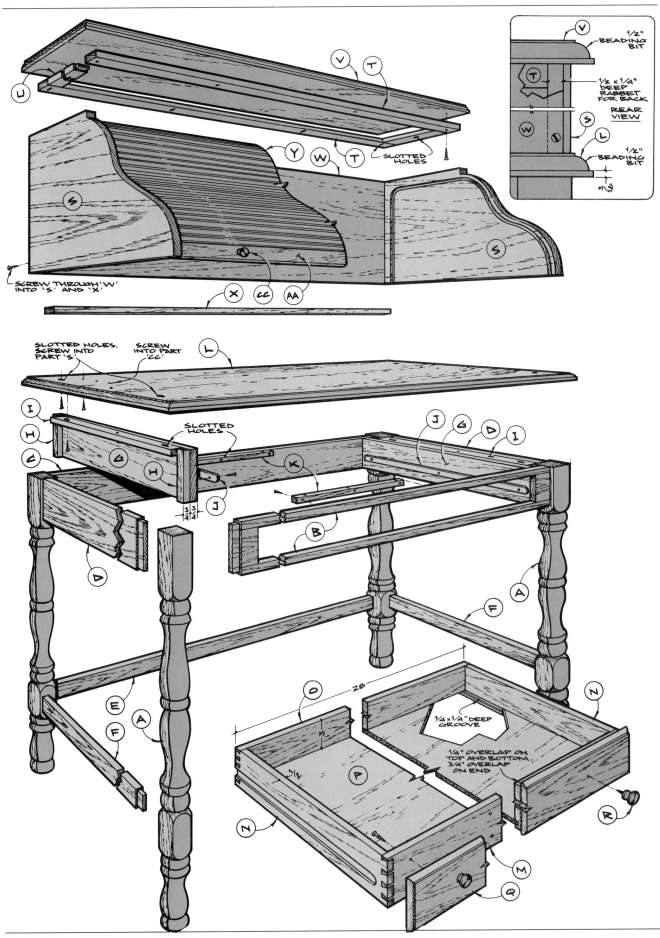

½"
BEADING
BIT

½ x ¼"
DEEP
RABBET
FOR BACK

REAR
VIEW

½"
BEADING
BIT

SLOTTED
HOLES

SCREW THROUGH 'W'
INTO 'S' AND 'X'

SLOTTED HOLES.
SCREW INTO
PART 'S'

SCREW
INTO PART
'CC'

SLOTTED
HOLES

¼ x ¼" DEEP
GROOVE

¼" OVERLAP ON
TOP AND BOTTOM.
¾" OVERLAP
ON END

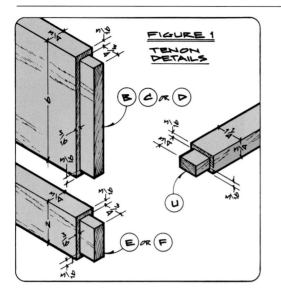

FIGURE 1
TENON DETAILS

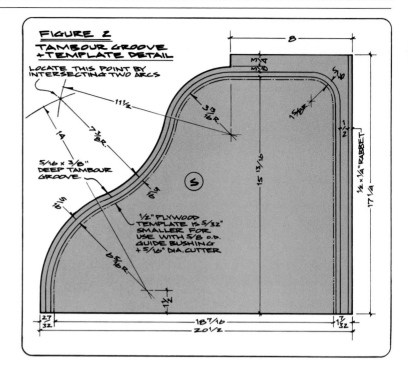

FIGURE 2
TAMBOUR GROOVE + TEMPLATE DETAIL

LOCATE THIS POINT BY INTERSECTING TWO ARCS

5/16 x 3/8" DEEP TAMBOUR GROOVE

1/2" PLYWOOD TEMPLATE IS 5/32" SMALLER FOR USE WITH 5/8 O.D. GUIDE BUSHING + 5/16" DIA. CUTTER

1/2 x 1/4 RABBET

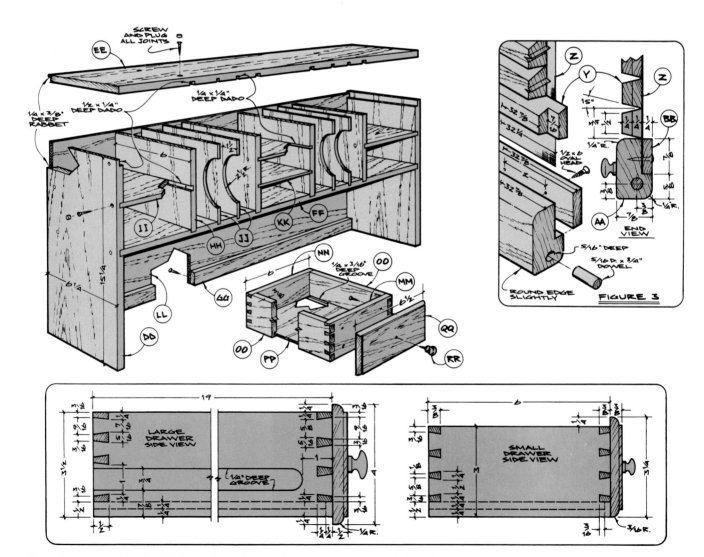

SCREW AND PLUG ALL JOINTS

1/4 x 1/4" DEEP DADO

1/2 x 1/4" DEEP DADO

1/4 x 3/8" DEEP RABBET

1/4 x 3/16" DEEP GROOVE

ROUND EDGE SLIGHTLY

FIGURE 3

5/16" DEEP

5/16 D. x 3/4" DOWEL

1/2 x 6 OVAL HEAD

END VIEW

LARGE DRAWER SIDE VIEW

1/4" DEEP GROOVE

SMALL DRAWER SIDE VIEW

Figure 4. Securely clamp the template and side to the workbench. Install a straight bit along with guide bushing on your router to cut the groove for the tambour. Work counterclockwise and obtain final depth in about three passes.

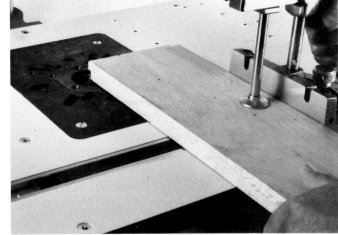

Figure 5. An alternative method to cutting the tenons on a table saw is to cut them on a router table equipped with miter gauge. Install a straight bit and set it to the appropriate depth. Make narrow cuts first, then the wider cuts (shown).

Tip◆ Place a spacer stick between the carcass sides to help keep them parallel.

Next, insert the organizer and screw it to the writing surface. Finally, screw the entire top assembly to the base.

Mount the various drawer knobs (parts R and RR) and the tambour handle knobs (CC) to complete this project. □

BILL OF MATERIALS — Desk with Tambour Top

Finished Dimensions in Inches

Base Section

A	Leg	1¾ x 1¾ x 29½	4
B	Front Apron Assembly	¾ x 5½* x 32½**	1
C	Back Apron	¾ x 5 x 32½**	1
D	Side Apron	¾ x 5 x 18½**	2
E	Back Stretcher	¾ x 2 x 32½**	1
F	Side Stretcher	¾ x 2 x 18½**	2
G	Liner	¾ x 5 x 18½	2
H	Filler Block	¾ x ¾ x 5	4
I	Side Cleat	¾ x 1½ x 17	2
J	Drawer Guide	¼ x ¾ x 18	2
K	Apron Cleat	¾ x ¾ x 12	2
L	Writing Surface	¾ x 22 x 36	1
M	Drawer Front	½ x 3½ x 28	1
N	Drawer Side	½ x 3½ x 19	2
O	Drawer Back	½ x 3 x 28	1
P	Drawer Bottom	¼ x 27½ x 18¾	1
Q	Drawer Face	½ x 4 x 29½	1
R	Drawer Knob	Brass, 1 in. dia.	2

Top Section

S	Side	¾ x 17¼ x 20½	2
T	Front/Back Cleat	¾ x 1¼ x 33	2
U	End Cleat	¾ x 1¼ x 6¾**	2
V	Top	¾ x 9½ x 36	1

W	Back	¼ x 17¼ x 34	1
X	Tambour Stop	½ x 1½ x 33	1
Y	Tambour	½ x ¾ x 33¾	30
Z	Canvas	as needed	1
AA	Handle	⅞ x 1½ x 32⅞	1
BB	Backing Strip	¼ x ⅞ x 32⅞	1
CC	Handle Knob	Brass, ¾ in. dia.	2
DD	Organizer Side	½ x 6¼ x 15¼	2
EE	Organizer Top	½ x 6¼ x 32½	1
FF	Organizer Shelf	½ x 6 x 32½	1
GG	Back Strip	½ x 1½ x 32	1
HH	Vertical Divider	½ x 6 x 7	4
II	Drawer Divider	½ x 6 x 6½	2
JJ	Separators	¼ x 6 x 7	4
KK	Horizontal Divider	¼ x 6 x 6½	2
LL	Divider Back	¼ x 15 x 32½	1
MM	Drawer Front	⅜ x 3 x 6	4
NN	Drawer Back	⅜ x 2½ x 6	4
OO	Drawer Side	⅜ x 3 x 6	8
PP	Drawer Bottom	¼ x 5⅝ x 5¹³⁄₁₆	4
QQ	Drawer Face	⅜ x 3¼ x 6½	4
RR	Drawer Knob	Brass, ½ in. dia.	4

*Width allows extra stock.
**Length includes tenons.

Designed and built by Dennis Watson

End Table

Simple and elegant describe this walnut and white oak contemporary end table. Its small, almost hidden drawer makes the table very practical if placed near a couch or easy chair.

Walnut and white oak give the end table a striking appearance. You can substitute other wood if you desire. The legs are the first order of business. Begin by selecting 1¾ in. thick walnut. Rip the leg 1¾ in. square and crosscut to 22 in. in length; the extra length will be trimmed off after turning. The next step is to rip the leg on the diagonal. This is done easily on the band saw with a "V" guide board. Remove the saw marks by either hand planing or running the edges over the jointer, removing as little wood as possible.

Rip a piece of white oak ⅛ in. thick by 2¾ in. wide, then hand plane or joint to remove the saw marks. Apply glue and clamp the white oak strip between the walnut sides; there is a tendency for the boards to slip when clamping pressure is applied, so try to keep the leg square in cross section. After the glue has dried, trim the oak strip flush with the walnut sides on your band saw.

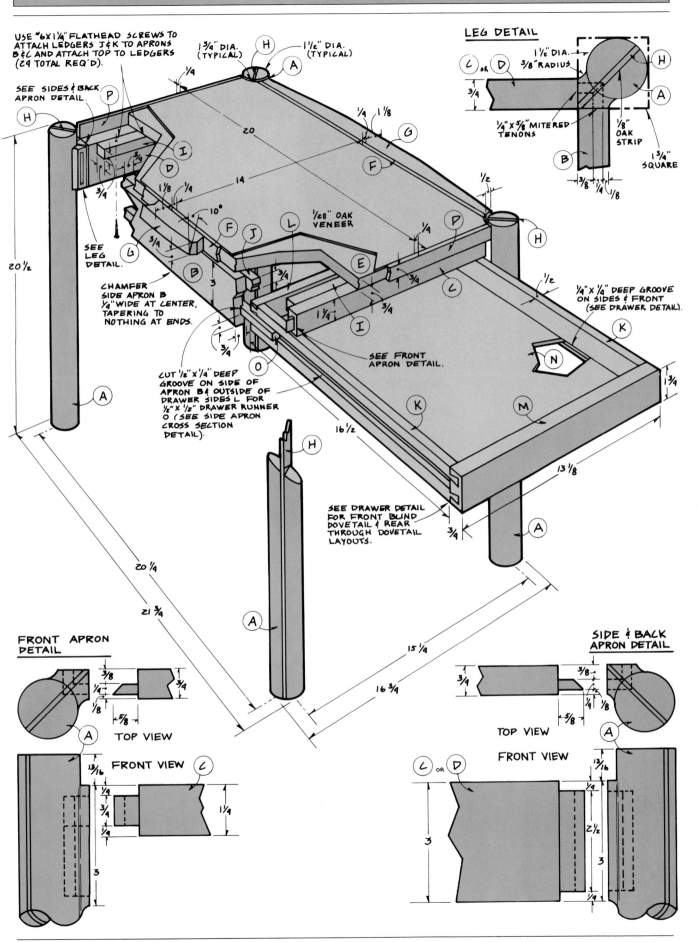

USE #6x1¼" FLATHEAD SCREWS TO ATTACH LEDGERS J&K TO APRONS B&C AND ATTACH TOP TO LEDGERS (29 TOTAL REQ'D).

SEE SIDES & BACK APRON DETAIL.

1¾" DIA. (TYPICAL)

1½" DIA. (TYPICAL)

¼

20

14

1⅛
¼

1⅛ ¼

10°

3

⅛" OAK VENEER

¼

½

¼

¾

¾

¾

¾

1¼

20½

SEE LEG DETAIL.

CHAMFER SIDE APRON B ¼" WIDE AT CENTER, TAPERING TO NOTHING AT ENDS.

CUT ½" X ¼" DEEP GROOVE ON SIDE OF APRON B& OUTSIDE OF DRAWER SIDES L FOR ½" X ½" DRAWER RUNNER O (SEE SIDE APRON CROSS SECTION DETAIL).

SEE FRONT APRON DETAIL.

¼" X ¼" DEEP GROOVE ON SIDES & FRONT (SEE DRAWER DETAIL).

½

16½

SEE DRAWER DETAIL FOR FRONT BLIND DOVETAIL & REAR THROUGH DOVETAIL LAYOUTS.

13⅛

1¾

¾

20¼

21¾

20½

15¼

16¾

LEG DETAIL

1½" DIA.
3/8" RADIUS

¾

¼" X ⅝" MITERED TENONS

⅛" OAK STRIP

1¾" SQUARE

⅜ ¼ ⅛

FRONT APRON DETAIL

⅜
¼
⅛

¾

⅝

TOP VIEW

FRONT VIEW

13/16

¼
¾
¼

1¼

3

3

SIDE & BACK APRON DETAIL

¾

⅜
¼ ⅛

⅝

TOP VIEW

FRONT VIEW

13/16

¼

2½

3

¼

3

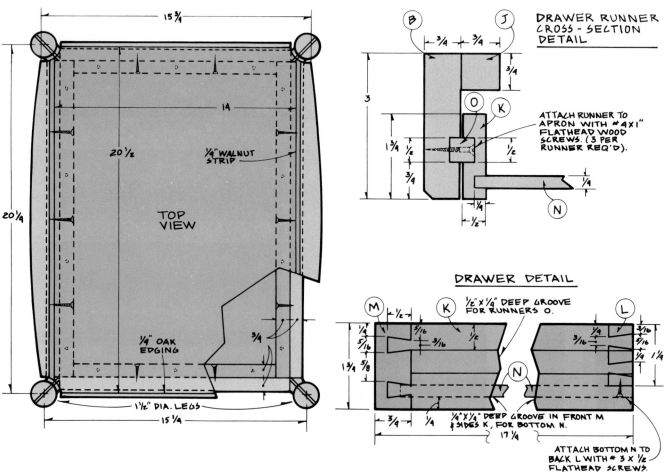

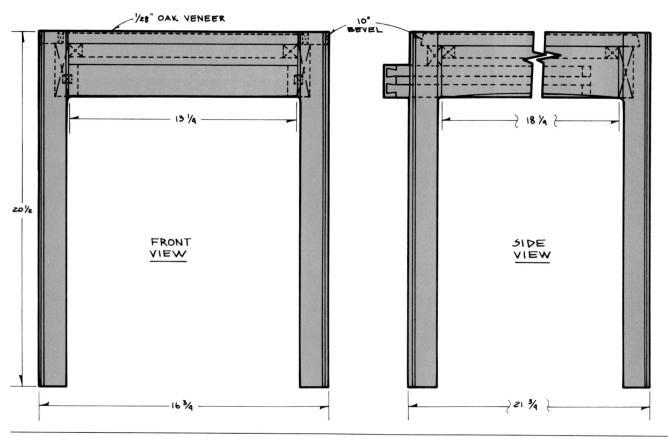

DRAWER RUNNER CROSS-SECTION DETAIL

ATTACH RUNNER TO APRON WITH #4X1" FLATHEAD WOOD SCREWS. (3 PER RUNNER REQ'D).

DRAWER DETAIL

½"X¼" DEEP GROOVE FOR RUNNERS O.

¼"X¼" DEEP GROOVE IN FRONT M & SIDES K, FOR BOTTOM N.

ATTACH BOTTOM N TO BACK L WITH #3 X ½ FLATHEAD SCREWS.

15¾

1A

20½

¼"WALNUT STRIP

20¼

TOP VIEW

¼" OAK EDGING

¾

1½" DIA. LEGS

15¼

1/28" OAK VENEER

10° BEVEL

13¼

18¼

20½

FRONT VIEW

SIDE VIEW

16¾

21¾

68

Figure 1. Each of the four walnut legs includes a strip of white oak laminated in the middle. Saw the leg across the leg blank's diagonal using a V-notched jig. Use a ½ in. wide band saw blade.

BILL OF MATERIALS — End Table

Finished Dimensions in Inches

A	Walnut Leg	1¾ x 1¾ x 20½	4
B	Walnut Side Apron	¾ x 3 x 19½	2
C	Walnut Front Apron	¾ x 1¼ x 14½	1
D	Walnut Front Apron	¾ x 3 x 14½	1
E	Plywood Top	¾ x 14 x 20	1
F	Walnut Strip	¼ x ¾ x 20½	2
G	White Oak Edging	¾ x 1⅛ x 20½	2
H	White Oak Strip	⅛ x 2¾ x 20½	4
I	Oak Ledger	¾ x ¾ x 11¾	2
J	Oak Ledger	¾ x ¾ x 18¼	2
K	Oak Drawer Sides	½ x 1¾ x 17	2
L	Oak Drawer Back	½ x 1¼ x 13⅛	1
M	Walnut Drawer Front	¾ x 1¾ x 13⅛	1
N	Plywood Drawer Bottom	¼ x 12⅝ x 17	1
O	Drawer Runner	½ x ½ x 16½	2
P	White Oak Strip Top	¼ x ¾ x 14	2

Figure 2. Also band saw a ⅛ in. thick strip of white oak for the leg lamination. Use a homemade edge guide to keep the workpiece parallel to the saw blade.

Mark the center of the leg accurately and install between centers in the lathe. When turning the leg, turn about 1½ in. in length on the top. Leave a square section about 4 in. long, then turn the remaining bottom portion.

After turning all four legs, lay out the location of the mortises and mark the exact length of the leg. Cut the mortises on a radial arm saw with a ¼ in. bottoming end mill in the right hand chuck. Cut the legs to length, being careful because the wood has a tendency to splinter. You can knife around the leg or wrap it with masking tape to reduce the splintering.

Cut the aprons to length; be sure to allow for the length of the tenons. Cut the tenon in a scrap piece and try the fit; it should be snug but not so tight that you have to drive it home.

Lay out the location of the drawer runner on the side rail and run a ½ in. by ¼ in. groove. Chamfer the bottom edge of the side apron with a spokeshave. Now dry-fit the base

Figure 3. Shape the lower edge of the apron sides (B) with a spokeshave. The chamfer is ¼ in. at the middle and tapers off to nothing at the ends. You can also use a coarse half-round file.

together. When all the joints pull up tightly, apply glue and allow to dry overnight, making sure the base is square.

The next step is to shape the square portion of the leg. Remove the bulk of the wood with a carving gouge. A round Surform is handy for smoothing the gouge marks out and final shaping. Finish up with sandpaper. When shaping the leg use some masking tape to protect the turned part of the leg and apron.

The drawer is the next order of business. Construction is typical, with blind dovetails used for the front and through dovetails for the rear. The dovetails can be hand cut or machine cut. Rip the sides and back from ½ in. oak, maple or poplar, and crosscut to length. The drawer front should be cut from the same board as the front apron so the grain matches. Run a ¼ in. by ¼ in. groove in the front and sides for the ¼ in. plywood bottom, and a ½ in. by ¼ in. groove in the side for the runner. Glue and clamp the drawer together using the bottom to keep it square. After the glue has dried, screw the bottom to the back with several small flathead screws.

Install the drawer runner in the side apron using No. 4 by 1 in. flathead screws. Try the drawer; you can adjust the runner out by adding paper or cardboard shims, or if necessary, plane a little off the runner if the drawer is too tight. Add some paraffin to make the drawer slide smoothly. Push the drawer in all the way, then plane or sand the front so it lines up with the apron.

The top is made from ¾ in. plywood veneered with white oak and edged with hardwood. If you choose to use solid wood for the top be sure and make the gap between the leg and top large enough to allow the top to move with humidity changes. The plywood should be similar to birch or

Figure 4. Laminate and turn the leg except where it is to join the table. Use a carving gouge to rough shape the leg where it joins the apron. Firmly secure the workpiece to prevent accidents.

Figure 5. Use a Surform file to smooth the carving marks left by the gouge. Apply masking tape as shown to protect the leg and apron during this filing operation.

Figure 7. Remove the wood for the legs, staying outside of the marking; finish up with a drum sander. Make sure you test-fit as you approximate the leg shape.

Figure 6. Band saw the side of the top, staying just to the outside of the line. Use a spokeshave to taper the sides and remove the saw marks. Take long strokes with the spokeshave.

Figure 8. Use a sharp cabinet scraper to finish the white oak top. This is a much safer method than using a belt sander on ⅟₂₈ in. thick wood veneer.

mahogany. Stay away from fir because the wild grain pattern will telegraph through the white oak veneer. Before applying the veneer, glue a ¼ in. by ¾ in. solid white oak strip to the front and rear edges and plane or sand flush with the plywood. Apply the veneer and trim flush with the plywood. Using a fine-tooth blade, rip a little off each side of the top to arrive at the final size.

Rip two strips of walnut ¼ in. wide and two strips of white oak 2 in. wide, and glue to each edge of the top. Very carefully plane or sand flush with the veneer.

The sides of the top are curved slightly, which is cut easily on the band saw or with a saber saw. Smooth up the edges with a spokeshave. Set the top in place and very accurately mark the location of each leg. Using a band saw or saber saw, cut just at the outside of the lines. Try the top and make small adjustments to the cutout using a small drum sander, about 1¼ in. diameter. Try the fit frequently. Attach the ¾ in. by ¾ in. square ledger strip to the apron with No. 6 by 1¼ in. flathead screws, then screw the top to the ledger strip using the same size screws.

Give the table a thorough sanding with 220 grit paper. Two coats of natural Watco Danish Oil were applied. The second coat was wet sanded with No. 600 grit wet/dry paper. A coat of paste wax finishes the project. □

Project courtesy of *The Woodworker's Journal* magazine

MICROWAVE CART

This cart is crafted in white oak and moves to where you need it. Build your own butcher block by following the techniques in the Tips section.

There is no questioning the tremendous popularity of microwave ovens, yet in most conventional kitchens counter space is at a premium. Since placing a microwave oven on the counter means a sacrifice of valuable space, and given the fact that the counter is not exactly an ideal location, microwave carts have become nearly as popular as the ovens themselves.

In developing the design of our cart, we looked at a variety of other carts and tried to incorporate the best features. We placed the oven up high, over a convenient butcher block work surface, yet not so high it will be above eye level or beyond the easy reach of a five foot tall person. There are storage shelves below and casters for easily moving the cart about. The cart is designed for stability, and the microwave shelf is large enough to accommodate a full-size oven.

We suggest that you use a close-grained hardwood for this project. White oak and rock maple are the best choices. Cut all the hardwood component parts from 3/4 in. thick stock. Additionally, use about one-third of a sheet of 3/4 in. thick hardwood plywood for the top and bottom shelves (D and H).

A good place to start is with making the butcher block. To make the butcher block use 37 identical pieces, each 3/4 in. by 1 3/4 in. by 24 1/2 inches. The 1/4 in. extra width and the 1/2 in. additional length on each piece are necessary to allow for trimming and surfacing after the glue-up is complete.

For more information on making butcher block, including tips, refer to the accompanying butcher block Tips feature

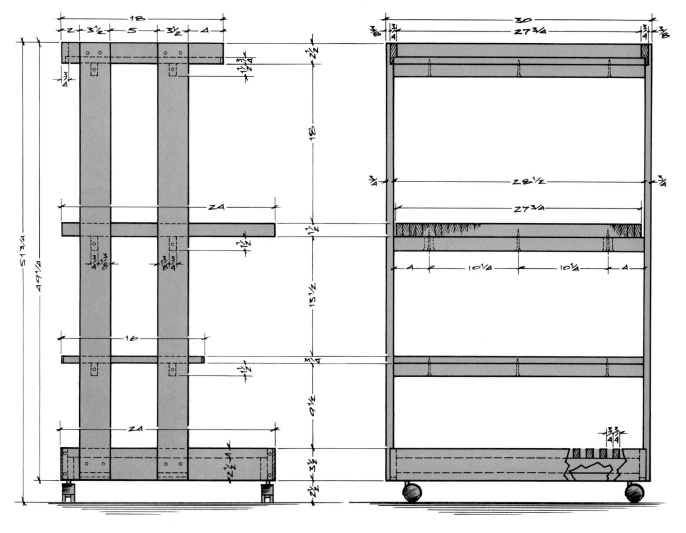

SIDE VIEW   FRONT VIEW

BILL OF MATERIALS — Microwave Cart

Finished Dimensions in Inches

A	Leg	¾ x 3½ x 49¼	4
B	End Retainer	¾ x 2½ x 18	2
C	Back Retainer	¾ x 2½ x 29¼	1
D	Top Shelf	¾ x 17⅜ x 28½	1
E	Top Shelf Edging	¼ x ¾ x 28½	1
F	Shelf Support	¾ x 1½ x 28½	6
G	Butcher Block Shelf	1½ x 27¾ x 24*	1
H	Lower Shelf	¾ x 15½ x 28	1
I	Lower Shelf Side Edging	¼ x ¾ x 15½	2
J	Lower Shelf Front Edging	¼ x ¾ x 28½	1
K	Base Apron End	¾ x 3½ x 23½	2
L	Base Apron Front & Back	¾ x 3½ x 29¼	2
M	Stretcher	¾ x 3½ x 29¼	2
N	Cleat	¾ x 2½ x 27¾	2
O	Rib	¾ x 1 x 22½	18
P	Caster**	2½ in. height	4

*Final Dimensions
**Available from: The Woodworkers' Store, 21801 Industrial Blvd., Rogers, MN 55374. Order part No. C1141.

shown on this and the next page. Butcher blocks can also be purchased from many local lumberyards as well.

Glue and clamp the butcher block and go to work on the rest of the cart. First, cut to length and width all the remaining hardwood parts (A, B, C, E, F, I, J, K, L, M, N and O). Also cut the two plywood shelves (D and H) to length and width. Rabbet parts A, B and C, and L and M, as shown in the appropriate details. Miter both ends of part C and the corresponding ends of parts B. Glue these three pieces up around the top shelf, adding the edging (E) to complete the top shelf assembly. Next, glue up the lower shelf edging (I and J) around the lower shelf.

Now make the base section. Notch parts K to accept the rabbeted ends of parts M, and assemble parts K, L and M using glue and screws as shown. Glue the two cleats (N) to the inside of parts L and add the 18 ribs (O) spaced ¾ in. apart. Also, drill the four holes to accept the casters (P), sizing the holes as necessary to accommodate the caster shank sockets. As you will note in the bottom view detail, locate these holes 2½ in. from the ends and exactly on the seam between parts L and N.

Now assemble the cart with glue and screws. Counterbore and plug the screw holes that mount the four legs to the top shelf and base assemblies and to the various shelf supports (F). Use plugs that match the wood you've chosen for the cart construction. Next, mount the top shelf, butcher block and lower shelf to their respective supports, counterboring the mounting screws. Slot the outer holes in the supports below the butcher block to accommodate seasonal movement as the butcher block responds to changes in the relative humidity.

Fine sand the cart. Soften all sharp corners and edges and finish the cart (except the butcher block) with several applications of a good quality penetrating oil such as Watco. As noted in the Tips sidebar on butcher block construction, apply a natural, nontoxic salad bowl finish to the butcher block. ☐

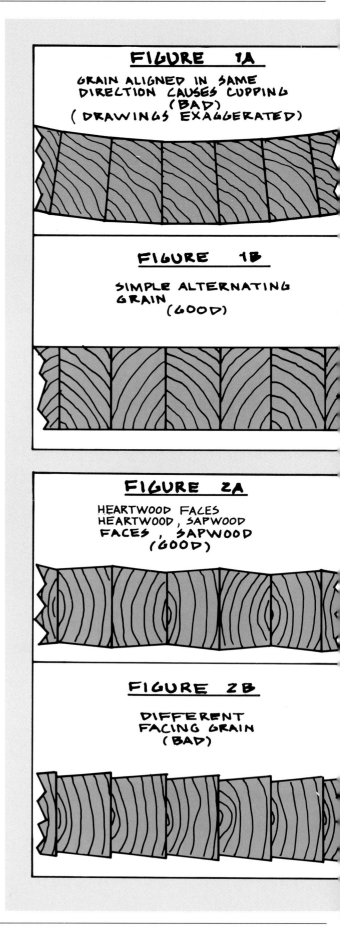

FIGURE 1A
GRAIN ALIGNED IN SAME DIRECTION CAUSES CUPPING (BAD) (DRAWINGS EXAGGERATED)

FIGURE 1B
SIMPLE ALTERNATING GRAIN (GOOD)

FIGURE 2A
HEARTWOOD FACES HEARTWOOD, SAPWOOD FACES, SAPWOOD (GOOD)

FIGURE 2B
DIFFERENT FACING GRAIN (BAD)

Making the Butcher Block

Butcher block is an attractive surface and comes in handy for a variety of projects. Although well-made butcher block is exceptionally strong, stable and durable, there are several problems that may be encountered in making it. The basic procedure of ripping sufficient boards to achieve the desired width, gluing and clamping them together, squaring the ends and then planing, sanding and finishing is simple and straightforward. But preparing and arranging the boards, along with the gluing and clamping process itself, requires careful planning and accuracy. As anyone who has attempted it knows, making butcher block requires a rather special technique.

The first point to consider is grain direction. Although true butcher block has short lengths of board arranged vertically so that the exposed end grain serves as the cutting surface, butcher block today is usually comprised of boards laid up horizontally. If you use plainsawn boards on edge, as most of us do, avoid facing all the boards with the grain running in the same direction. This may result in the butcher block cupping (Figure 1A).

There are three basic, commonly accepted methods for laying up butcher block. First, the boards can be arranged with a simple alternating grain pattern (Figure 1B). Second, you may arrange the boards with facing grain (heartwood to heartwood, sapwood to sapwood) as shown in Figure 2A. This method effectively eliminates the problem of small steps from uneven shrinkage, which is often encountered when boards are laid up with different facing grain (Figure 2B). The third method of creating butcher block is to utilize quartersawn boards and alternate the grain as shown in Figure 3. The method you select may depend on the type of boards (quartersawn, flatsawn, etc.) available to you.

Whichever technique you use, the three important elements to remember are: stock selection, flat glue surfaces and ade-quate clamp pressure. The material should have straight, even grain with no knots, burls or other defects.

The easiest way to make butcher block is to take ¾ in. thick mill planed boards and then rip them into widths equal to the butcher block's intended thickness. Because the flat, factory surface on the board now becomes the edge to be glued, you need not joint the stock. If, however, you use roughsawn lumber, it is necessary to joint all surfaces to be edge-glued. A power jointer speeds the work, though the material can also be jointed by hand, as our ancestors did. In any case, when cutting the stock, allow extra board length so the butcher block ends may be squared later.

Gluing and clamping the butcher block also requires care. Use a good carpenter's glue. Apply a thin coat to each mating surface making certain the coverage is complete. Closely space the clamps to provide even pressure. As you tighten the clamps, notice a slight glue squeeze-out along the length of each joint.

One clamping trick is to insert small headless brads in each board, as illustrated in Figure 4. Clip the brad heads with wire snips. The brads prevent slippage along the glue lines when clamp pressure is applied. Do not place these brads too close to the edge to be trimmed. An alternative is to use waxed cleats clamped on either side of the butcher block to keep the pieces aligned (Figure 5).

If you have a handheld power planer, the task of surfacing is a breeze. However, you can also glue up the butcher block in sections that a thickness planer can accommodate and then later glue these sections. For the rest of us, a sharp plane, belt and pad sanders and a healthy measure of elbow grease get the job done.

Use only a nontoxic finish on the butcher block. ◆

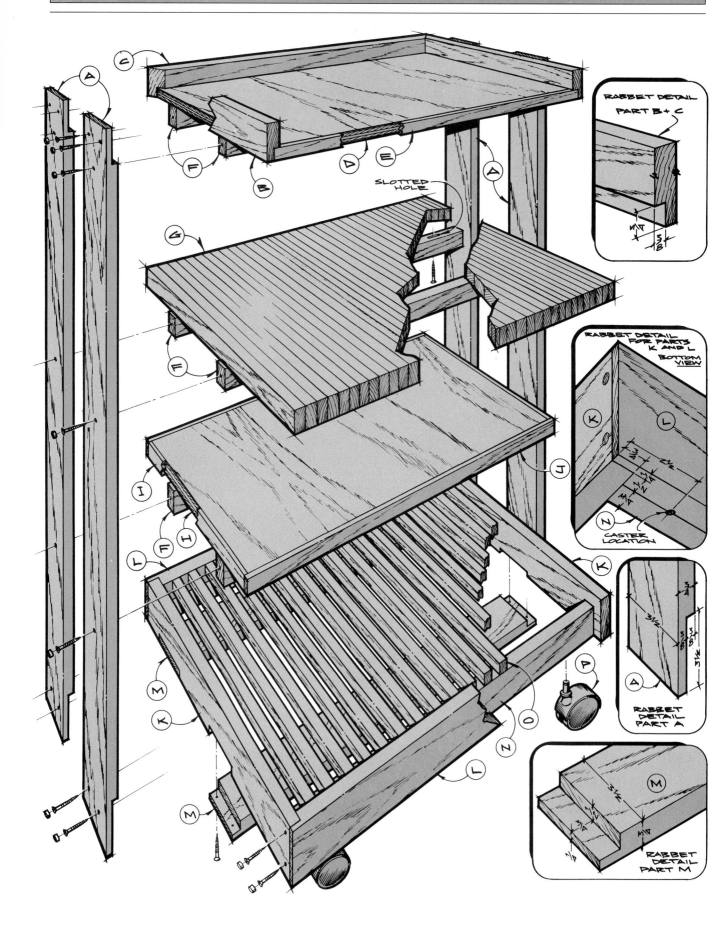

RABBET DETAIL
PART B + C

SLOTTED
HOLE

RABBET DETAIL
FOR PARTS
K AND L
BOTTOM
VIEW

CASTER
LOCATION

RABBET
DETAIL
PART A

RABBET
DETAIL
PART M

Project courtesy of *The Woodworker's Journal* magazine

Joiner's Tool Chest

It combines a sensible design with one other vital element — easy construction.

The tool chest is essentially a large box as the detail illustration indicates (the case box being ripped to form the chest front and chest case parts).

Begin by laying out the top and bottom (A) and sides (B), as shown in the cutting detail, on an 8¾ in. wide by 93 in. long board. Laying out these parts in the sequence shown and cutting them from a single length of board provides the case with an interesting visual grain continuity. Note that the width of the board includes an allowance for a ⅛ in. wide saw kerf. Now crosscut the board to create the 26 in. long top and bottom parts and the 18 in. long side parts.

While the designer used native Connecticut cherry for all the hardwood parts in the project, any hardwood will suffice. The ¼ in. plywood front, back and drawer bottom parts should match the hardwood you select and can all be obtained from a half sheet of plywood.

Lay out the dovetails following the procedure detailed below. Take careful note that the second dovetail pin from the front edge (and the corresponding space between the tails) is an additional ⅛ in. wide to allow for the saw kerf when the chest front is cut from the box.

Begin by laying out the dovetails on the ends of parts B, referring to the drawings for all dimensions. Ideally, the length of the tail should be equal to the thickness of part A plus about ⅓₂ inch. Later, when the joint is assembled, the tails will stick out ⅓₂ in., allowing them to be sanded perfectly flush with the sides. As you lay out the dovetail locations, work accurately, and use a hard, sharp pencil.

Once you have laid out the tails, mark the area to be removed between dovetails with an **X**. Scribe the tail location not only on the face surface of the board, but also on the end grain. Secure parts B in a vise, and use a fine-tooth saw to make the angled cuts. Work carefully, cutting on the waste side of the line, just grazing but not removing it.

Bring the cuts almost — but not quite — to the scribed bottom line. Use a coping saw to cut across the grain, removing the waste. Remove the workpiece from the vise, and

clamp it flat on the bench over a scrap board. Then use the chisel to dress the sides and bottom of the cutouts. The pins on parts A can best be laid out and scribed by using the finished dovetails as a template. To do this, clamp part A end up in the vise. Lay the dovetailed parts B in their proper position on parts A, and trace the dovetails with a sharp knife or pencil. Use a square to carry the scribed lines to the face of the board. As explained earlier, this distance should be equal to the thickness of B plus 1/32 inch. Once again, mark the waste portions with an X; then cut out in the manner used to cut the dovetails. A well-fitted joint should go together with only light tapping from a mallet and scrap block. If needed, trim further with the wood chisel.

As for final fit, remember that while a loose, sloppily cut dovetail is neither strong nor attractive, a dovetail that requires hammering to assemble is also unacceptable. When dry-fit, the joint should mate easily with only the slightest resistance. If the joint fits any tighter than this, you will find that with the application of glue, the wood will swell, and the joint will be impossible to assemble.

Now use either a table saw and a dado head (set for 1/4 in. width and 1/4 in. depth) or router table equipped with a 1/4 in. diameter straight cutter to establish the 1/4 in. by 1/4 in. grooves in both sides (A, B) for the front and back plywood panels

(C). Stop the 1/4 in. by 1/4 in. grooves in the top and bottom parts 1/2 in. from the ends. This requires that stop blocks be used on the router table. Note that the grooves are located 3/16 in. from the front and back edges respectively.

After a final test-fit of the top, bottom and sides with the 1/4 in. thick plywood front and back in place, glue up the case, making sure to check for squareness. Allow to dry overnight. Next, with the table saw and fence set up as shown in the detail, rip the case on all four sides to create the chest lid or front. Position 1/8 in. spacer slips in the kerf, and apply tape across the chest to keep all parts in relation when you make the final pass to sever the front. Use a block plane to clean up the saw marks along the edges.

To make the drawers, first cut a 1/2 in. by 9 in. by 24 1/2 in. long board from which to cut the fronts (D and E). Similarly, cut a 3/8 in. by 8 in. by 38 in. long board from which to cut the backs (H and I) and sides (F and G) as shown in the cutting plan. Lay out and crosscut the drawer divider grooves in both drawer fronts and backs. Locate these grooves to accommodate your tool collection. Bore 1 1/4 in. diameter holes for the finger pulls in the front stock, and use a table saw to rip the boards to create the individual drawer front, back and side parts. Now, cut the box joints (see front and side elevation for layout) and cut a 1/4 in. by 1/4 in. rabbet on the

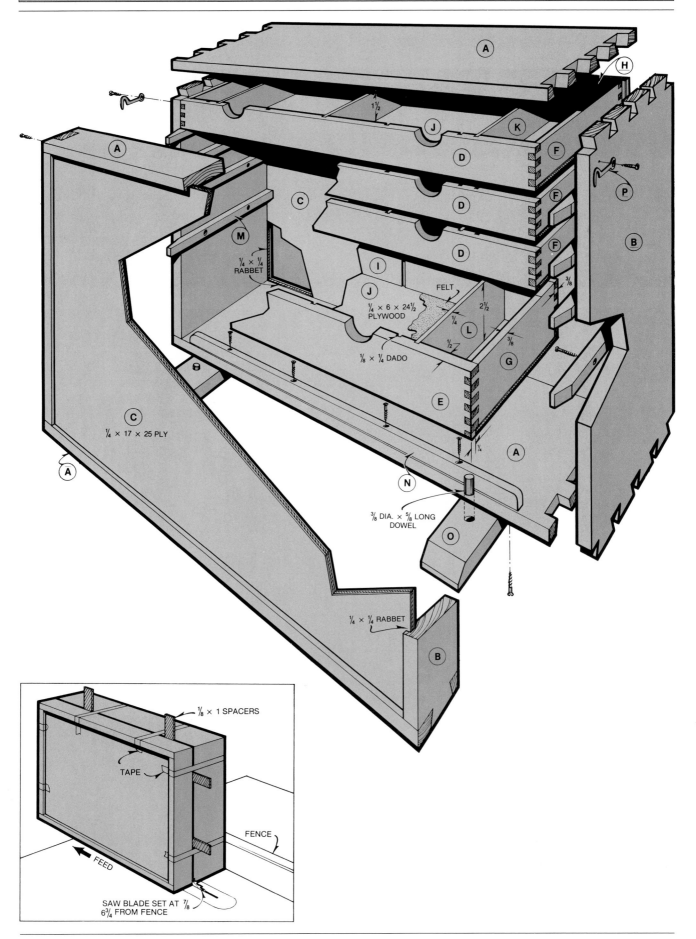

A

H

A

J

K

D

F

C

M

F

D

F

¼ × ¼
RABBET

B

P

D

⅜

I

J
¼ × 6 × 24½
PLYWOOD

FELT

2½

¼

L

⅜

G

½

⅛ × ¼ DADO

E

C
¼ × 17 × 25 PLY

N

A

A

⅜ DIA. × ⅝ LONG
DOWEL

O

¼ × ¼ RABBET

B

⅛ × 1 SPACERS

TAPE

FENCE

FEED

SAW BLADE SET AT ⅞
6¾ FROM FENCE

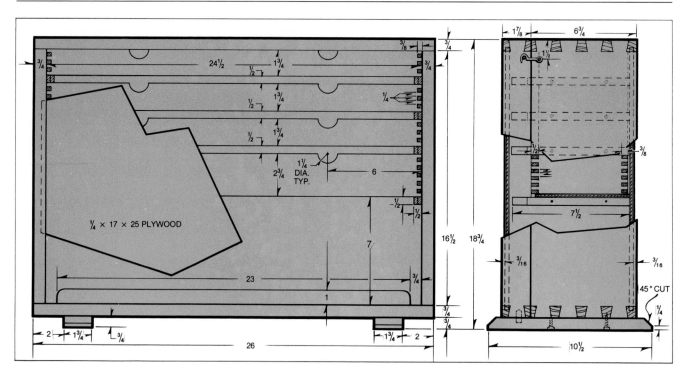

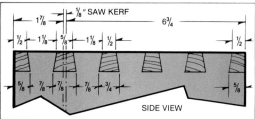

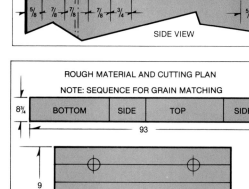

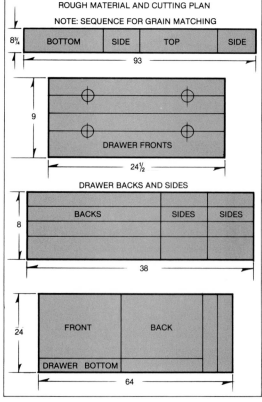

BILL OF MATERIALS — Joiner's Tool Chest

Finished Dimensions in Inches

A	Top/Bottom	¾ x 8¾ x 26*	2
B	Side	¾ x 8¾ x 18*	2
C	Front/Back	¼ x 17 x 25	2
D	Drawer Front (sm.)	½ x 1¾ x 24½**	3
E	Drawer Front (lg.)	½ x 2¾ x 24½**	1
F	Drawer Side (sm.)	⅜ x 1½ x 6¼	6
G	Drawer Side (lg.)	⅜ x 2½ x 6¼	2
H	Drawer Back (sm.)	⅜ x 1½ x 24½	3
I	Drawer Back (lg.)	⅜ x 2½ x 24½	1
J	Drawer Bottom	¼ x 6 x 24½	4
K	Drawer Divider (sm.)	¼ x 1½ x 5⅝	To Suit
L	Drawer Divider (lg.)	¼ x 2½ x 5⅝	To Suit
M	Drawer Runner	½ x ½ x 7½	8
N	Retainer	½ x 1 x 23	1
O	Feet	¾ x 1¾ x 10½	2
P	Hook Latch	1½ in. long***	2

*Note that the width dimension given is for the top, bottom and sides of the chest box *before* they are ripped to create the chest case and chest front (see detail).

**Note that the small and large drawer fronts are ripped from a single 9 in. by 24½ in. board (see drawer front detail).

***Available from: Klockit, P.O. Box 629, Highway H North, Lake Geneva, WI 53147. Order part No. 39008.

Figure 1. The easiest method of cutting a dovetail is with the aid of a jig. Guide the router, equipped with dovetail cutter, along the jig with a guide bushing.

Figure 2. If you do not have the luxury of a table saw, make the finger joints with a band saw or saber saw. Use an extra wide blade (for stability), and cut short of the cutting line. Then use a thin wood chisel to square the finger perimeter.

inside bottom edge of all the drawer fronts to accept the drawer bottoms (J). Glue up the drawer fronts, sides, backs and bottoms. If the drawer bottoms are cut perfectly square, you can use them to square up the drawer carcasses during the glue-up process.

To make the drawer runners (M), rip stock to ½ in. by ½ in. by 64 in. long, and cut into 7½ in. lengths. Taper one end, and drill and countersink the screw holes. Lay out the drawer locations, and mount the drawer runners to the case. Also cut the retainer strip (N), round the ends as shown, and drill and countersink and screw in place. Cut the feet (O) to size and shape, drill and countersink. Finally, mount the feet to the assembly.

You may want to construct wooden turnbuttons and block mounts to secure various tools on the inside of the chest lid (see lead photo).

Add drawer dividers (K and L) as needed to compartmentalize the drawers to suit your tool collection.

Drill and install dowel pins for each foot. These pins mate into corresponding holes drilled into the bottom edge of the chest lid. Chamfer the dowel ends to facilitate entry. These dowels serve to index and anchor the lid to the chest.

Install hook latches on either side of the chest to secure the lid at the top. A hasp and lock set could be substituted, if you prefer, for security. Should you plan to transport the chest, we suggest that thin wedges be used on the sides of each drawer to hold them tightly closed during the move.

After final sanding, apply several coats of penetrating oil. Drawers may be lined with felt if desired. For portability add chest handles on either side. □

Project courtesy of *The Woodworker's Journal* magazine

18th Century Tilt-Top Table

This mahogany tilt-top table is a reproduction of a table built in Philadelphia in the mid-18th century.

This project is a fine example of how period furniture can mix practicality with elegance. Traditionally brought out for serving tea, tilt-top tables of this type feature a top that both pivots to a vertical position and swivels around like a lazy Susan. With the top tilted vertically, the table can be stored flat against a wall or in a corner. This saves space yet allows the table to remain on display, showing off the elegance of its shapely legs and pedestal and its decorative figured top.

The table top with moulded rim (A), known as a dish top, is glued up from wide mahogany planks and shaped on a lathe as if it were a very large plate with a raised edge. The dish top can also be shaped by hand or with a router, though neither of these methods works as well as the lathe. We've included an alternate pattern for a flat top with a moulded edge. Some

tea tables from this period had flat tops, and such construction will save time and simplify the project.

For either style of top, two cleats (B) are screwed under the top perpendicular to its grain. The cleats prevent cupping and are drilled to form the upper half of the tilting mechanism's hinge. The top rests on a contraption usually called a birdcage (also known as a gallery or crow's nest), which consists of two horizontal squares (C, D) drilled through their centers and separated by four small turnings (E) — the pillars at each corner of the cage. The birdcage serves three functions. It completes the tilt-top hinge, allows the swivel action, and fastens the top to the pedestal. A wooden key (F), resting on a turned washer (G), locks the top and birdcage to the base. The base consists of an urn-shaped pedestal (H) with three legs (I). The legs are attached with dovetails that slide up into the pedestal from below.

Construction

Begin the project by laying out all the table parts, except the top and key, full size. Make patterns (out of stiff cardboard or 1/8 in. plywood) for the central pedestal, the cleats, the side profile of the leg and the birdcage turnings. Also make a cross-sectional pattern of the table rim.

Turn the 36 in. diameter dish top on the lathe's outboard side. The larger a top is, the more vibration there will be when turning. A top this size requires an industrial lathe. The lathe should be bolted to the floor and wall. Additional diagonal bracing will further help subdue the vibrations. Because the turning is done outboard, it requires a freestanding tool rest designed for this purpose.

Choose the boards for the top for their beauty. The tilting top is a natural show-off, so ribbony, richly colored mahogany is desirable. To obtain the 37 in. width, join two 18 1/2 in. wide pieces or three pieces that are each about 12 1/2 in. wide. Assemble the pieces so that the wood matches well at the joint and disguises the seams. If possible, arrange the boards to carry the grain from one to the next.

After the glue-up, plane the approximately 37 in. by 37 in. square blank (for the top) flat on the underside. Then rough cut the diameter with a jigsaw or band saw. Before turning this mahogany circle you need to cut an additional 3/4 in. thick plywood circle (Baltic birch is good) with a diameter of about 24 inches. The bigger this circle the better, since it helps to support the mahogany during turning. Screw the outboard faceplate to the center of this circle, attach it to the lathe and flatten (using scraping tools only) the face of the plywood. Now remove the faceplate from the lathe but keep it attached to the plywood, and glue the planed side of the mahogany circle to the newly flattened plywood, sandwiching a layer of kraft paper between the two. Brown paper bags work well. Use enough glue for a good glue joint, but don't saturate the paper or you will never get it cleanly apart. Clamp this up overnight leaving the outboard faceplate attached throughout. (If you take the plate off, it's almost impossible to put it back in the same place.)

Turn the top at your slowest speed but no more than 300 to 400 rpm. True up the edge with freshly sharpened scrapers, and shape the underside of the rim. Removing thickness from the underside gives the table edge a lighter, more delicate look. Move to the face or top side of the mahogany and shape

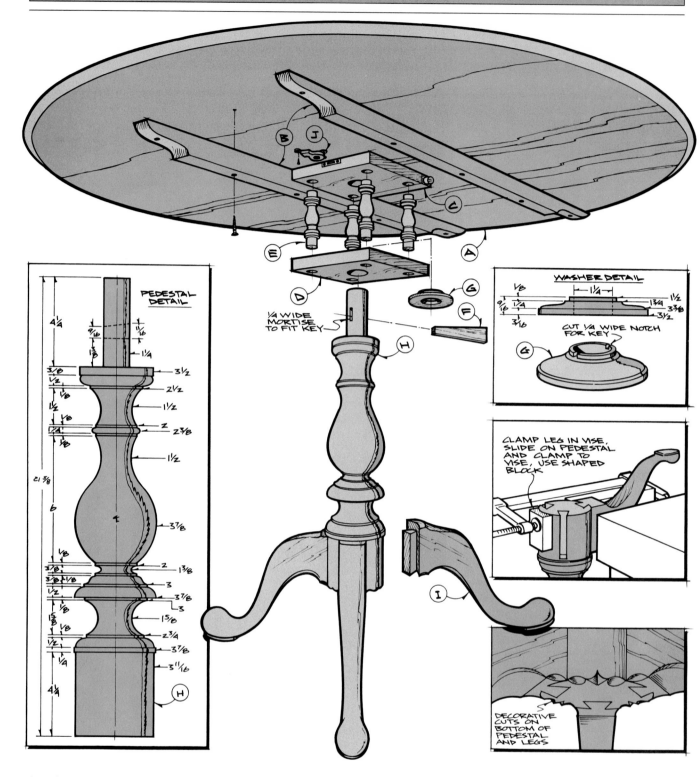

PEDESTAL
DETAIL

¼ WIDE
MORTISE
TO FIT KEY

WASHER DETAIL

CUT ¼ WIDE NOTCH
FOR KEY

CLAMP LEG IN VISE,
SLIDE ON PEDESTAL
AND CLAMP TO
VISE, USE SHAPED
BLOCK

DECORATIVE
CUTS ON
BOTTOM OF
PEDESTAL
AND LEGS

the edge according to the pattern. Then sand the entire rim, including the underside, to 220 grit.

Next, hollow out the table top. Because so much wood is removed from one side only, the top tends to progressively cup as more and more of the wood is cleared out. To minimize this problem, work on only a 3 in. area at a time. Start at the rim and move toward the center. Use a parting tool with a masking tape marker to establish the depth of cut. Using either the parting tool or a gouge, with a scraping action only,

clear the wood out back to the shaped rim. Then sand to 220 grit with sandpaper wrapped over a flat wood block. Move in another 3 in. and repeat. Watch that you don't cut below the previous area. If cupping occurs, do not retrace your steps. Any unevenness will have to be corrected later by clamping the top flat to your bench and using a hand plane and cabinet scraper.

When the turning is complete and the top is smooth, take the top off the lathe and remove the plywood using a chisel

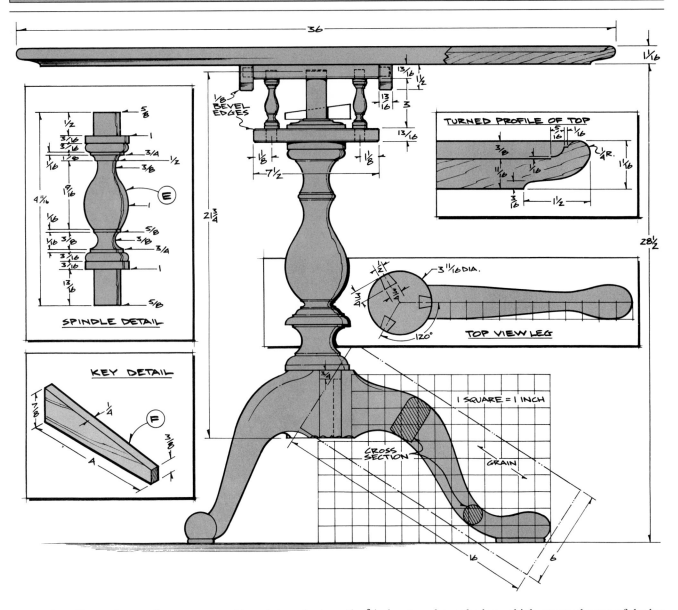

SPINDLE DETAIL

KEY DETAIL

TURNED PROFILE OF TOP

TOP VIEW LEG

1 SQUARE = 1 INCH

CROSS SECTION

GRAIN

as a wedge. Clamp the top flat on your workbench in order to scrape the paper from its underside. Keep it clamped flat to prevent warping while working on other parts of the table.

Historically, dish tops were also crafted by hand. You can use this method or use a router. However, with either of these methods you are likely to encounter the same cupping problem as with the turning method. Our alternate pattern uses a flat top and a panel raising router bit to create an elegant top without the fuss. The panel raising bit, part No. 54118, is available from the Amana Tool Company, 1250 Brunswick Avenue, Far Rockaway, NY 11691. If you select the alternate top and use the panel raising bit shown in the alternate top profile detail, you'll need to round the edges of the table top perimeter as shown.

The central pedestal (H) is made from a 4 in. by 4 in. by 21¾ in. turning block. Mount this block in your lathe, and mark the position to allow for identical remounting when needed. Turn the upper end of the pedestal to loosely fit a sample 1¼ in. diameter hole drilled in a scrap piece. The cylinder at the lower end of the pedestal must be turned very straight for a good leg fit. Check it with a straightedge. Note

the 3⁄32 in. step above the leg, which covers the top of the leg and hides any discrepancy in its fit. After turning the rest of the pedestal shape, mark out the leg placement by dividing the circle on the underside of the pedestal into thirds. Draw three equally spaced lines from the circumference to the circle center. These lines will later match up with the center lines drawn on the legs. These operations are covered in depth in the story titled Making Tripod Legs. Aesthetically, it is most pleasing if you mark out leg placement so that the grain bull's-eye (the concentric circles formed by the annular rings) of the pedestal is centered between two of the legs on one side and centered on the third leg on the opposite side.

Cut the legs from 2 in. stock or by resawing from 4 in. stock. The latter choice results in an extra leg which is useful for practice. Refer to the Making Tripod Legs story for detailed instructions on how to lay out and shape the legs and how to lay out and cut both the leg dovetails and the corresponding mortises in the pedestal.

With the legs and pedestal now substantially complete, proceed work on the remaining details. For the birdcage, make four matching spindle turnings with dowel ends (see

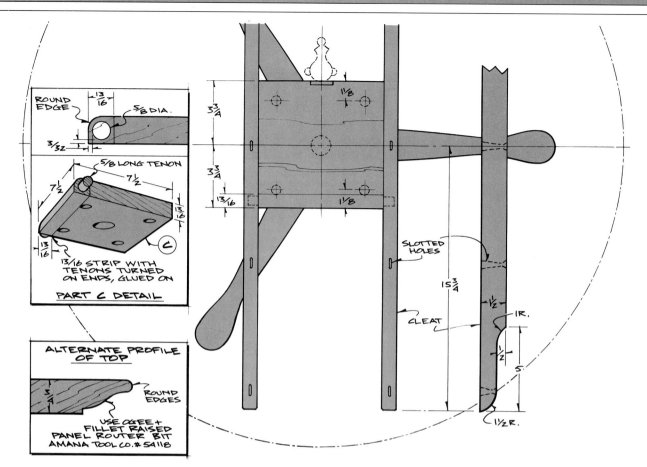

BILL OF MATERIALS — Tilt-Top Table

Finished Dimensions in Inches

A	Top	1 1/16 x 36 in. dia.*	1
B	Cleat	13/16 x 1 1/2 x 31 1/2	2
C	Birdcage Top	13/16 x 7 1/2 x 8 3/4**	1
D	Birdcage Bottom	13/16 x 7 1/2 x 7 1/2	1
E	Spindle	see spindle detail***	4
F	Key	1/4 x 7/8 x 4	1
G	Washer	see washer detail***	1
H	Pedestal	see pedestal detail***	1
I	Leg	see leg detail***	3
J	Catch	3 in. long****	1

*Alternate top thickness is 3/4 in.

**Length includes dowel pins.

***Turning blanks for spindles measure 1 x 1 x 4 11/16, turning blank for pedestal measures 4 x 4 x 21 11/16, turning blank for washer measures 9/16 thick x 4 1/2 dia., leg blanks measure 2 x 6 x 16.

****Available from Horton Brasses, Nooks Hill Rd., P.O. Box 95, Cromwell, CT 06416. Order part No. H-43.

spindle detail) that snugly fit 5/8 in. diameter test holes. The turnings must be the same length from shoulder to shoulder. Now cut the top (C) and bottom (D) of the birdcage. Both the top and bottom sections of the birdcage appear to measure 7 1/2 in. square, but the top piece is actually longer. It includes the two 5/8 in. diameter by 5/8 in. long dowel pins that are turned on either end and that fit into the cleats mounted to the tilting top. Also, this top piece must start out at 7 5/8 in. wide

to allow for the 1/8 in. kerf when it is resawn to form the section that includes the dowel pins. Cut off the 13/16 in. wide strip, turn the dowel pin tenons on either end, and then glue the strip back into place. Center the dowel pins across the thickness of part C so that the diameter's edge is 3/32 in. from the edge (see part C detail). Also, rout the top edge of part C between the pins to a curve. This allows for clearance when the table top is pivoted. Clamp or pin the top and bottom (C and D) together, and drill through both pieces at once. Use a 5/8 in. diameter bit for the four spindle turnings and a 1 1/4 in. diameter bit for the pedestal turning. Note that the holes in the birdcage top for the spindle turnings and pedestal are 1/2 in. deep. Forstner bits are best for drilling these holes. Now assemble the birdcage.

Once more, return the pedestal to the lathe. With the pencil jig (see Making Tripod Legs, step 10, for this jig), scribe for the 1/4 in. wide through mortise to accept the key (F). Outline the ends of the key mortise slot on opposite sides of the pedestal. Note that the slot outline is longer on one side because the key is tapered. The dimensions for the key mortise are shown on the detail of the pedestal. Drill to the pedestal center from each side with a drill bit smaller than 1/4 inch. Then clear out to the pencil line with a wood chisel. Make the key just slightly under 1/4 in. thick and fit it to the mortise.

The key holds the top to the pedestal, and the wooden washer (G) below it prevents the key from scratching the birdcage. To make this washer, rough cut both a 9/16 in. thick by 4 1/2 in. diameter disk of mahogany and a 3/4 in. thick by 5 in. diameter plywood backing piece. Glue these together

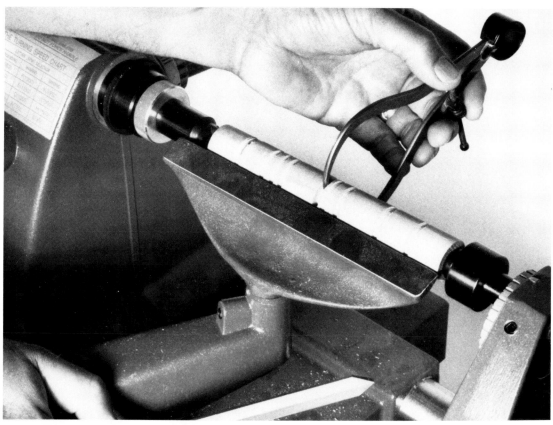

Figure 1. Use a parting tool to establish the turning points and use calipers to check diameters.

Figure 2. Turn the tenon required for the birdcage top (C) on the lathe. Then edge-glue to the larger birdcage workpiece as shown in part C detail.

this way are sometimes called *sloppy screws*. Use the birdcage to determine the placement of the cleats; clamp the cleats to the top and drill *very carefully* for those screws. Use a stop or a piece of tape on the drill bit to insure proper depth. It would be a shame to miscalculate at this point and drill through the top.

Attach one cleat, slide the birdcage into place and attach the second cleat. To keep the top horizontal when the table is in use, the top latches to the birdcage with a teardrop-shaped brass catch (J). Screw the catch to the underside of the table and mortise the latch plate into the birdcage top.

Finally, now that all cutting and fitting work is done, glue the legs onto the pedestal. It's easiest to glue on one leg at a time. Clamp a leg in the bench vise and then slide the pedestal up onto the dovetail. As shown in the clamping detail, a concave clamping block shaped to fit the curve of the pedestal is used with a bar clamp to achieve a tight joint. The block should be narrow enough to fit the space between the legs. You may need to reposition the bar clamp in order to clamp the second and third legs in place.

Once the legs are attached, use a rasp and a file to shape the top of the legs to match the curve of the pedestal. Then shape the bottom of the pedestal, between the legs, to the decorative shape shown. As the illustration shows, this detail is simply a little scalloping into the edges.

Finish by sealing the project with shellac to keep the filler from coloring the wood, fill the pores with colored filler, seal again (the sealer keeps the filler from getting muddy) and complete with several coats of shellac or oil varnish. Be sure the filler you select matches the color of the wood. You may need to mix several colors to achieve the right shade. □

using kraft paper in between (keep it clamped overnight) and mount on the lathe faceplate. Turn a flattened donut shape whose center hole loosely fits the upper cylinder of the pedestal. Then notch the raised edge around the hole to receive the key (see washer detail).

The cleats (B) are the last item to make. Drill the inner sides of the cleats to receive the dowel pivots on the ends of part C. Also, drill and countersink for the screws that will attach the cleats to the top. Allow for wood movement by enlarging all but the center screw holes into slots — about 5/16 in. — at the end adjacent to the table top. Screws put in

Designed and built by Dennis Watson

Walnut Foot Stool

This contemporary walnut foot stool is the perfect complement to your favorite chair.

Construction needs include conventional blind mortise and tenon joints, and spline-strengthened miter joints. The really fun part of the project starts when you get out the gouges and Surform to shape and blend the legs and rails. Upholstering the seat is not difficult; it's a simple cover

sewn together at the corners, pulled over a foam covered plywood board and stapled in place.

The legs and top rail require a 2½ in. by 1¾ in. piece of walnut, which is expensive and difficult to find, so we used 1¼ in. thick walnut and glued a ¾ in. thick strip 3 in. long to the top of the legs and each end of the top rails. We also used a ½ in. by 3 in. back to the legs where the seat rail joins. The additional strips of wood provide enough thickness to cut the radius or curved corners. Miter the ends of the legs and top rail, then cut the mortises for the lower rail and seat rail. Cut the mortises on the radial arm saw using a ¼ in. bottoming end mill and a shopmade jig. The mortises could also be cut with a router or by hand with a chisel. If you prefer, dowels could be substituted for the mortise and tenon joint.

Rip the stock for the stretcher from ½ in. walnut and the seat rail from ½ in. walnut. Cut to length and don't forget to allow for the tenons. Cut the tenons on the table saw or radial arm saw a little fat, then trim with a sharp chisel to fit snugly in the mortises.

At this time you can band saw the interior radius of the legs and upper rail. Don't band saw the exterior radius until after glue-up; the square corners aid in clamping. If you don't

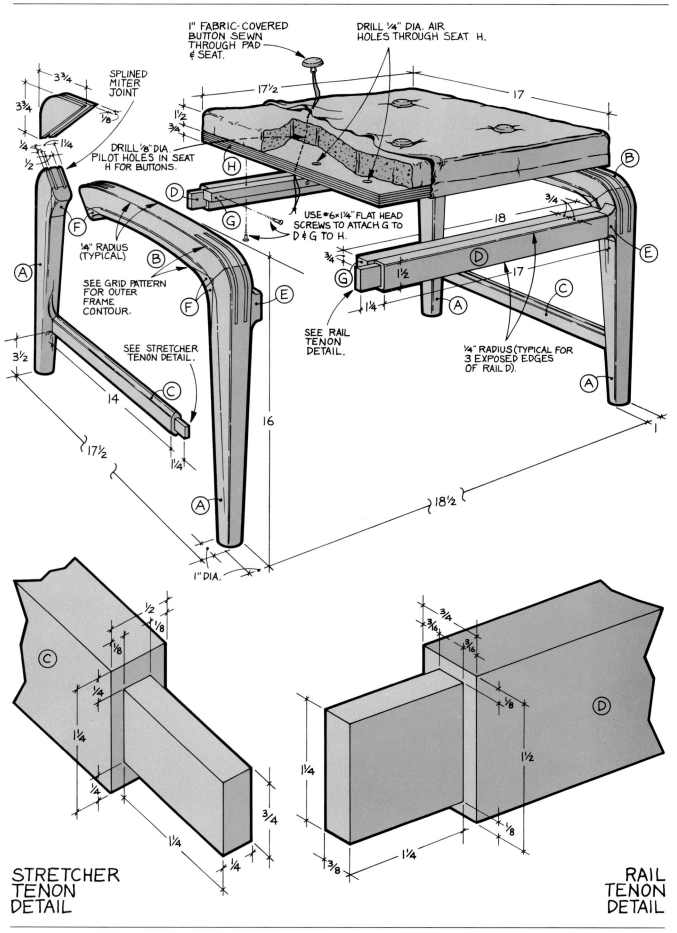

1" FABRIC-COVERED BUTTON SEWN THROUGH PAD & SEAT.

DRILL ¼" DIA. AIR HOLES THROUGH SEAT H.

SPLINED MITER JOINT

3¾

3¾

⅛

¼

1¼

½

17½

1½

¾

DRILL ⅛" DIA. PILOT HOLES IN SEAT H FOR BUTTONS.

17

H

D

B

G

¼" RADIUS (TYPICAL)

SEE GRID PATTERN FOR OUTER FRAME CONTOUR.

USE #6×1¼" FLAT HEAD SCREWS TO ATTACH G TO D & G TO H.

¾

18

F

B

E

A

F

E

¾

A

G

1½

C

SEE RAIL TENON DETAIL.

17

D

1¼

3½

SEE STRETCHER TENON DETAIL.

¼" RADIUS (TYPICAL FOR 3 EXPOSED EDGES OF RAIL D).

14

C

16

A

1¼

17½

1

A

18½

1" DIA.

½

⅛

⅛

¼

C

1¼

¼

¾

¾

3/16

3/16

3/16

⅛

D

¼

1¼

1½

¼

1¼

3/8

⅛

STRETCHER TENON DETAIL

RAIL TENON DETAIL

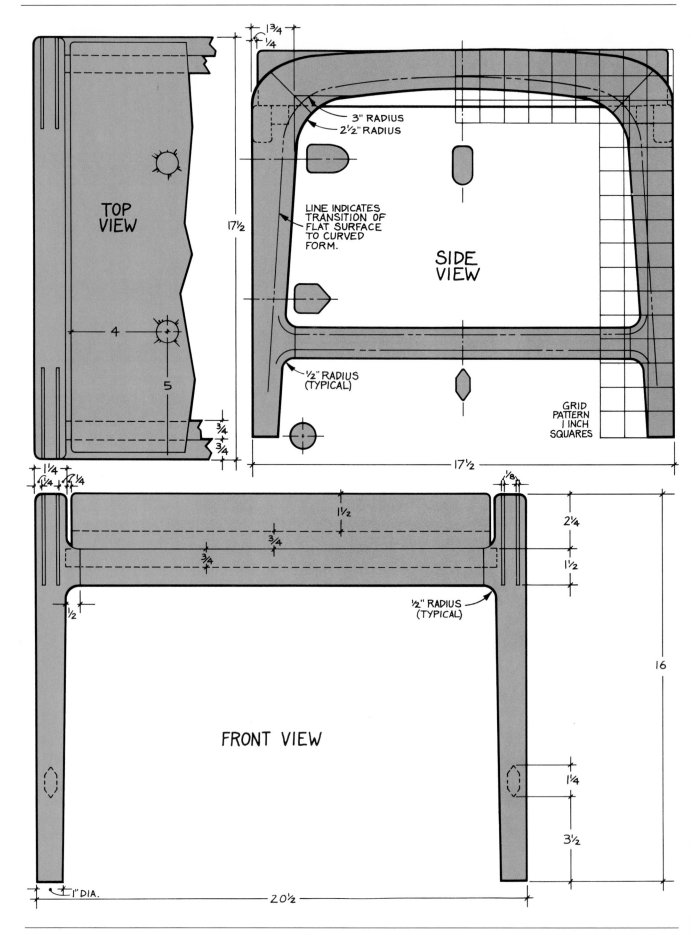

TOP VIEW

1¾
¼

3" RADIUS
2½" RADIUS

LINE INDICATES
TRANSITION OF
FLAT SURFACE
TO CURVED
FORM.

SIDE VIEW

17½

½" RADIUS
(TYPICAL)

4

5

¾
¾

GRID
PATTERN
I INCH
SQUARES

17½

1¼
¼ ¼

1½

¾
¾

⅛

2¼

1½

½" RADIUS
(TYPICAL)

½

16

FRONT VIEW

1¼

3½

I" DIA.

20½

Figure 1. Glue small blocks of walnut to the legs to provide enough wood from which to cut the radiused corners.

BILL OF MATERIALS — Walnut Foot Stool

Finished Dimensions in Inches

A	Walnut Leg	1¾ x 1¼ x 16	4
B	Walnut Top Rail	1¾ x 1¼ x 17½	2
C	Walnut Stretcher	½ x 1¼ x 16½	2
D	Walnut Seat Rail	¾ x 1½ x 19½	2
E	Walnut Block	½ x ¾ x 3	4
F	Walnut Block	¾ x 1¼ x 3	8
G	Walnut Ledger	¾ x ¾ x 18	2
H	Fir plywood seat	¾ x 17½ x 17	1

have a band saw and are using a saber saw, it's just as easy to wait and make the interior cuts after glue-up. Dry-fit the ends together and make sure the joints pull up tight, then add glue and clamp overnight.

The real strength of the miter joint lies in the two ⅛ in. triangular splines. Cut the ⅛ in. slots for the splines using a 10 in. carbide tip combination blade on the table saw. A shopmade tenoning jig is used to hold the end frame vertical. The frame is clamped to the jig, and the jig and frame slide along the rip fence past the saw blade. Cut two slots in each corner. The splines should fit snugly in the groove. If they're too tight, the wood will swell when glue is applied, and you'll not be able to drive in the splines. The splines could be made

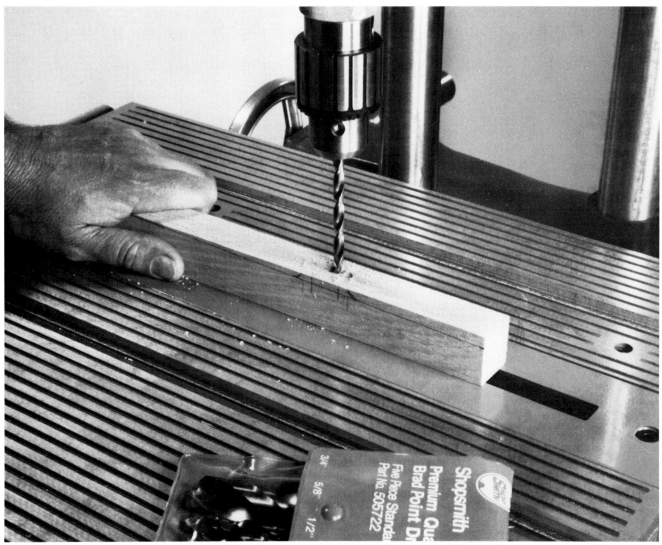

Figure 2. Form the cavity for the leg mortises with a Forstner bit or spur bit installed in your drill press. Use a depth stop and finish the mortise with wood chisels. Wear eye protection.

Figure 3. After gluing the leg assemblies, cut the spline slots with a homemade jig to hold the assembly at a 45 degree angle. Cut two spline slots on the table saw. Make sure the workpiece is held securely.

from contrasting wood, such as oak or cherry, for an interesting visual effect. Glue the splines in place. Use a C-clamp across the face with small blocks to prevent the clamp from marring the surface and to distribute the pressure.

Now comes the fun part, the shaping. We used carving gouges and a round Surform to rough out the work. The rough surfaces were smoothed using a small flap type sander and a ½ in. diameter drum sander, both mounted in a ¼ in. drill. Final sanding was done by hand using 220 grit sandpaper.

With the ends finished, the seat rail is next. It's made from ¾ in. thick stock. Cut the tenon on each end and dry-fit the seat rail to both end frames; check to make sure the joints pull up tight. Apply glue and clamp. Check to be sure the assembly is square. Use a Surform and a ½ in. sanding drum to smooth the corner between the end frame and seat rail.

Cut a piece of ¾ in. plywood to size and drill several holes in it to allow air to escape from the cushion. Glue medium density foam to the plywood using rubber cement. Now cut the upholstery to size and sew the box corners. Next, stretch the fabric over the foam and plywood, and staple in place. Have 1 in. buttons covered at a local upholstery shop

Figure 4. Cut the side's general shape with a saber saw on the inside cuts. Make the outside cuts on the band saw.

Figure 5. A rotary rasp chucked to the drill is a quick way to smooth the radiused corner between the leg and lower rail.

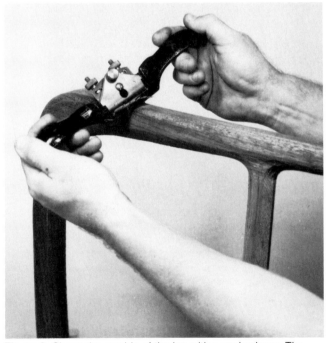

Figure 6. Shape the outside of the leg with a spokeshave. The top of the leg is rectangular in cross section, circular at the bottom.

Figure 7. Use a round Surform file to smooth the tool marks left by the carving gouge.

with the same upholstery fabric used to cover the stool. Drill a ⅛ in. hole in the plywood bottom at the location of the button. Attach heavy weight string to the button, and using a long upholstery needle, probe for the hole. Pull the string through and tie off. For a professional looking job, use tack strip to apply upholstery to the underside of the bottom. It covers the exposed wood and stapled edges.

Attach a ¾ in. by ¾ in. ledger strip to the seat rails using No. 6 by 1¼ in. flathead screws. Then screw the seat to the ledger with No. 6 by 1¼ in. flathead screws.

The stool is finished using two coats of Watco Danish Oil, with the second coat wet sanded using No. 600 wet/dry sandpaper. The oil is followed with a coat of paste wax to finish the project. □

Project reprinted from *Woodworking Techniques and Projects* by Rosario Capotosto

Rotating Centerpiece

This attractive server, mounted on a lazy-Susan bearing, gently brings the item you want to your side of the table with a flick of a finger.

You can make the piece by turning the parts on a lathe, but this tool is by no means essential. You can achieve the same result using a saber saw and router, and buying ready-made gallery spindles.

To make the server on the lathe, you do faceplate turning — so the base is screwed directly to the faceplate. Screw the stock for the ring to a scrap board of the same size, which is in turn secured to the faceplate. Make sure to locate the screws in the backup board and the work so they will be centered within the confines of the ring to avoid cutting into a screw with the turning chisel. If your lathe can't handle an 18 in. diameter disk, the turning will have to be done outboard. Although your roughing cuts to round the pieces are correctly made from the face side of the work, it is advisable to pre-saw the squares to a rough round form for safety. Accidentally touching spinning square corners can result in serious injury. After sizing the diameter of the base and ring with a parting chisel, shape the workpiece with a spear-point chisel.

So much for the lathe procedures; the rest of the text explains how to make the server without a lathe.

The circular base and the ring are made with ¾ cherry stock or other hardwood of your choice. Both are 17½ in. in diameter, so you'll have to glue up stock to obtain workpieces of sufficient size.

The simplest way to obtain the 18 in. by 18 in. square required is to edge-glue two 9 in. by 18 in. boards together, but this won't work. Such a board would be prone to warp. The ring in particular would be weak and apt to split in the end-grain areas. Also, end grain is always somewhat difficult to shape to a moulded edge and to sand and finish-coat satisfactorily. Additionally, the end-grain pattern would run off the edges — not particularly attractive for a circular design.

The alternative is to make the board by gluing together four triangular segments. The result is a warp-resistant piece featuring an interesting symmetrical grain pattern, minimal end-grain throughout, and a structurally sound ring and base.

The square for the base is made by cutting four 45/45/90 degree triangles from a piece of stock measuring 9¼ in. by 48 inches. Set the radial arm or a miter gauge for a 45 degree miter cut. Flip the board over front to back after each pass, cutting each triangular segment so it has an 18 in. base.

Follow the same procedure in preparing the stock for the ring. However, here you can economize on lumber by making truncated triangles. These pieces, with the same 18 in. base, can be cut from a piece of 4½ in. by 60 in. stock. When these four segments are joined, a square opening will result in the waste area in the center.

Several kinds of edge joint can be used effectively to join the segments, including tongue and groove, dowel or the spline-reinforced edge joint illustrated. A plain butt joint should be avoided because it would be rather weak, particularly for the ring.

When the pieces have been cut, arrange them with the best side up and mark them for identification. This is important whenever grooves (tongues) are to be cut or when holes for dowels are to be drilled for a joint. The same surface of the parts should face the guide fence, be it on the saw or drill press. The same applies when using any one of a variety of doweling jigs.

This approach allows some leeway in centering — if the grooves (or dowels) are slightly off center it won't matter since the error will be consistent. A point to remember if you

Figure 1. Set the saw for a 45 degree miter cut. Then make the first cut and use the cutoff as a stop. Clamp it in place so its point just touches the blade. After each succeeding cut, flip the workpiece over so the mitered end butts against the stop.

Figure 2. Cut the splines by setting the saw blade to the correct depth of cut. Move each workpiece as shown, while firmly keeping the workpiece against the saw fence. Watch out for your fingers in case of binding or finger slippage!

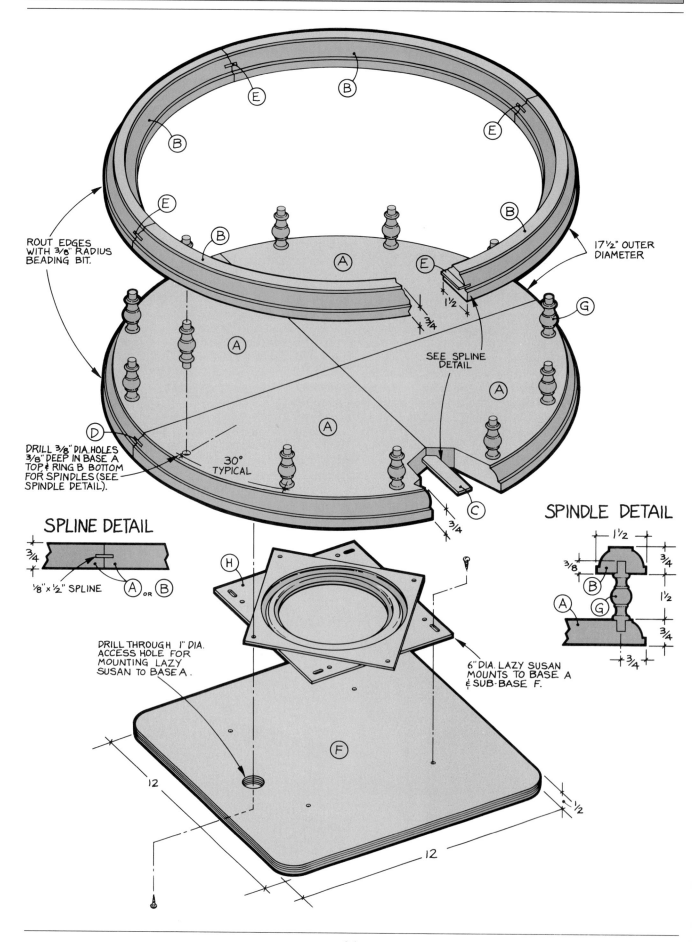

ROUT EDGES
WITH ³⁄₈" RADIUS
BEADING BIT.

E

B

B

E

E

E

B

B

A

A

A

A

A

A

G

17½" OUTER
DIAMETER

1½

¾

SEE SPLINE
DETAIL

D

DRILL ³⁄₈" DIA. HOLES
³⁄₈" DEEP IN BASE A
TOP & RING B BOTTOM
FOR SPINDLES (SEE
SPINDLE DETAIL).

30°
TYPICAL

C

¾

SPINDLE DETAIL

1½

³⁄₈

¾

B

A

G

1½

¾

¾

SPLINE DETAIL

¾

⅛" x ½" SPLINE

(A) or (B)

H

DRILL THROUGH 1" DIA.
ACCESS HOLE FOR
MOUNTING LAZY
SUSAN TO BASE A.

F

6" DIA. LAZY SUSAN
MOUNTS TO BASE A
& SUB-BASE F.

12

½

12

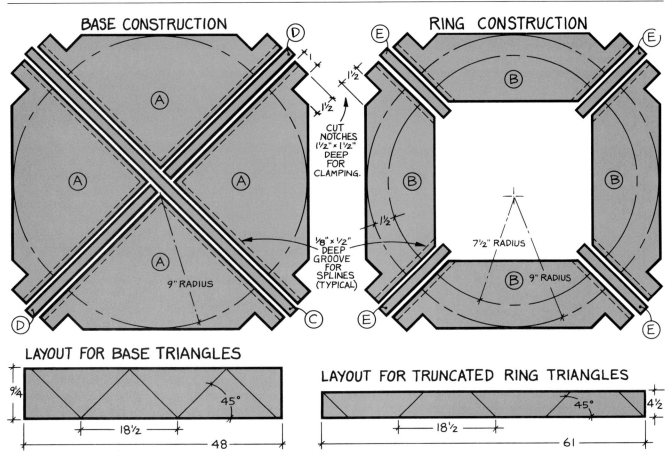

BASE CONSTRUCTION

RING CONSTRUCTION

CUT NOTCHES 1½" × 1½" DEEP FOR CLAMPING.

⅛" × ½" DEEP GROOVE FOR SPLINES (TYPICAL)

9" RADIUS

7½" RADIUS

9" RADIUS

LAYOUT FOR BASE TRIANGLES

9¼

45°

18½

48

LAYOUT FOR TRUNCATED RING TRIANGLES

45°

4½

18½

61

decide to use dowel joints: locate the dowels so they won't be in the path of the cutting line.

Cut the grooves centered on the edges of each joint surface, then cut the splines and check them for a good fit; they should be neither too tight nor too loose. Cut them from the same stock so they won't be prominent in the finished work.

Regardless of the kind of joint used, gluing four triangular segments ordinarily could prove quite trying. But the task is readily accomplished in the manner illustrated, using four C-clamps and two bar clamps. Cut two flats at the corners

as indicated in the illustration to provide positive bearing surfaces for the clamps. The C-clamps apply pressure to the outer sections of the joints while the bar clamps exert pressure on the center area. When assembling, apply the C-clamps to the corners first, then add the bar clamps.

Use a saber saw with a circle cutting pivot guide to make the circular cuts. In order to track perfectly true, the pivot point must be in precise lateral alignment with the front edge of the blade. You can check the alignment by carefully measuring with a rule, then confirm the accuracy by making a test cut in a piece of cardboard.

Figure 3. Cut clamp notches into the corners of each triangular segment, and cut the splines to size and test-fit before gluing.

Figure 4. Apply glue to all joint surfaces, then assemble by joining the two pairs of segments along with the longer spline. Attach the C-clamps to the corners with moderate pressure and add the two bar clamps. Keep the assembly flat.

BILL OF MATERIALS — Rotating Centerpiece

Finished Dimensions in Inches

A	Base	¾ x 9¼ x 18½	4
B	Ring	¾ x 4½ x 18½	4
C	Base Spline	⅛ x ½ x 26	1
D	Base Half-Spline	⅛ x ½ x 12	2
E	Ring Spline	⅛ x ½ x 6	4
F	Sub-Base	½ ply x 12 x 12	1
G	Spindle	⅜ dia. x 1½*	12
H	Lazy Susan Bearing	6" dia.**	1

*Constantine's Part # SP 101, 2050 Eastchester Rd., Bronx, NY 10461.
**Constantine's Part # 49Q6

If your guide does not feature an adjustable pivot, and should your test cut prove erratic (spiral in or out), it may be possible to correct the problem by using a blade with a different width or by boring a new pivot hole in the guide.

Bore a blade entry hole in the waste area, adjacent to the cutting line, and large enough to permit the blade to be positioned tangent to the cutting line. Set the radial distance between blade and pivot, use a smooth-cutting blade and feed slowly.

When cutting the ring it is necessary to insert a strip of wood across the center of the opening to provide a base for the circle guide pivot. This can be toenailed with a few brads or held in place with a spot of glue. The outer circle must be cut first in order to preserve the pivot support.

Sanding follows sawing. The pivot-guided cuts result in fairly smooth edges free of saw blade ripples, so you won't have to do too much sanding. Use a stationary disk sander for

the outside curves and a large diameter (3 in.) sanding drum for the inside curve. If neither of these tools is available, you can do an adequate job by hand. Use segments of the cut-off waste as shaped sanding blocks.

A router with a ⅜ in. radius beading bit is used to form the decorative edge. Rout clockwise on the outer edge and counterclockwise on the inside edge. Otherwise the blade will gouge the wood and spoil the work.

A protractor is used to locate the twelve positions for the spindle holes. Turn the base upside down and make a pencil line across the center. Place the protractor's center mark in the dead center of the disk and tick off pencil marks spaced 30 degrees apart. Shift the protractor to the other side of the line to continue the marks. With a rule, draw radial lines from the center point through each tick mark. You can use a marking gauge or a compass to make hole marks on the radial lines, ¾ in. from the edge.

To assure perfect alignment of the spindles, tape the ring to the base and drill ¹⁄₁₆ in. pilot holes through the bottom of the base and partly into the ring. Make an identifying mark on both pieces for later rematching, then take them apart. Drill the holes for the spindles. Apply glue sparingly to the holes in the base and insert the spindles. Then apply glue to the holes in the ring. Do not apply glue to the spindle ends; it would be smeared onto the surface during the fitting operation. Flip the base over and guide the spindles into the holes in the ring.

A 4 in. lazy-Susan bearing is used to permit the server to turn effortlessly. Attach the bearing to a piece of ½ in. plywood 12 in. square. Drill a 1 in. diameter screw access hole in this sub-base, centered over the screw holes in the bearing plate. Attach the bearing first to the sub-base, then to the server base. □

Figure 5. Use a circle guide to cut the upper ring. The center strip is added to support the pivot. Cut the outer circle first.

Figure 6. Shape both edges of the ring with your router as shown. Keep the frame well supported and make in sections until you work your way around the ring.

Vienna Regulator Clock

The Vienna regulator clock was and still is considered to be one of the finest of the classic European clock designs.

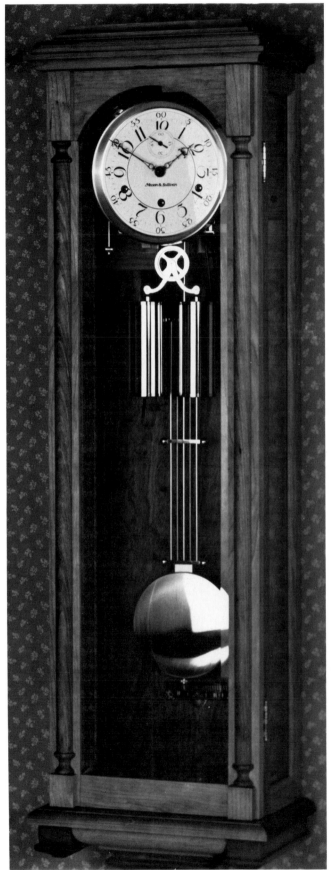

The Vienna regulator clock style was developed and perfected in Austria and Germany during the 19th century and has changed little over the years. This particular model is representative of a traditional Vienna regulator from the 1850's.

With thick beveled glass on the front and both sides, the Vienna regulator case is intended to fully expose the handsome solid brass movement, weight shells and pendulum that characterize this design. While the model pictured was crafted in cherry, walnut would be an excellent alternate choice. We have arranged with the Mason and Sullivan Company to provide a single kit including all the hardware, glass and movement parts that you will need to build the clock exactly as shown (see bill of materials). Although the specified hardware, glass and movement represent an expense of about $400, this cost should be balanced by the fact that the identical finished clock retails for about $1,200.

The construction of the clock case involves basic woodworking skills; however, because of the need for precision, this is a project that is best undertaken by those with a moderate to advanced level of experience. It is strongly recommended that the hardware, glass and movement (see bill of materials) be purchased *before* beginning the assembly to insure proper fit of all the parts.

Cabinet Construction

The best method to build the case is to construct the individual assemblies of the side frames first. The stiles (A, B, C) and rails (D) are of a mitered moulded type. First, use a ⅜ in. radius ball bearing guided router bit to apply the ⅜ in. radius detail, then cut the ⅜ in. by ⅜ in. rabbet for the glass. Tenon the ends of D, and mortise A, B and C to fit. Note that although the tongue cut on parts D (which fits into the corresponding groove cut in parts F and E) is stepped on the ends, this in no way affects the strength of the construction. Parts A and B are identical except in the hardware application, where A is mortised for the hinges and B is mortised for the latches. After mitering the bead as shown (note that the stile bead must be mitered and cut back to accept the rails), glue and assemble the side frames. Now cut the parts for the base (E), top (F), upper top (G), crown (H), pediment base (I), lower pediment (J), pediment moulding (K), base blocks (L) and base moulding (M). Use a ½ in. bearing guided cove cutter to

Project courtesy of *The Woodworker's Journal* magazine

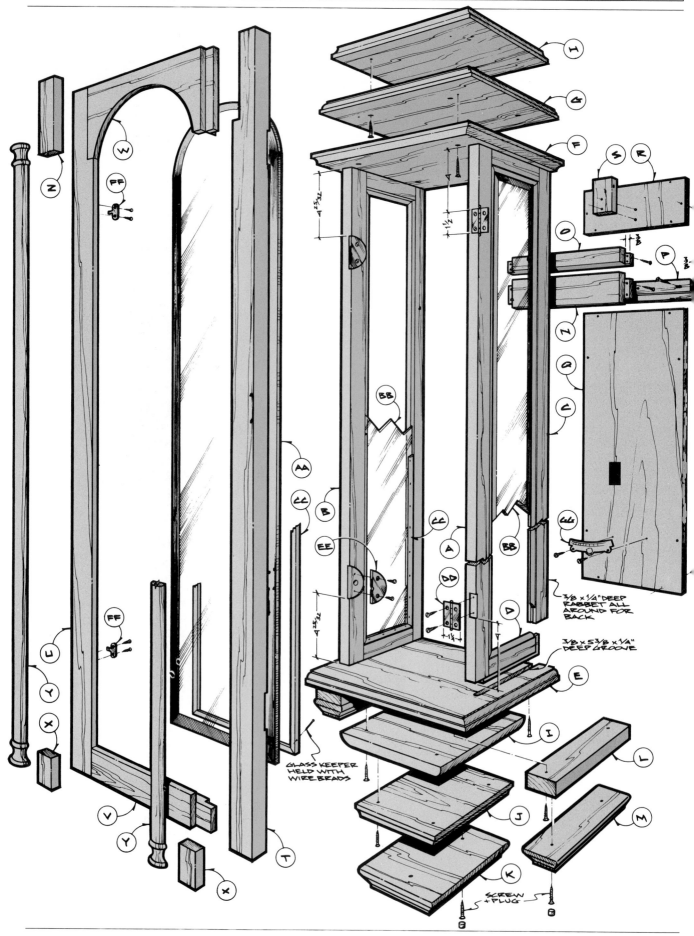

3/8 x 1/4" DEEP RABBET ALL AROUND FOR BACK

3/8 x 5 3/8 x 1/4" DEEP GROOVE

GLASS KEEPER HELD WITH WIRE BRADS

SCREW + PLUG

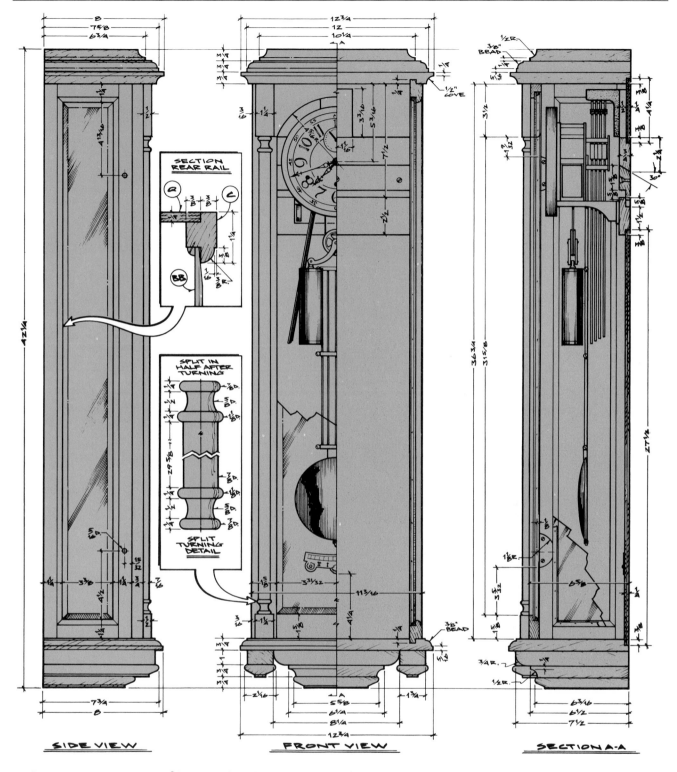

SIDE VIEW FRONT VIEW SECTION A-A

profile parts H, F and J, and a ⅜ in. beading bit to mould the edges of parts E and G. Rout part I with a ¾ in. radius round over bit. Follow the simple four-step process shown in the moulding detail to establish the pediment mouldings on parts K and M. Don't forget to rout the ⅜ in. by ¼ in. grooves in the base and top to accept the tongue on parts D.

Now assemble the case. Begin by mounting the base and top to the side frame assemblies. Bore, countersink and screw parts E and F to reinforce the tongue-and-groove glue joint.

Screw part G to part H as shown and then mount to part F. No glue is needed here, but finish sand all parts before assembly. Screw the lower mouldings and pediments in place, one over the other, as shown. Drill and countersink for all the screws; keep all edges flush at the back as indicated and plug the screw holes in parts K and M.

Next, using the router equipped with a ⅜ in. rabbeting bit, rabbet the case back to accept the various back and hanger parts. Square the rabbet corners with a wood chisel. Now cut

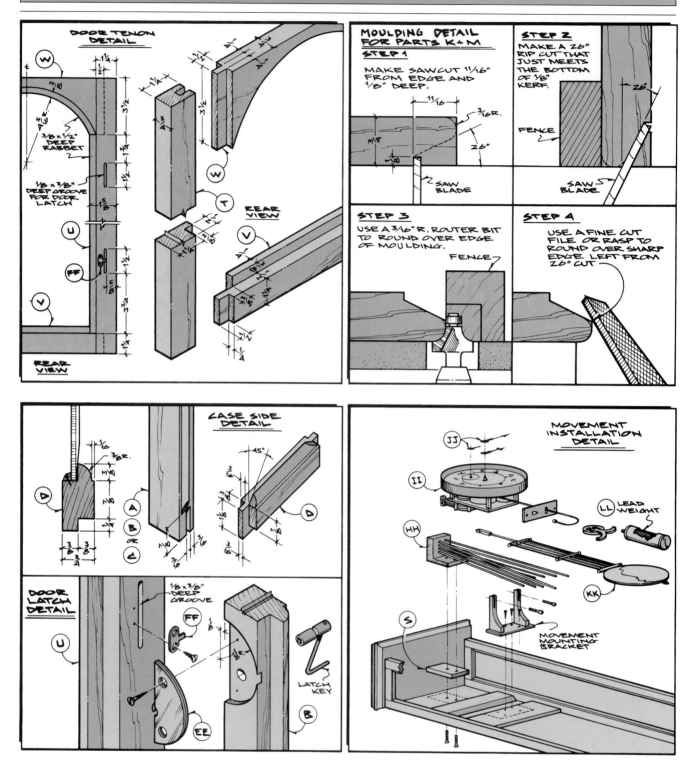

and fit the lower and upper back (Q and R), the case back rail (N), case hanger (O) and wall hanger (P). Note that the case hanger and wall hanger are both beveled at 30 degrees where they join one another. When complete, lower the case onto part P, which is mounted securely to the wall with toggle bolts or other screw-type fasteners. Glue and screw the case back rail and case hanger in place, but secure the upper and lower back with screws only. All these parts are best final mounted *after* the side glass has been fixed in place, to provide clear access through the back for a drill.

Make the door, consisting of parts T, U, V and W, as shown in the door tenon detail. Note that tenons on the ends of the upper and lower door rails fit into corresponding mortises in the stiles. Use a ⅜ in. rabbeting bit to cut the ⅜ in. by ½ in. deep rabbet to accept the glass in the door rails and stiles. Several passes are needed to achieve the ½ in. depth. Make certain that you understand the door construction and the fact that stiles T and U must be notched (see exploded view) to receive the top rail, before laying out and cutting the door parts. Work carefully.

Figure 1. When routing decorative cuts around square or rectangular workpieces, cut the end grain edges first and then the long grain edges. This should eliminate tear-out.

BILL OF MATERIALS — Vienna Regulator Clock

Finished Dimensions in Inches

A	Right Side Front Stile	¾ x 1¼ x 36¾	1
B	Left Side Front Stile	¾ x 1¼ x 36¾	1
C	Rear Stile	¾ x 1¼ x 36¾	2
D	Side Rail	¾ x 1½ x 4⅞*	4
E	Base	¾ x 8 x 12¾	1
F	Top	¾ x 8 x 12¾	1
G	Upper Top	¾ x 7⅝ x 12	1
H	Crown	¾ x 6¾ x 10¼	1
I	Pediment Base	1 x 7½ x 8¼	1
J	Lower Pediment	¾ x 6½ x 6¼	1
K	Pediment Moulding	¾ x 6³⁄₁₆ x 5⅝	1
L	Base Blocks	1 x 1¾ x 7½	2
M	Base Moulding	¾ x 2¹⁄₁₆ x 7¾	2
N	Case Back Rail	¾ x 2½ x 10⁷⁄₁₆	1
O	Case Hanger	¾ x 2¼ x 10⁷⁄₁₆	1
P	Wall Hanger	¾ x 2¼ x 10⁷⁄₁₆	1
Q	Lower Back	¼ x 10⁷⁄₁₆ x 27½	1
R	Upper Back	¼ x 10⁷⁄₁₆ x 4¼	1
S	Chime Spacer	½ x 2⅛ x 3³⁄₁₆	1
T	Door Stile Right	¾ x 1⅝ x 36¾	1
U	Door Stile Left	¾ x 1⅝ x 36¾	1
V	Lower Door Rail	¾ x 1⅝ x 9¹¹⁄₁₆*	1
W	Upper Door Rail	¾ x 3½ x 9¹¹⁄₁₆*	1
X	Lower Stile Block	½ x 1¼ x 1⅝	2
Y	Stile Turning	see detail	split
Z	Upper Stile Block	½ x 1¼ x 3½	2
AA	Door Glass (beveled)	8⅝ x 34¹¹⁄₁₆**	1
BB	Side Glass (beveled)	4¹⁄₁₆ x 35**	2
CC	Keeper Strip	¼ x ¼**	20 ft.
DD	Hinge	1¼ x 1½**	2
EE	Latch	as shown**	2
FF	Catch	as shown**	2
GG	Regulator Plaque	1½ x 3⅝ brass**	1
HH	Chimes	Westminster**	1
II	Movement	solid brass, cable drive**	1
JJ	Hands	as shown**	3
KK	Pendulum	5½ in. diameter brass**	1
LL	Lead Weight	as shown**	2

*Includes tenons.

**Parts AA-LL are all available as a kit from Mason & Sullivan, 586 Higgins Crowell Road, West Yarmouth, MA 02673. Request current prices by calling 800-227-7418 and specifying Vienna Regulator Clock.

Assemble the door frame, and cut the upper and lower stile blocks (X, Z). The stile turning (Y) is a simple split turning if you have access to a lathe. If not, order the split turnings from the Mason and Sullivan Company (see bill of materials for address; order part No. 2247). The split turning is only available in walnut. The cost is $12.95 per piece (two required). Locate and glue the stile blocks and split turnings in place. *Note:* Cut the ⅛ in. by ⅜ in. groove in part U to accept the door latch (see door latch detail) and the hinge mortises in part T before you mount the stile blocks and split turnings.

Secure the door and side panel glass (AA and BB) with the plastic keeper strip (CC) included in the clock kit. You will need to pre-drill for the wire brads (also included) to avoid bending them or breaking the glass.

Mount the clock movement (II) to the case back rail, and mount the chime assembly to the chime spacer (S), which has been screwed in place to the case back as shown. Further instructions on mounting and adjusting the movement are included in the kit.

Note: Final sanding of the clock case and door, and application of the finish, should be accomplished before inserting the glass and mounting the movement.

Our clock was finished with several coats of a linseed oil/varnish mixture. Take care not to get finish on the area of the rabbets where the case back rail and case hanger will be glued in place. These parts, in addition to the upper and lower back and chime block, should be finished *after* they are mounted. Touch-up finishing will probably be needed after the glass, door and movement have been mounted. ☐

Project courtesy of *The Woodworker's Journal* magazine

Shaker Sewing Desk

It has enough room for storing thread, cloth and much more.

This fine example of a Shaker sewing desk was measured and photographed at Hancock Shaker Village in Hancock, Massachusetts. On the original, the legs and various frame members were made from maple while the panels and drawers were made from pine stained a deep red. As a final finish, the Shakers used a clear varnish on the entire piece.

We included Fig. 1 in the artwork to show the basic framework of the piece. In order to show it with a minimum of confusion, we did not include the various panels, drawers, runners, guides, etc. The basic framework with all these parts added on is shown in Fig. 8. The point to keep in mind is that Fig. 1 is not intended as an assembly drawing; in fact, when the basic framework is glued up later on, the panels must be assembled as part of that framework.

Make the two front legs (A and B) and the two back legs (C and D) first. Rip stock to 1 ½ in. square before cutting each leg to the length shown in the bill of materials. Using the lathe, turn the bottom end of each leg to the dimensions specified in the turning detail. As indicated in the front elevation, note that the turning starts at a point 8 ¼ in. from the leg bottom.

Next, lay out the location of the various mortises that need to be cut for each of the legs. To locate the mortises and

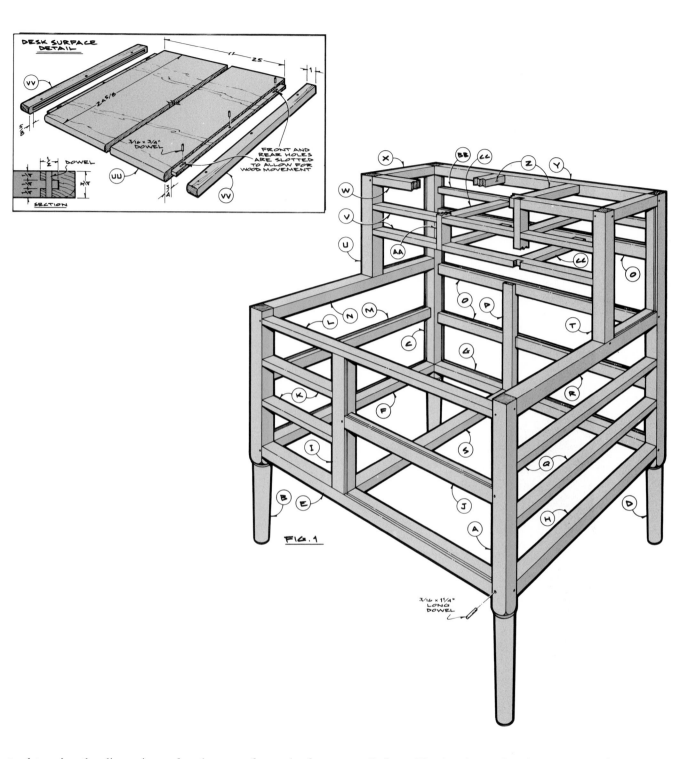

DESK SURFACE DETAIL

25

24 5/8

3/16 x 3/4" DOWEL

FRONT AND REAR HOLES ARE SLOTTED TO ALLOW FOR WOOD MOVEMENT

DOWEL

SECTION

FIG. 1

3/16 x 1 1/4" LONG DOWEL

to determine the dimensions of each one, refer to the four elevation drawings in addition to Figs. 1 and 2. Lay out the mortises with care and double-check the size and location of each one. One miscalculation can ruin all the previous work that went into the leg. Once you are satisfied with the layout, use a sharp wood chisel to chop out each mortise. Later, after the framework is dry-assembled, you need to lay out and cut additional mortises for parts DD, MM and PP (see Fig. 8), but for now you do not need to deal with them.

Refer to Fig. 1 and note that the legs have a ¼ in. deep by ¼ in. wide groove cut to accept the panels (see panel section typical). Lay out the various groove locations on the legs. Then use the router or, better yet, a router table to make the groove cuts. Use a ¼ in. straight bit and make the cut in two passes, with each cut removing ⅛ in. of stock. Next, rip stock to thickness and width for parts E through Z plus BB (see Figs. 2 and 4). Refer to the bill of materials for the cut lengths of all these parts. Note that the lengths include a tenon

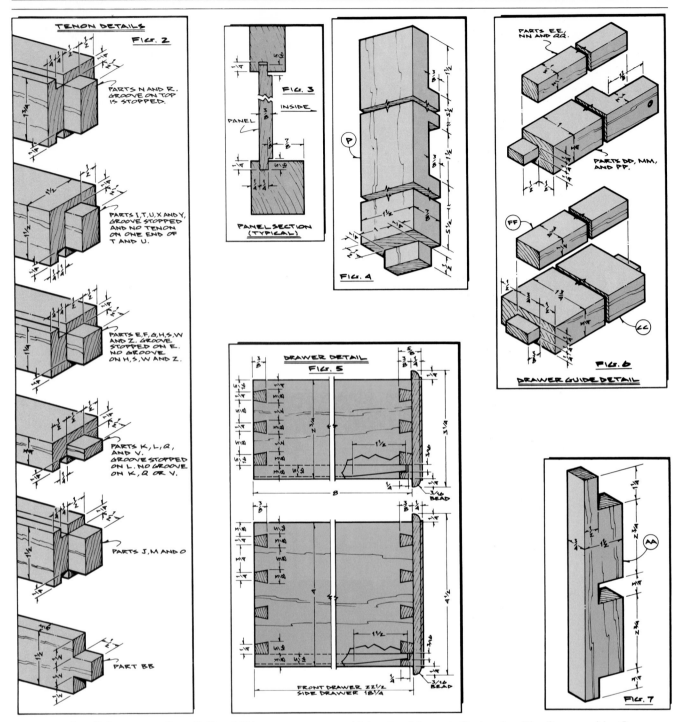

or tenons for all these parts. Parts P, T and U have a tenon on only one end while all others have a tenon on each end. At this point, it would be a good idea to label each piece with its proper part number — it will come in handy later on. Now, referring to the elevation drawings and to Figs. 1, 2 and 4, lay out the location of the various mortises in each of the parts. As with the legs, lay out each mortise with care and double-check the size and location of each one. Once you have chopped out all the mortises, cut the ¾ in. wide by ½ in. deep notches in parts V and W to accept parts AA.

The tenons are best cut using the table saw with a dado head. Use a spacing block to establish the ½ in. tenon length and set the dado head to make a ¼ in. deep cut. Make all the ¼ in. shoulder cuts first, using Fig. 2 as a guide. Once you make all the ¼ in. deep cuts, raise the blade to ½ in. and make the ½ in. deep shoulder cuts.

Refer to Figs. 1 and 2 to lay out the location of the various ¼ in. deep by ¼ in. wide grooves. Cut them in the same manner used to cut the grooves on the legs.

Next, make parts AA (Fig. 7) and the four parts CC (Fig. 6). Use the dado head to cut the notches in parts AA and the tenons on each end of parts CC.

You'll need ⅜ in. thick stock to make the panels (parts GG, HH, II and JJ). Most lumberyards don't carry ⅜ in. material, so you'll need to start with thicker stock and reduce it. Some lumberyards have thickness planers and are willing

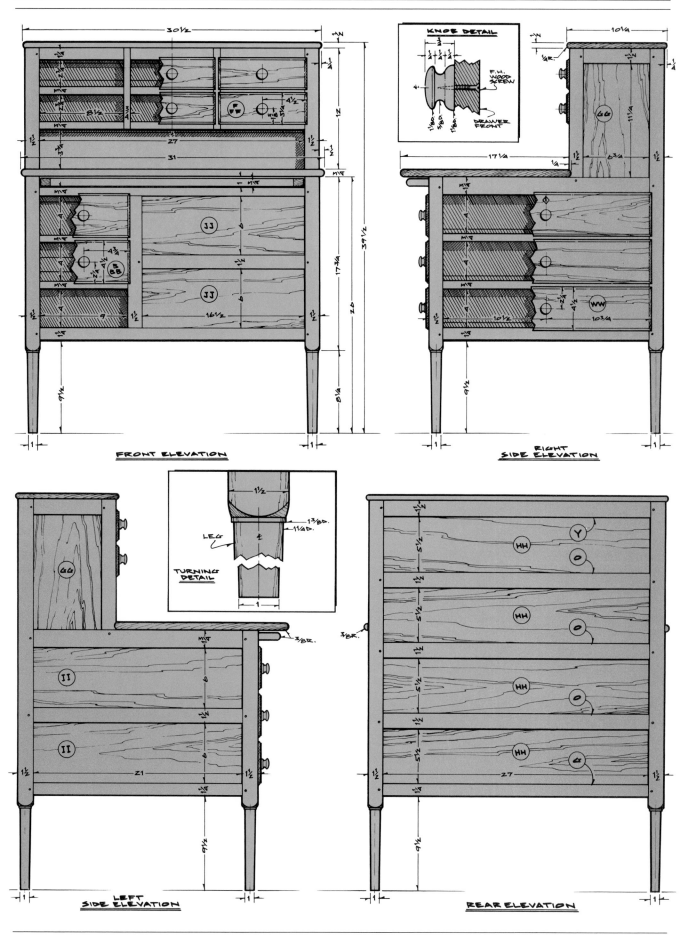

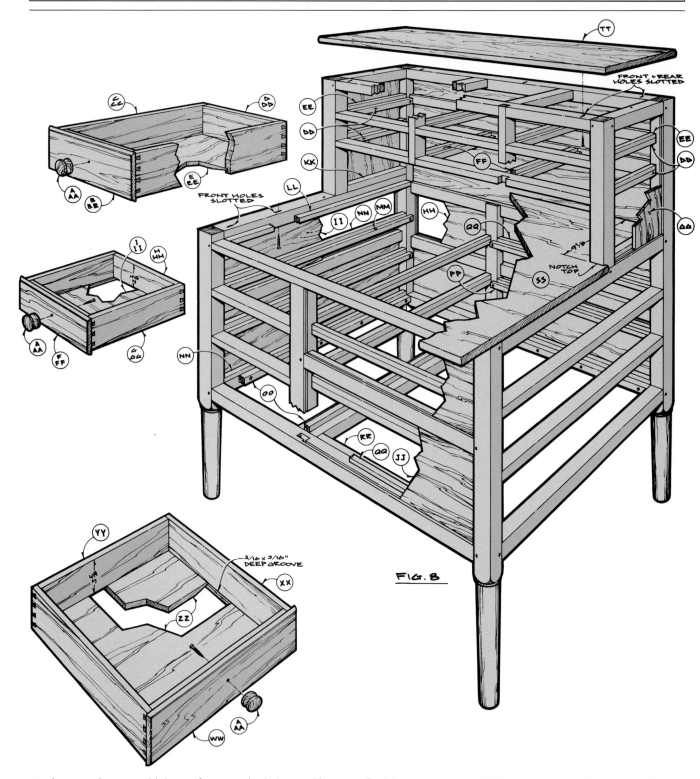

FIG. 8

to plane stock to any thickness for a nominal charge. If your lumberyard doesn't do this, check some local millwork shops, as they often offer this service.

Cut the panels to the overall length and width shown in the bill of materials, then use the table saw and dado head to cut the 1/8 in. deep by 5/16 in. wide rabbet (see Fig. 3) all around. The panel length and width dimensions given in the bill of materials do not allow any clearance inside the grooves. When you dry-assemble the framework you may

find it necessary to lightly hand plane the panel edges to provide room for them to expand and contract with seasonal changes in humidity.

At this point dry-assemble all parts (A through Z, plus AA, BB, CC, GG, HH, II and JJ). The dry assembly is important to insure that all parts fit correctly. Since so many pieces are involved, a specific sequence of assembly must be followed. If you labeled each of the parts earlier, it will make this step somewhat easier.

Figure 9. It is imperative that the components making up the frame be dimensionally correct, otherwise you will spend a great deal of time custom fitting individual parts. Use a jointer or thickness planer to dress the lumber. Work with long workpieces, and keep fingers and clothes well away from the cutting blade.

Begin the dry-assembly by putting together the front subassembly (parts A, B, E, K, L, I, J and JJ). You may need a clamp or two between the legs to hold everything together. Next, as a second separate subassembly, join the back (parts C, D, G, O, P, BB, Y and HH), again using clamps between the legs. Now, as a third separate subassembly, join the upper drawer front face (part N, R, T, U, V, W and AA).

To complete the dry-assembly, join the front to the back by adding the upper drawer front face plus all the remaining front to back stretchers (parts F, H, M, Q, S, X, Z, CC, GG and II). Add clamps as necessary to keep the assembly together while you check for general fit-up and squareness. While the framework is still dry-assembled, lay out and mark the mortises to be cut for parts DD, MM and PP (Fig. 6).

Now disassemble the framework. Once apart, use a wood chisel to cut out the mortises for parts DD, MM and PP. Sand all the disassembled parts, finishing with 220 grit.

The framework is now ready for final assembly glue-up. For final assembly, follow the same sequence used for the dry-assembly. And to provide for the extra assembly time needed, be sure to use plastic resin glue. This glue, which is available at most hardware stores, comes in the form of a brown powder that is mixed with water just before assembly. Plastic resin glue dries slower than white or yellow glue, and

BILL OF MATERIALS — Shaker Sewing Desk

Finished Dimensions in Inches

A	Front Leg	1½ x 1½ x 26	1	**GG**	Top, Side Panel	⅜ x 7¼ x 11¾	2
B	Front Leg	1½ x 1½ x 26	1	**HH**	Back Panel	⅜ x 6 x 27½	4
C	Back Leg	1½ x 1½ x 38¾	1	**II**	Side Panel	⅜ x 6½ x 21½	2
D	Back Leg	1½ x 1½ x 38¾	1	**JJ**	Front Panel	⅜ x 6½ x 17	2
E	Front Stretcher	1¼ x 1½ x 28*	1	**KK**	Top, Side Brace	¾ x ⅞ x 6¾	2
F	Side Stretcher	1¼ x 1½ x 22*	1	**LL**	Cleat	¾ x ½ x 21	2
G	Back Stretcher	1¼ x 1½ x 28*	1	**MM**	Drawer Guide	¾ x 1 x 22	4
H	Side Stretcher	1¼ x 1½ x 22*	1	**NN**	Drawer Guide	½ x ½ x 21	6
I	Front Stile	1½ x 1½ x 14½*	1	**OO**	Drawer Guide	¾ x ½ x 21	2
J	Front Stretcher	1 x 1½ x 17½*	1	**PP**	Drawer Guide	¾ x 1 x 17½	4
K	Front Stretcher	¾ x 1½ x 10*	2	**QQ**	Drawer Guide	½ x ½ x 16½	6
L	Front Stretcher	¾ x 1½ x 28*	1	**RR**	Cleat	¾ x ½ x 16½	2
M	Side Stretcher	1 x 1½ x 22*	1	**SS**	Top	¾ x 26⅜ x 31	1
N	Side Stretcher	1½ x 1¾ x 22*	1	**TT**	Upper Top	½ x 10¼ x 30½	1
O	Back Stretcher	1 x 1½ x 28*	3	**UU**	Pull Out Surface	¾ x 24⅝ x 26*	1
P	Back Stile	⅞ x 1½ x 14½*	1	**VV**	Breadboard End	¾ x 1 x 24⅝	2
Q	Side Stretcher	¾ x 1½ x 22*	2	**WW**	Side Drawer Face	⅝ x 4½ x 21½	3
R	Side Stretcher	1½ x 1¾ x 22*	1	**XX**	Side Drawer Side	⅜ x 4 x 18¼	6
S	Bottom Stretcher	1¼ x 1½ x 22*	1	**YY**	Side Drawer Front & Back	⅜ x 3⅝ x 21	3
T	Top, Side Stile	1½ x 1½ x 13¼*	1				
U	Top, Side Stile	1½ x 1½ x 13¼*	1	**ZZ**	Side Drawer Bottom	5/16 x 18⅛ x 20⅝	3
V	Top, Front Stretcher	¾ x 1½ x 28*	2	**AAA**	Drawer Knob	see detail	12
W	Top, Front Stretcher	1¼ x 1½ x 28*	1	**BBB**	Front Drawer Face	⅝ x 4½ x 9½	3
X	Top, Side Stretcher	1½ x 1½ x 7¾*	2	**CCC**	Front Drawer Side	⅜ x 4 x 22½	6
Y	Top, Back Stretcher	1½ x 1½ x 28*	1	**DDD**	Front Drawer Front & Back	⅜ x 3⅝ x 9	3
Z	Top, Top Stretcher	1¼ x 1½ x 7¾*	2				
AA	Top, Front Stile	¾ x 1½ x 8¼	2	**EEE**	Front Drawer Bottom	5/16 x 8⅝ x 22⅜	3
BB	Top, Back Brace	⅜ x 1½ x 28*	1	**FFF**	Top Drawer Face	⅝ x 3¼ x 9	6
CC	Top, Brace	¾ x 1¾ x 8*	4	**GGG**	Top Drawer Side	⅜ x 2¾ x 8	12
DD	Drawer Guide	¾ x 1 x 7¾*	4	**HHH**	Top Drawer Front & Back	⅜ x 2⅜ x 8½	6
EE	Drawer Guide	½ x ½ x 6¾	4	**III**	Top Drawer Bottom	5/16 x 7⅞ x 8⅛	6
FF	Drawer Guide	½ x ¾ x 7¼	4	*Includes tenons.			

that's helpful when you are facing a time consuming clamping operation like this one.

Glue and clamp the front subassembly first (don't forget the panels). Then check for squareness and set aside to dry. Repeat this process for the back and the upper drawer front face subassemblies, again checking for squareness. When dry, complete the assembly by joining the front, back, upper drawer front face and the remaining front to back stretchers and panels. Square everything up and allow it to dry thoroughly.

Lay out and bore holes for the 3/16 in. diameter by 1 1/4 in. long tenon dowel pins (see Fig. 1 and elevation views). Cut the pins slightly long, then glue them in place and sand flush. Also, referring to Fig. 8, lay out and bore the various holes in parts N, R, W, X and Y that are used later on to attach parts SS and TT. Note that some of these holes are slotted to allow parts SS and TT to expand and contract with seasonal changes in humidity. Make a slotted hole by boring a 1/4 in. diameter hole and elongating it with a rattail file.

Referring to Fig. 6 and the bill of materials, cut drawer guides DD, EE, FF, MM, NN, PP and QQ to thickness, width and length. On parts DD, MM and PP, note that a tenon is cut on one end while a notch is cut on the other. Also, using the bill of materials as a guide, cut parts KK, LL, OO and RR to size. Before cutting any of the above parts, though, be sure to first take the actual measurements from the assembled framework. Due to minor construction variances, the actual dimensions may change slightly.

Figure 10. Crosscut all components as square as possible. Check the saw for squareness by cutting a thick piece of scrap lumber on your table saw or radial arm saw. Use a tri-square to insure a perfect cut.

Figure 11. Cut stopped grooves for the breadboard ends (VV) on your router table. Use tape with start and stop marks to visually align the workpiece for cutting. This method works on overhead and under the table routers. Unplug the router during this setup to prevent accidents.

Assemble the various drawer guides as shown in Fig. 8. The 1⅛ in. long notch on the back end of parts DD, MM and PP allows the tenon to be inserted in the mortise without interference. Then glue and screw the notch in place.

Make the sliding desk surface, consisting of parts UU and VV, next. Part VV, called a breadboard end, helps to keep the desk surface flat while providing a finished look to the ends. It's a technique common to many Early American and Shaker pieces.

Cut part UU to overall length and width from ¾ in. thick wood stock. Then use the table saw and dado head to cut the tenons on each end. Cut parts VV to size, then use a router table with a ¼ in. diameter straight bit to cut the ½ in. deep mortise. Make the cut in four passes, each pass removing ⅛ in. of stock. Note that the mortise is cut longer than the tenon is wide to accommodate seasonal movement.

Once you cut the mortises and tenons, dry-assemble part UU to parts VV using pipe clamps to hold them together. Now, bore the three 3/16 in. diameter dowel pin holes. Then remove the pipe clamps and separate the parts. Using a rattail file, elongate the two end holes in each tenon as shown. Reassemble the parts, then apply glue to the 3/16 in. dowel pins and drive them in place. Remember to glue only the pins, not the mortise and tenon joints.

Final sand parts UU and VV. Then cut a ¾ in. by ¾ in. by 12 in. long cleat, and screw it to the underside of part UU flush with the back edge. When part UU is installed, the cleat acts as a stop to keep the desk surface from sliding out.

Next, glue up stock for parts SS and TT. After cutting both parts to final length and width, lay out the location of the cutout and notch on each back corner of part SS (see elevation views and Fig. 8). Make the cutout so that the back of part SS fits between parts T and U and extends all the way back to panel HH.

Final sand parts SS and TT before applying two coats of a good penetrating oil as a final finish. Finish parts UU and VV at the same time.

Install part TT using wood screws driven up through the slotted holes in parts W, X and Y. Place parts UU and VV in position on the frame, then add part SS by driving screws up through parts N and R. Driving the screws in such tight quarters is a chore that can be greatly simplified if you have a ratchet wrench with a screwdriver blade attachment. If you don't have one, you'll probably find it necessary to crank the handle of a short screwdriver with an adjustable wrench or pair of pliers. Once part SS is added, cut and fit parts KK, which serve as filler blocks.

Make the drawers. All drawers have the same knob (AAA). Turn them to the dimensions shown in the knob detail. Drive a flathead wood screw through the inside of the drawer front to hold the knob in place.

The original desk had a brass lock on the upper right side drawer. If you can't get a lock locally, purchase one from Carolina Craftsmen, 975 South Avocado Street, Anaheim, CA 92805. Order part No. S-2. The diamond shaped escutcheon measures ¾ in. across the points and 1 in. top to bottom. Cut it from .032 in. thick brass stock, then bore the keyhole and file the slot. Secure it to the front with two small brass brads.

Apply two coats of penetrating oil to all unfinished surfaces. Allow to dry, then buff with a soft cloth for a warm satin finish. Apply a thin coat of beeswax on the drawer guides to help the drawers slide easily. □

Old-Fashioned Coffee Mill

Wake up each morning to the aroma of fresh ground coffee beans.

	BILL OF MATERIALS — Old-Fashioned Coffee Mill		
	Finished Dimensions in Inches		
A	Side	½ x 4½ x 5¼ cherry	2
B	Back	½ x 4½ x 5¼ cherry	1
C	Front	½ x 2⅜ x 5¼ cherry	1
D	Base	½ x 6½ x 6½ cherry	1
E	Drawer Front	½ x 2⅛ x 4³⁄₁₆ cherry	1
F	Drawer Side	½ x 1⅞ x x 4¾ cherry	2
G	Drawer Back	½ x 1⅞ x 4³⁄₁₆ cherry	1
H	Drawer Bottom	⅛ x 3¹⁵⁄₁₆ x 4½ plywood	1

The coffee mill is designed to accommodate a mechanism from a mail order source. Make sure you have the mechanism in hand before you build this project in order to insure proper fit.

The box and drawer are assembled with finger or box joints. The increased glue area makes this a very strong joint, though it's used here primarily for visual appeal.

The joint is not difficult to make. Use a simple jig on the table saw to insure accurately spaced notches and fingers of uniform width. Once you learn the procedure, you can apply it to a variety of other projects such as drawers, chests and boxes.

To begin, cut all the stock to size, then replace the saw blade with a dado head set up for a ¼ in. wide and ½ in. deep cut. Attach a fresh piece of wood to the miter gauge with screws and nuts, then make a pass to cut a notch into it.

Next, apply a piece of masking tape to the table, positioned so it bridges the notch in the fence. Accurately mark the tape to indicate the cutting path. Unscrew the fence from the miter gauge and draw a pencil mark exactly ¼ in. away from the edge of the notch (towards the end opposite the miter gauge). Position this mark on the tape mark so you can make a second notch cut spaced ¼ in. from the first. Make the cut, then erase the pencil mark.

Turn the fence upside down and glue a ¼ in. by ½ in. block into the second notch. This block should be long enough so it projects a little more than twice the thickness of the work. Use a square to accurately draw two pencil lines, one through the center of the first notch and a second centered between each notch. Attach the fence to the miter gauge so that it is in its original position. This completes the setup of the jig.

Make test cuts in two scraps of wood by placing the previously cut notch over the guide block. If the test pieces mate properly, you can proceed with the work. If not, it is an indication that the guide block is not correctly located.

Break off a finger from the test piece to use as a spacer. Hold a back and side member together, offset side to side by the thickness of the spacer. Use a few strips of masking tape to keep the mated pieces from shifting. Place them against the fence.

Align the edge of the projecting back member with the centerline between the notches in the fence; then clamp the work to the fence. Make a pass to cut a notch in both pieces simultaneously. Remove the clamp. The remainder of the cuts are made without clamping because the guide block will prevent the work from sliding laterally. Note that by starting on the centerline between the notches, a half notch and finger are formed. This is optional. To start with a full notch, simply

Figure 1. Attach a fresh wood fence to the miter gauge, make a pass over the dado head to cut a notch, then mark the notch location on a strip of tape.

Figure 2. Detach the fence and shift it ¼ in. to the right, using the tape mark for a guide. Use tape to hold the fence to the miter gauge temporarily. Cut this second notch.

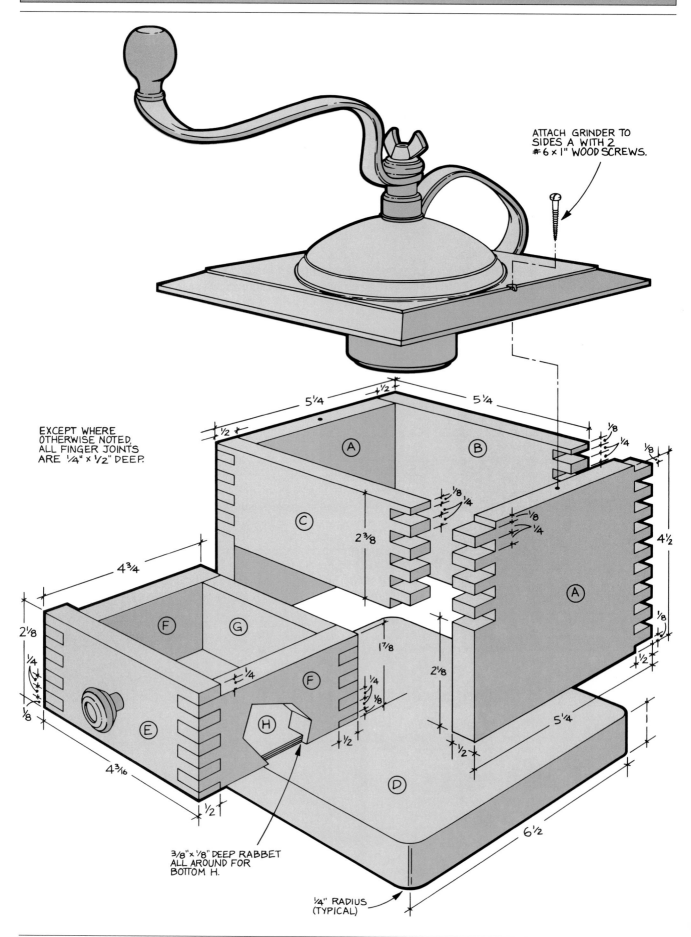

ATTACH GRINDER TO
SIDES A WITH 2
#6 × 1" WOOD SCREWS.

EXCEPT WHERE
OTHERWISE NOTED,
ALL FINGER JOINTS
ARE ¼" × ½" DEEP.

5¼

5¼

½

½

⅛

¼

⅛

A

B

⅛

¼

C

2⅜

⅛

¼

4½

⅛

¼

A

⅛

4¾

2⅛

½

F

G

¼

1⅞

F

¼

⅛

2⅛

¼

½

⅛

5¼

½

E

H

½

4³⁄₁₆

D

½

6½

3/8" × ⅛" DEEP RABBET
ALL AROUND FOR
BOTTOM H.

¼" RADIUS
(TYPICAL)

Figure 3. Glue a guide block into the second notch. Then offset a back and side coffee mill workpiece ¼ in., using a ¼ in. scrap finger cut from a test piece as a guide.

Figure 4. Align the edge to the centerline nearest the guide block. Make a pass to cut the first notch. Use a C-clamp to secure the two workpieces during this operation.

disregard the line and snug the work up to the guide block to make the first cut.

Place the previously cut notch over the guide block to position the work for the next cut. Continue this step until all the notches have been cut.

Detach the side members from the back member. Tape the second side member to the back to make the second set of cuts. This time the offset position will be reversed — the member away from the fence will extend; therefore, align the edge of the setback member with the other centerline, the one directly over the notch in the fence.

Repeat the procedure with the front piece, alternately taped to one side member, then to the other. Here you must be sure to cut only enough notches to span the width of the front member.

Since glue must be applied to so many surfaces, a slow-setting hide glue is recommended for assembling the joints.

The bottom of the drawer is rabbeted to receive a plywood panel. Use a router with a ⅜ in. rabbeting bit for this cut. The resulting rounded inside corners can be squared with a chisel, but this is optional. You can leave the corners round, rounding the corners of the insert panel to match.

Sand the box and base panel before assembly, then apply the finish of your choice. We used two coats of clear satin finish. This imparts a light amber tone which enhances the natural color of the wood.

Attach the grinding mechanism to the box with two screws. Made of cast iron which has a rich gray-black color, it can be used as is or you may opt to give it an antique white finish.

To obtain the antiqued finish, apply several light coats of Krylon's spray enamel (Antique White #1503) to the cast iron, allowing each coat to dry thoroughly. Follow with a brushed-on coat of UGL gold paint (United Gilsonite

Figure 5. Place the notch in the workpiece over the guide block to position it for the next cut. Repeat the steps until all the notches are cut using this method.

Laboratories). Do not allow the gold paint to dry. Dampen a cloth lightly with a paint thinner, roll it into a small, tight pad and wipe the gold paint off the high spots of the relief design and the wood handle. Treat the drawer knob in the same manner. The result will be a warm, white highlighting, nicely complemented by the gold in the depressed areas. If you can't obtain the brand of paint we used, test a substitute first for compatibility.

The coffee mill mechanism is available from The Woodworkers' Store, 21801 Industrial Blvd., Rogers, MN 55374. Consult their catalog or write for current price. □

Designed and built by Fergus Retrum

Lumber Storage Rack

This unique lumber storage rack features removable brackets and a design that can be adapted to virtually any garage.

This design adapts to garages with open and covered walls. Basically, 2 x 2 brackets insert in spacers to support lumber. The spacers along with an additional stud are nailed on the outside of an existing stud. Brackets can be inserted and removed. This system makes the rack ideal for wood storage.

If your garage or shop wall is covered, build an inner stud frame complete with plate and sill. Space the studs no more than 24 in. on center. Nail the plate to the ceiling joists through the cover material and toenail to studs in the covered wall. Use angle irons if needed. Such a structure will require an additional stud for each vertical bracket series plus the plate and sill.

You must determine the height and length of the storage rack you can build. Then systematically mark and cut the parts as diagrammed. Note that the 2 x 2 brackets can be cut square, while the spacing blocks must be cut at a 5 degree angle on both ends. It is best to cut all the workpieces in groups. That is, cut all the required brackets at one time. A power miter box or radial arm saw works best.

Installation

Begin installation with the lowest bracket. Install one bracket and one spacer at the base. Rest the first bracket on the sill, firmly against the outer wall and against the first stud. Place the first spacer on top of it, against the wall and the stud. Tilt the bracket so that it fits snugly against the entire angled end of the spacer above and hold tightly in place. Drive two prestarted 10d common nails through the spacer, securely into the wall stud (do not nail the bracket). Shape and drive a 5 degree wedge between the sill and the first bracket.

Place the second bracket immediately over the first spacer and the second spacer over it. Snug the bracket and spacer so that the bracket assumes the 5 degree angle. Drive the prestarted 10d nails in the center one-third of the spacer, securely into the wall stud. Repeat this procedure for bracket and spacer three through six. Custom fit and install the top spacer as well.

Work the first new 2 x 4 stud between the sill and plate and tap tightly against the installed spacers and the outer wall. Drive 20d common nails through the new stud and through the top and bottom one-third of each of the spacers, into the wall stud, seating the nails firmly. Toenail the new stud into

BILL OF MATERIALS — Lumber Storage Rack

Finished Dimensions in Inches

The following is for one vertical bracket system with 6 brackets

A	Bracket	1½ x 1½ x 16 pine	6
B	Spacer	1½ x 3½ x 12 pine	5
C	Stud	1½ x 3½ x 96 pine	1
D	Wedge	1½ x 1½ x 5 pine	1

the sill and plate. Continue installation, repeating the steps, on the same side of each stud in your lumber storage system.

Remember: do not nail through the brackets (2 x 2s). This precaution leaves the brackets free to be removed if more than one vertical rack space is needed to accommodate larger stored items.

When all the brackets are in place you can stack your lumber by species, grades and sizes. Approximately ten boards can be stored on a bracket tier with the weight evenly distributed and without outward impediment. □

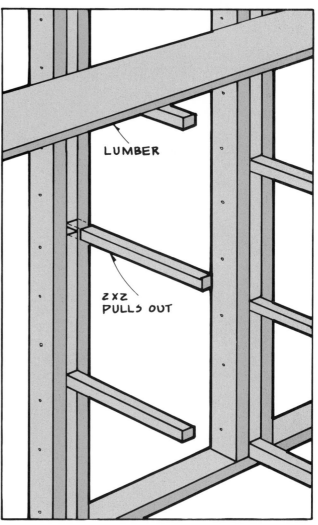

Figure 1. The 2 x 2 bracket fits between spacers. The spacers, in turn, are secured to an existing stud and one new wall stud.

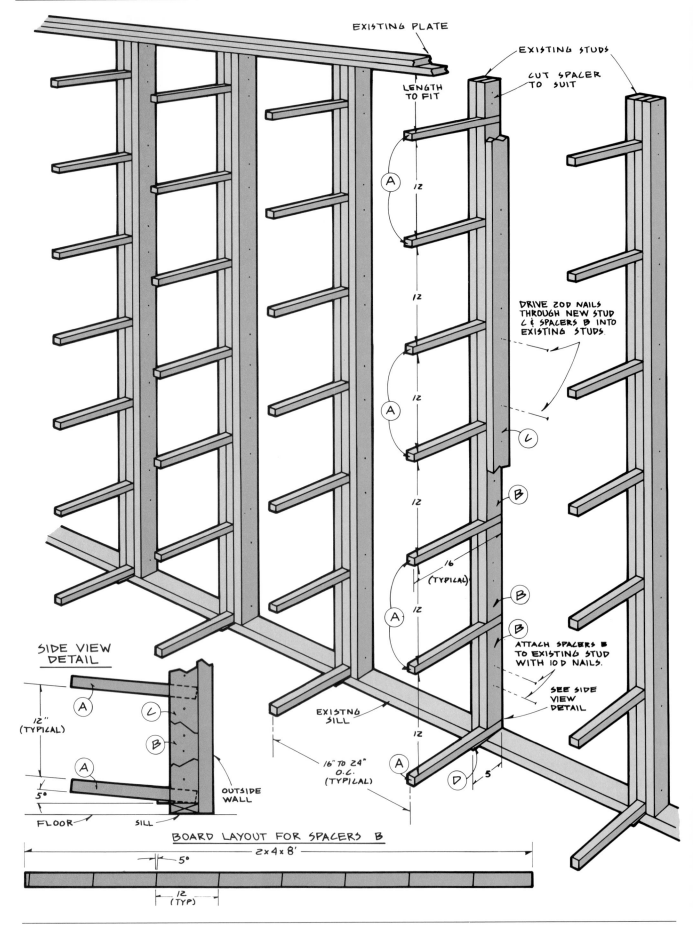

EXISTING PLATE

EXISTING STUDS

CUT SPACER TO SUIT

LENGTH TO FIT

Ⓐ 12

12

DRIVE 20D NAILS THROUGH NEW STUD C & SPACERS B INTO EXISTING STUDS.

Ⓐ 12

Ⓒ

12

Ⓑ

16 (TYPICAL)

Ⓑ

Ⓐ 12

Ⓑ

ATTACH SPACERS B TO EXISTING STUD WITH 10 D NAILS.

SEE SIDE VIEW DETAIL

EXISTNG SILL

12

SIDE VIEW DETAIL

12" (TYPICAL)

Ⓐ

Ⓒ

Ⓑ

Ⓐ

5°

FLOOR

SILL

OUTSIDE WALL

16" TO 24" O.C. (TYPICAL)

Ⓐ

Ⓓ 5

BOARD LAYOUT FOR SPACERS B

2 x 4 x 8'

5°

12 (TYP)

Project designed and built by George Campbell

Gateleg Table

Warm spring and summer evenings make outdoor dining an attractive idea.

This gateleg table will add a touch of elegance to your deck or patio. It is based on a traditional Early American design, modified for outdoor use.

Designed to seat four when open, it quickly folds into a compact package for easy storage. The table can also be used against a wall with just one leaf unfolded. All-heart redwood gives it a warm look that will blend with any outdoor setting.

After cutting all the components to the rough sizes shown in the diagram, lay out the table top components on a flat surface. Mark the centers of the top slats, then draw lines to locate the positions of the battens and cleats. Use a 1/2 in. thick piece of scrap to space the slats 1/2 in. apart.

Secure the battens to the slats with resorcinol glue and No. 8 by 1 1/4 in. screws. Drill countersunk pilot holes for the screws using a combination pilot bit and countersink. Check the adjustment of the bit to prevent drilling through the wood.

Screw the cleats to the center board next, then attach the leaves to the center cleats with strap hinges. Use a depth stop

Figure 1. If you do not have access to a table saw or radial arm saw to form the half laps in the legs, cut them with a saber saw by making two cuts to the depth and width of the half lap. Then use a wide, sharp wood chisel with a mallet to remove the waste.

Figure 2. Use self-locking, nylon-insert nuts to secure the pivot bolts. Tighten these just enough to allow easy pivot movement.

on the drill bit when boring pilot holes to prevent drilling through the wood. Check the alignment and spacing of the leaves before attaching them.

Place the completed top assembly, face up, on sawhorses, and lay out the 42 in. diameter circular profile. Use a bar compass, or make a simple compass with brads, 21 in. apart, in a piece of long thin scrap.

Cut out the circle with a fine-toothed blade in your saber saw. Work slowly and keep the blade centered in the saw's base slot to prevent the blade from creeping off a vertical line.

Round over the top edge of the table top with a 1/4 in. round over bit, with pilot, in your router. Round over the bottom edge, carefully, by resting the router's base on the edge of the table top. Be especially careful when rounding over near the gaps in the table top. It is easy to let the tool slip into the gaps, marring the top.

Add the stop blocks to the leaves. Make these parts from scrap, forming the rabbets with a router or dado blade. Form the rabbets on a long piece of stock, then cut the parts off. This helps avoid working close to the tool's blade.

Next, begin building the base. Cut the notches in the lower stretcher as shown in the diagram, then attach both stretchers to their leg cleats using screws and glue. Attach the braces to the legs, along with the stretcher and cleat assemblies, to complete the base. Using a framing square, check squareness carefully as you work.

Round over the edges of the base, as you did for the table top, avoiding the notches and the top ends of the legs.

Form notches for the lap joints in the components of the gateleg assemblies. Use multiple passes with a dado blade on your table or radial arm saw. Measure carefully for a perfect fit. You can help yourself make identical parts by clamping the parts together and making the notches with one pass of the dado blade.

Before assembling the legs, drill the pivot holes as shown in the diagram. Use a portable drill guide or drill press to make the holes line up correctly.

Assemble the legs using screws and resorcinol glue, then round over the edges with a router.

Place each gateleg into the base, with the longer leg resting in the notches of the lower stretcher. Mark the positions of the pivot holes, then drill through with a 5/16 in. bit. Use a backup board to prevent splintering.

Install the carriage bolts with washers and self-locking, nylon-insert nuts. Tighten the nuts to provide easy swinging action of the legs without excess play.

Before final assembly, sand the table components thoroughly, starting with 120 grit garnet paper and working down to 220 grit paper. Use a straight line power sander or a hand-sanding block, and always sand with the grain. This is especially important with a soft wood like redwood.

Attach the table top to the base assembly, using standard chair leg braces to provide additional stability. The screws furnished with the braces are too long, so substitute No. 10 by 5/8 in. screws.

Finally, apply two coats of a clear wood sealer, such as Thompson's Water Seal. Allow 24 hours between coats, and sand lightly for best results.

If you are tempted to apply varnish to this project, think twice. Redwood, when exposed to sunlight, undergoes a chemical change that will break the bond between the wood and the varnish. This causes blistering. □

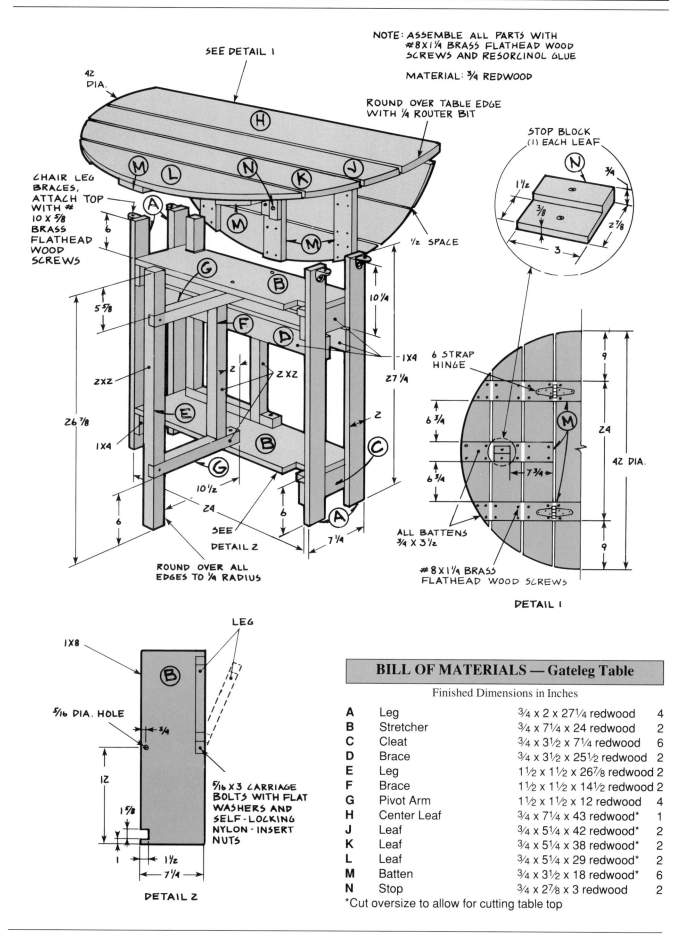

SEE DETAIL 1

42 DIA.

NOTE: ASSEMBLE ALL PARTS WITH #8×1¼ BRASS FLATHEAD WOOD SCREWS AND RESORCINOL GLUE

MATERIAL: ¾ REDWOOD

ROUND OVER TABLE EDGE WITH ¼ ROUTER BIT

CHAIR LEG BRACES, ATTACH TOP WITH # 10 × ⅝ BRASS FLATHEAD WOOD SCREWS

½ SPACE

STOP BLOCK (1) EACH LEAF

1½   ¾   ⅜   2⅞   3

6

5⅝

10¼

2×2

2×2

2

26⅞

1×4

E

27¼

2

6 STRAP HINGE

9

6¾

7¾

6¾

24

42 DIA.

9

10½

24

6

7¼

ROUND OVER ALL EDGES TO ¼ RADIUS

SEE DETAIL 2

ALL BATTENS ¾ × 3½

#8×1¼ BRASS FLATHEAD WOOD SCREWS

DETAIL 1

1×8

B

5/16 DIA. HOLE

LEG

¾

12

1⅝

1

1½

7¼

5/16 × 3 CARRIAGE BOLTS WITH FLAT WASHERS AND SELF-LOCKING NYLON-INSERT NUTS

DETAIL 2

BILL OF MATERIALS — Gateleg Table

Finished Dimensions in Inches

A	Leg	¾ x 2 x 27¼ redwood	4
B	Stretcher	¾ x 7¼ x 24 redwood	2
C	Cleat	¾ x 3½ x 7¼ redwood	6
D	Brace	¾ x 3½ x 25½ redwood	2
E	Leg	1½ x 1½ x 26⅞ redwood	2
F	Brace	1½ x 1½ x 14½ redwood	2
G	Pivot Arm	1½ x 1½ x 12 redwood	4
H	Center Leaf	¾ x 7¼ x 43 redwood*	1
J	Leaf	¾ x 5¼ x 42 redwood*	2
K	Leaf	¾ x 5¼ x 38 redwood*	2
L	Leaf	¾ x 5¼ x 29 redwood*	2
M	Batten	¾ x 3½ x 18 redwood*	6
N	Stop	¾ x 2⅞ x 3 redwood	2

*Cut oversize to allow for cutting table top

Project courtesy of *The Woodworker's Journal* magazine

Garden Bench And Table

This handsome bench and table set is an adaptation of traditional English garden-style furniture.

Both projects were designed to be used outdoors but are refined enough in appearance to be displayed inside too. They were crafted of clear premium grade redwood (at a material cost exceeding $200). However, by purchasing construction grade redwood you may well cut that cost in half. There will, however, be some knots in the construction grade material.

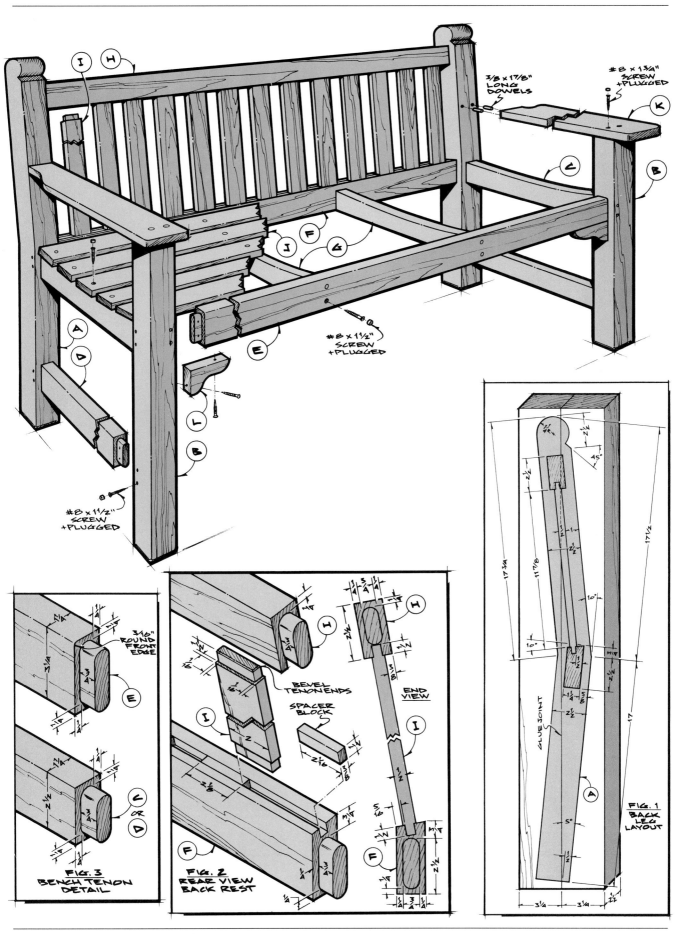

3/8 x 1⅞"
LONG
DOWELS

#8 x 1¾"
SCREW
+PLUGGED

#8 x 1½"
SCREW
+PLUGGED

#8 x 1½"
SCREW
+PLUGGED

3/16"
ROUND
FRONT
EDGE

FIG. 3
BENCH TENON
DETAIL

BEVEL
TENON ENDS

SPACER
BLOCK

END
VIEW

FIG. 2
REAR VIEW
BACK REST

GLUE JOINT

FIG. 1
BACK
LEG
LAYOUT

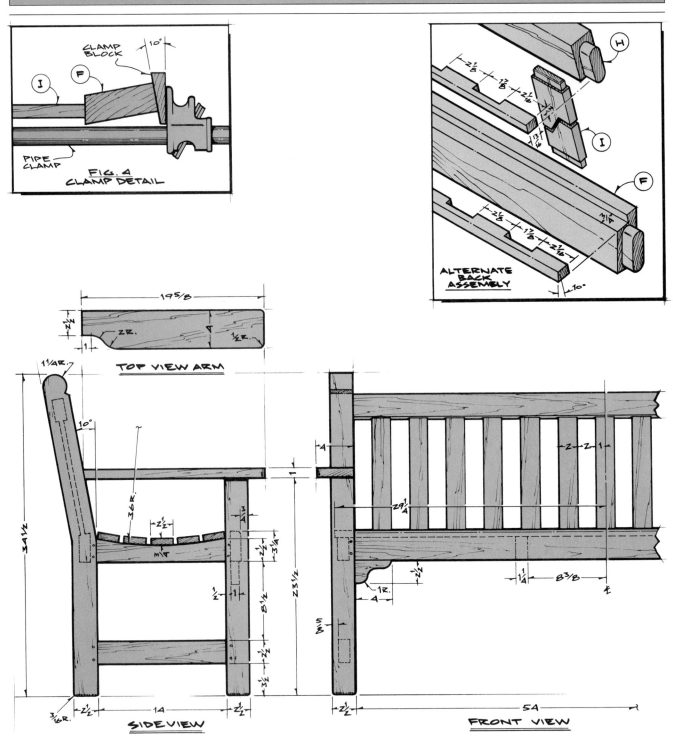

If you opt for the construction grade redwood, make all parts except for the legs, corner brace and chair arm from 2 x 4 stock, thicknessed, ripped and crosscut as needed. The table legs and front bench legs can be cut from 4 x 4 stock, the bench back legs from 4 x 6 stock and the chair arms and corner brace from 2 x 6 stock. The back and seat slats are resawn from 4 x 4 stock.

We selected redwood for this project because it is an easy-to-work material with good decay resistance when properly treated. An even better choice, if you have access to it, would be teak. Buying teak from a hardwood retailer will

probably be somewhat more expensive than redwood. However, by purchasing the teak from a marine construction supplier you may find the actual price difference to be negligible. Teak is very hard, heavy and has excellent water and moisture resistance due to the natural oils in the wood. These same characteristics make teak virtually impossible to machine with standard High Speed Steel (HSS) cutters, so you will need all carbide knives, blades and bits for the planer, table saw and router. Other hardwoods such as cherry, oak or walnut can also be used if you intend to use the garden bench and table only indoors.

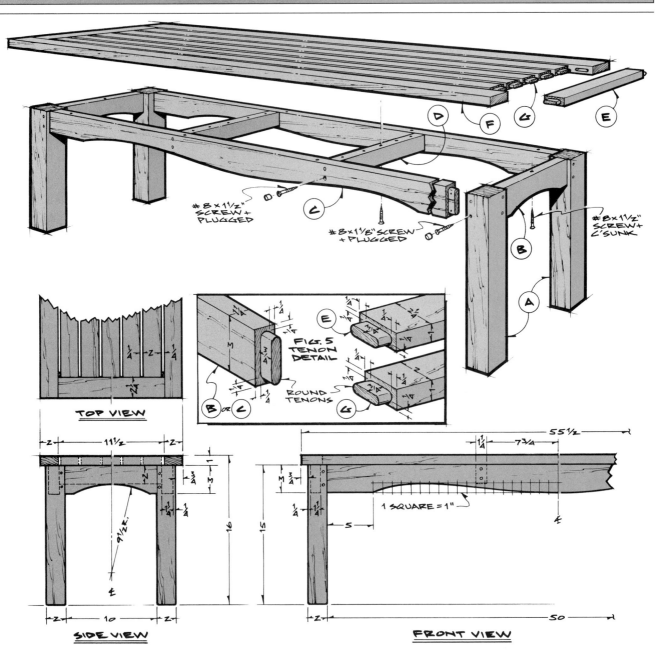

#8 x 1½"
SCREW +
PLUGGED

#8 x 1⅛" SCREW
+ PLUGGED

#8 x 1½"
SCREW +
C'SUNK

FIG. 5
TENON
DETAIL

ROUND
TENONS

TOP VIEW

1 SQUARE = 1"

SIDE VIEW

FRONT VIEW

For exterior use, apply a good waterproof adhesive such as plastic resin glue. With teak use epoxy, wiping the mating surfaces of the glue joints with acetone first to clean away oils that could affect adhesion.

Bench

A good place to start is with the bench back leg (A). If you must glue up stock to obtain the necessary width, the back leg layout detail (Fig. 1) shows the ideal location of the glue line. Referring to the back leg detail, lay out and then band saw the back leg profile. Clean up the band saw marks with a disk sander.

Next, cut the front legs (B) to size, and thickness plane the stock for the various rails (E, F and H) and stretchers (C, D and G), which are all cut from 1¼ in. thick material. Rip the front rail and all the stretchers to width and crosscut to overall length. However, do not cut the tenons on these pieces

until you machine their corresponding mortises. Note that a ³⁄₁₆ in. radius round over is required for the top edge of the front rail.

Bore the ¾ in. wide mortises in the front and back legs (to accept the stretchers and rails) on the drill press using a ¾ in. diameter Forstner bit. Cut the stretcher and rail tenons now (see Fig. 3 tenon details).

To make the back and top rails (F and H), allow a little extra material width on what will be the grooved edge of the stock. Make the top rail about 2¾ in. and the bottom rail 3½ inches. This extra width enables you to cut the grooves, assemble the spacer blocks and then make the final rip cuts (establishing the 10 degree bevel on the back rail and the square edge on the top rail). Following this sequence insures that the spacer blocks are perfectly flush with the grooved edges of the top and back rails. Cut and fit the rail tenons (Fig. 2) before making the groove and final rip cuts.

Use a dado head to cut the ³⁄₈ in. wide slat grooves in the top and back rails. For the top rail, if your stock is 2³⁄₄ in. wide, set the dado for a ³⁄₄ in. deep cut. To cut the back rail groove, first refer to the back leg and Fig. 2 end view details and pencil the groove location on the end of the back rail. Now incline the dado head 10 degrees, and adjust the dado

head height and rip fence as needed to position them to match the penciled groove. Make a test cut on a piece of scrap wood to insure accuracy.

After establishing the slat grooves in the top and back rails, cut 28 spacer blocks. While the Fig. 2 spacer block detail shows the final ¹⁄₂ in. block height, start with the spacers slightly oversize or about ³⁄₄ in. high. Note that while the spacers are shown as 2¹⁄₈ in. long, the end spacers must be 2¹⁄₁₆ in. long. Use a steel measuring tape to lay out the location of these spacer blocks and then glue them in place. Now rip cut the top rail to width and establish the 10 degree bevel on the back rail. The spacer blocks serve to locate the back slats and fill spaces that would otherwise trap moisture.

In order to lay out the 36 in. radius on the end and center stretchers (C and G), tie a string to a pencil so there are 36 in. between the pencil and the end of the string. Tack the end of the string at a point perpendicular to the centerpoint of the stretcher (clamped crossways on the workbench) and scribe the seat curve radius. Band saw the radius and belt sand to smooth the curve.

Cut the back slats (I) and seat slats (J) to size, and use the dado head to establish the ³⁄₈ in. by 1⁷⁄₈ in. by ¹⁄₂ in. long tenons on the ends of the back slats. Also make the arm (K) and corner brace (L) at this time. Refer to the arm top view for the arm profile and to the bench front view for the corner brace profile. Use the band saw to cut both these profiles and then sand smooth.

Now assemble the bench. Start by joining the front and back legs with the end and bottom stretchers. Next, complete the back assembly (consisting of the top and back stretchers and slats). As shown in Fig. 2, bevel the slat tenon ends slightly. This helps them fit into the top and back rails. Apply glue and insert all the slats into the back rail. To add the top rail, you must start at one end and gradually fit the top rail into place by positioning one slat at a time. After starting all the slats into the top rail, force the completed back assembly up tight with bar clamps. As illustrated in the Fig. 4 clamping detail, you need to pre-cut some 10 degree clamp block wedges to back up the lower edge of the back rail. *You need to work quickly in order to complete the back assembly before the glue sets.* Having a friend help out with the assembly is strongly recommended.

Now join the two leg assemblies with the back assembly and front rail. Add the center stretchers, corner brace and seat slats as shown. Complete the bench by installing the arms. We recommend waterproof epoxy, both for the arm dowels and the various screw plugs. While we cut our plugs using the drill press and a ³⁄₈ in. diameter plug cutter, a ³⁄₈ in. diameter dowel stock cut to length and stained to match can also be used.

Bench assembly note: Since the mortises in the back legs to accept the top and back rail tenons are machined before the back assembly is completed, the fit of the back assembly to the back legs may be tricky. If necessary, pare the tenons as needed to ease the fit and accommodate any inconsistency. An alternate method that insures an exact fit is to machine these mortises after the back assembly is completed. While tenons are traditionally cut *after* the mortises, the standardized ³⁄₄ in. wide tenons used on the bench construction should enable you to achieve an accurate fit even though the

BILL OF MATERIALS — Garden Bench and Table

Finished Dimensions in Inches

Bench

A	Back Leg	see back leg layout	2
B	Front Leg	2½ x 2½ x 23½	2
C	End Stretcher	1¼ x 2½ x 15½*	2
D	Bottom Stretcher	1¼ x 2½ x 15½*	2
E	Front Rail	1¼ x 3¼ x 55½*	1
F	Back Rail	1¼ x 3¼ x 55½*	1
G	Center Stretcher	1¼ x 2½ x 15⅛	2
H	Top Rail	1¼ x 2½ x 55½*	1
I	Back Slat	½ x 2 x 12⁷⁄₈*	13
J	Seat Slat	¾ x 2½ x 58½	5
K	Arm	1 x 4 x 19⅝	2
L	Corner Brace	1 x 2½ x 4	2

Table

A	Leg	2 x 2 x 15	4
B	End Apron	1¼ x 3 x 11½*	2
C	Side Apron	1¼ x 3 x 51½*	2
D	Stretcher	1¼ x 2 x 11	2
E	Frame End	1 x 2¼ x 13*	2
F	Frame Side	1 x 2 x 55½	2
G	Rail	1 x 2 x 52½*	5

*Length includes tenons.

Figure 6. Cut rounded mortises by locating and drilling two stopped holes into the workpiece with a Forstner bit. Then draw lines connecting the outside circles, and chisel out the section in between.

mortises for the tenons on the back and top rails are cut *after* the tenons.

Alternate back assembly: A simpler back assembly is to rabbet the back and top rails as shown and mount the slats using notched retainer strips (see alternate back assembly detail). Note that with the lower strip you cut the 10 degree bevel after the notches are established. The advantage in this alternate method is that the back slats are added *after* the bench is assembled, eliminating any problem in gluing up and then fitting the back assembly to the back legs.

Table

The table construction is very straightforward. Cut the legs (A), aprons (B and C) and stretchers (D) to length and width. Make the ¾ in. thick apron tenons and the corresponding mortises in the legs following the same technique as used for the bench. Band saw the 9½ in. radius on the end aprons (use the string and pencil technique as explained with the bench instructions) and the side apron profile (see front view grid) *after* cutting the tenons on the ends of these pieces.

Assemble the table frame, using counterbored screws as shown to mount the stretchers and reinforce the mortise and tenon joints. Start by assembling the legs and end aprons, join these assemblies with the side aprons and then add the stretchers. As with the bench, use waterproof epoxy to secure the screw plugs.

Now make the table top, which is essentially a large frame with rails. As shown in the Fig. 5 tenon detail, note that the various frame end, frame side and rail mortises and tenons are ½ in. thick as opposed to the ¾ in. thick tenons used earlier. Assemble the top frame by first mounting the frame ends on the rails. Then add the frame side pieces. Secure the table top as shown in the exploded view, with screws inserted up through countersunk screw holes in the end aprons and stretchers.

After applying a ³⁄₁₆ in. diameter radius to the bottom end of the bench and table legs (to reduce the chance of chipping), final sand both projects. We recommend just breaking (rounding over) all sharp edges and corners to eliminate the chance of splinters and to reduce any discomfort such edges could cause. A pad sander does a good job of breaking these edges.

Figure 7. Form the tenon shoulders on the table saw. Mark their outside diameters with a circle template. Round the tenons with a sharp wood chisel.

Finishing

To provide our bench and table with maximum weather and decay resistance, we applied two generous coats of Cuprinol brand wood preservative. While the Cuprinol may be brushed on, a more effective and much quicker method is to spray it on with a common pump-type garden sprayer. The fine spray insures total coverage, laying on an even, heavy coat. After allowing it to penetrate fully, apply the second coat.

Note: By reapplying the Cuprinol once a year, you can be assured of long trouble-free service regardless of exposure to the elements. Of course, as with all finishing products, wear appropriate protective clothing and eye protection, use a particulate vapor mask and apply only in a well-ventilated work area — preferably outdoors. □

Courtesy of Jonathan Press

Dry Sink with Wall Unit

If you need a place to show off dishes or other treasures, display them in this Early American-style dry sink with elegant wall unit.

This dry sink is made from oak and oak veneer plywood. The overall size of this cabinet is 20¼ in. by 36 in. by 37½ inches. Use the back shelf for displaying decorative items and the two drawers for storing silverware and other necessities. The spacious lower cabinet features a half-shelf for storing items that do not stack easily.

We have gone a step further by designing a matching wall cabinet to display your treasured dishes and saucers. The cabinet is 10¼ in. by 22½ in. by 40 in. and is constructed from 1 in. oak. The grooved shelf allows dishes to be displayed upright.

Dry Sink

Lay out the patterns for the back and side panels and cut them out with a band saw. Prior to assembly, rout the appropriate edges on sides (B), shelf (C) and back (A). When cutting the sink bottom (E), use a fine-toothed saw blade. This will minimize wood splintering. Assemble with counterbored 1½ in. wood screws and cap with oak plugs. Place some soap on each screw to ease insertion into the hard oak.

Make the rabbet cuts on the sides (Q) and dadoes for the bottom (M). Assemble the sides and the top braces (S) to the

bottom (M) with wood screws and glue. Be sure to square the cabinet.

Cut the stiles (I) and rails (F, G, J) to fit to insure a tight joint.

Modify the half-shelf (N) to accommodate your dish collection. In any event, glue a strip of oak (O) onto the front of the oak plywood. Rout the brackets (P) and fasten to the inside of the cabinet with several counterbored screws. Cap with wooden plugs. Then glue or nail the half-shelf to the brackets.

Mount the back brace (R) after the drawer guide hardware has been chosen. Lay out the contours for the trim (K, L) and cut with a band saw, miter the corners and attach to the cabinet.

Both doors are constructed from solid oak material. The front (U) is cut from laminated stock and its edges are similarly routed before assembly. You may choose to modify the door by using a raised panel. Glue two stiles (U2) along with splines to the panel and allow it to cure. Now, measure the two rails (U1) and cut them to suit. To strengthen each door, peg the sides or secure with counterbored 2 in. wood screws. When the door is complete, rout the outside showing edges.

The drawer construction and assembly is straightforward. Rout the front showing edges of each drawer face (V). Make a rabbet cut along the back side of each side piece (V2) and a dado along the edge of the inside drawer (V1, V2, V3). After assembling three sides of the drawer, slip in the bottom (V4) and add the final side. These pieces are secured with glue and counterbored 1½ in. wood screws. Make sure the drawers are square.

Drill the holes for the drawer pull and recess the screws on the drawer face (V). Then attach the face to the front of the drawer support (V1) with several counterbored 1¼ in. wood screws. Do not use glue.

Mortise the doors only for mounting the hinges. The mortise depth should be the thickness of a folded hinge. Also, attach a magnetic latch for each door.

Mount the center drawer glides following the directions provided by the manufacturer.

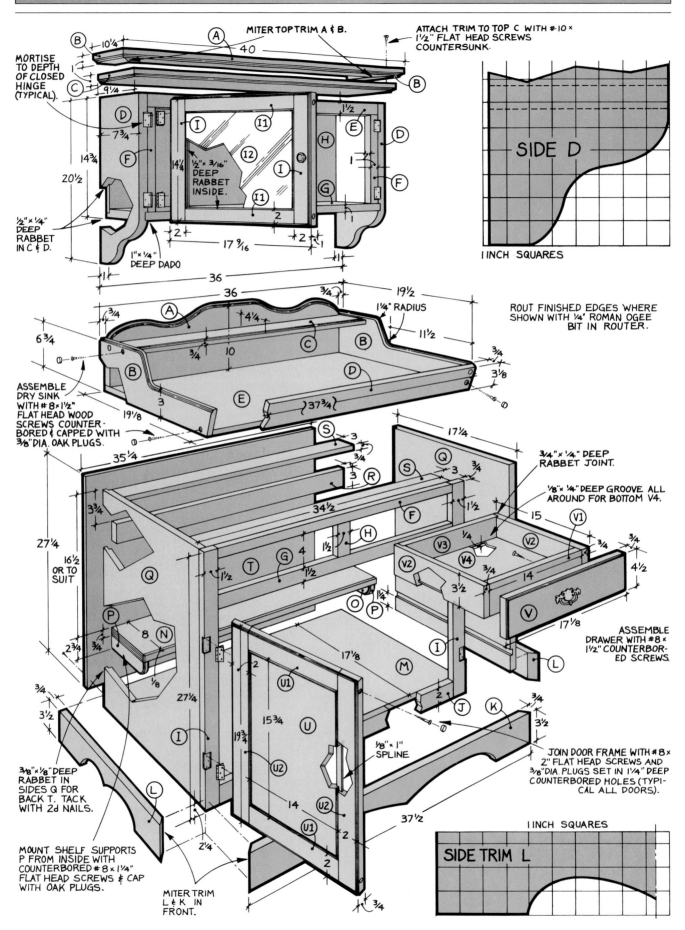

MITER TOP TRIM A & B.

ATTACH TRIM TO TOP C WITH #10 × 1½" FLAT HEAD SCREWS COUNTERSUNK.

MORTISE TO DEPTH OF CLOSED HINGE (TYPICAL).

10¼

40

9¼

7¾

14¾

20½

14¼

½" × 3/16" DEEP RABBET INSIDE.

1½

½" × ¼" DEEP RABBET IN C & D.

1" × ¼" DEEP DADO

36

2

17 9/16

2

36

SIDE D

1 INCH SQUARES

¾

19½

1¼" RADIUS

11½

4¼

6¾

10

ROUT FINISHED EDGES WHERE SHOWN WITH ¼" ROMAN OGEE BIT IN ROUTER.

¾

3⅛

ASSEMBLE DRY SINK WITH #8×1½" FLAT HEAD WOOD SCREWS COUNTER-BORED & CAPPED WITH ⅜" DIA. OAK PLUGS.

3

19⅛

37¾

35¼

3

¾

3

34½

¾" × ¼" DEEP RABBET JOINT.

⅛" × ¼" DEEP GROOVE ALL AROUND FOR BOTTOM V4.

15

17¼

1½

27¼

3¾

¼

14

4½

16½ OR TO SUIT

1½

1½

3½

17⅛

ASSEMBLE DRAWER WITH #8 × 1½" COUNTERBOR-ED SCREWS.

2¾

¾

8

⅛

¾

3½

27¼

19¾

15¾

14

⅛" × 1" SPLINE

2¼

2

¾

3½

JOIN DOOR FRAME WITH #8 × 2" FLAT HEAD SCREWS AND ⅜" DIA. PLUGS SET IN 1¼" DEEP COUNTERBORED HOLES (TYPI-CAL ALL DOORS).

⅜" × ⅛" DEEP RABBET IN SIDES Q FOR BACK T. TACK WITH 2d NAILS.

MOUNT SHELF SUPPORTS P FROM INSIDE WITH COUNTERBORED # 8 × 1¼" FLAT HEAD SCREWS & CAP WITH OAK PLUGS.

MITER TRIM L & K IN FRONT.

37½

1 INCH SQUARES

SIDE TRIM L

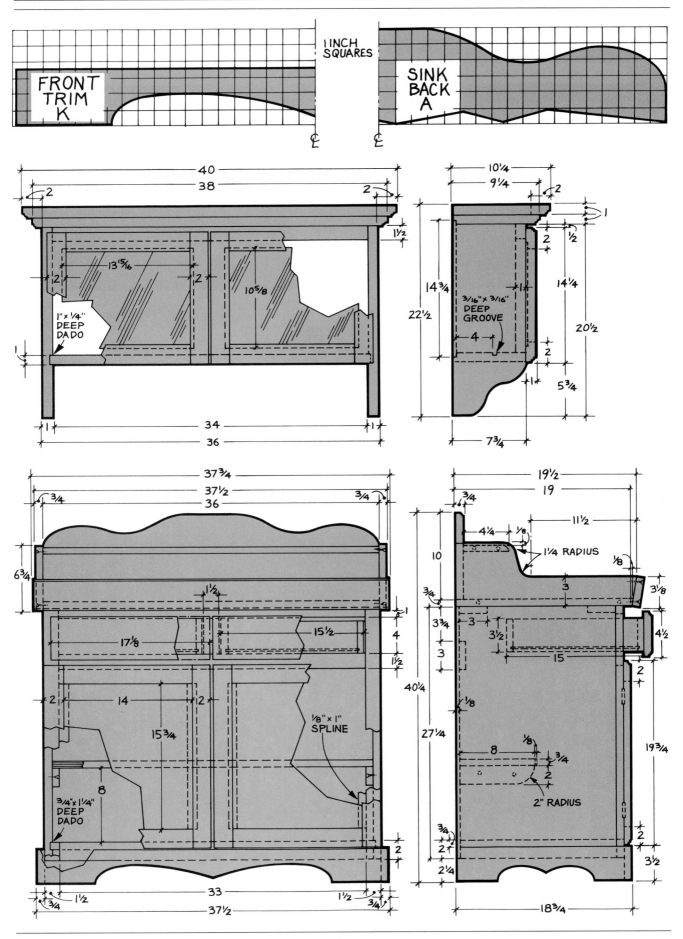

Figure 1. Cut splines in the door stiles, rails and front with a table saw. Keep the workpieces firmly against the fence.

Figure 2. A different, but acceptable, method of joining the doors, stiles and rails is shown. Here the adjoining pieces are secured with a long, counterbored and plugged wood screw.

BILL OF MATERIALS — Dry Sink with Wall Unit

Finished Dimensions in Inches

Dry Sink

A	Sink Back	¾ x 10 x 36 oak	1
B	Sink Side	¾ x 6¾ x 19½ oak	2
C	Sink Shelf	¾ x 4¼ x 36 oak	1
D	Sink Front	¾ x 3⅛ x 37¾ oak	1
E	Sink Bottom	¾ x 19⅛ x 36 oak plywood	1
F	Front Rail	¾ x 1 x 33 oak	1
G	Front Rail	¾ x 1½ x 33 oak	1
H	Rail Brace	¾ x 1½ x 4 oak	1
I	Stile	¾ x 1½ x 27¼ oak	2
J	Bottom Rail	¾ x 2 x 33 oak	1
K	Front Trim	¾ x 3½ x 37½ oak	1
L	Side Trim	¾ x 3½ x 18¾ oak	2
M	Bottom	¾ x 17⅛ x 35 oak plywood	1
N	Half-Shelf	¾ x 8 x 34½ oak plywood	1
O	Shelf Edge	⅛ x ¾ x 34½ oak	1
P	Shelf Bracket	¾ x 2 x 8 oak	2
Q	Side	¾ x 17¼ x 27¼ oak plywood	2
R	Back Brace	¾ x 3 x 34½ oak plywood	1
S	Top Brace	¾ x 3 x 34½ oak	2

T	Back	⅛ x 27¼ x 35¼ temp. hardboard	1
U	Door Front	¾ x 14 x 15¾ oak	2
U1	Door Rail	¾ x 2 x 14 oak	4
U2	Door Stile	¾ x 2 x 19¾ oak	4
V	Drawer Front	¾ x 4½ x 17⅛ oak	2
V1	Drawer Support	¾ x 3½ x 14 oak	2
V2	Drawer Side	¾ x 3½ x 15 oak	4
V3	Drawer Back	¾ x 3½ x 14½ oak	2
V4	Bottom	⅛ x 14 x 14½ temp. hardboard	2

Wall Unit

A	Top Trim	1 x 2 x 40 oak	1
B	Top Side Trim	1 x 2 x 10¼ oak	2
C	Top	1 x 9¼ x 38 oak	1
D	Side	1 x 7¾ x 20½ oak	2
E	Rail	1 x 1½ x 34 oak	1
F	Side Brace	1 x 1 x 12¼ oak	2
G	Shelf	1 x 7¾ x 34½ oak	1
H	Panel Back	¼ x 14¾ x 35 oak plywood	1
I	Door Frame	1 x 2 x 14¼ oak	4
I1	Door Frame	1 x 2 x 13⁹⁄₁₆ oak	4
I2	Door Glass	³⁄₁₆ x 10⅝ x 13¹⁵⁄₁₆ plastic glass	2

Figure 3. Dado the wall unit's sides (D) with a dado blade inserted in your table saw. Make the width of cut by first running a scrap piece across the blade. Return the scrap to the front feed position, turn off the saw and mark the width of cut on a piece of tape. This helps you align your cuts.

This cabinet was sealed with a light oak stain and coated with a satin finish tung oil varnish. Use a soft, lint-free cloth to apply the stain, but use a paintbrush around the door insert. Always complete these processes in well-ventilated areas.

Finally, attach the back panel with 2d common nails. Your dry sink cabinet is complete.

Wall Cabinet

Begin by transferring the design onto the sides (D). Cut with a band saw and rout the outside edge. A dado or V-groove is made on the shelf (G) for supporting the dishes upright. Make rabbet cuts along the inside backs of the sides, bottom and top sections (C). When assembled, square the corners of the rabbeted sections with a wood chisel. Then rout the top (C) and assemble the basic frame with counterbored 1½ in. wood screws and glue. Attach oak plugs to the bottom. Clamp on a flat surface, square and allow the glue to dry.

Fasten the rail from the top with screws. Mount the side braces (F) with 1½ in. wood screws from inside of the cabinet and cover the holes with oak plugs. Add the top trim pieces (A,B) after having routed the edge and join them with miters.

Assemble the door frame (I, I1) with the use of glue and counterbored wood screws (dowels will also suffice). Also, plug the recesses with oak dowels. Rout the outside and inside showing edges of both frames, making sure to allow room for a rabbet cut on the inside. Then use a rabbeting bit with a pilot guide to make the inside rabbet for the plastic panel (I2). Square each rabbeted corner with a wood chisel. Before mounting the glass with retaining buttons, finish the cabinet to match the dry sink. The rear panel (H) can be stained or cut from an existing oak wall panel.

Also mortise the door hinges the thickness of a folded hinge and use a magnetic latch for each door. Add two knobs

Figure 4. Cut out the project's profiles with a saber saw equipped with a fine-tooth blade. Work slowly, particularly in tight curves.

and this wall hutch will be ready to complement the dry sink. Mount it to a wall with four wood screws attached along the top of the inside panel. If the unit does not fit flat against the wall, locate two screws in both lower corners. □

Project reprinted from *How to Make Animated Toys* by David Wakefield

Tyrannosaurus Rex Toy

Watch out! The monstrous Tyrannosaurus Rex is extinct no more!

BILL OF MATERIALS — Tyrannosaurus Rex Toy			
Finished Dimensions in Inches			
A	Body	1¾ x 8 x 12	1
B	Head Spacer	1⅞ x 1 x 2¼	1
C	Head Side	⅜ x 1⅞ x 4	2
D	Arm	½ x 1⅜ x 3½	2
E	Upper Leg	½ x 1⅞ x 3⅜	2
F	Lower Leg	½ x 1⅞ x 3⅜	2
G	Work Dowel	⅜ in. dia. x 7¾	1
H	Axle	¼ dia. x 3⅛	1
J	Peg	7/32 dia. x 1 1/16 shaft	10
K	Cam	½ x 1¼ dia.	1
L	Wheel	⅝ x 2¼ dia.	2
M	Cam Pin	⅛ dia. x ⅞	1

The diagonally opposed, offset wheels give this monstrous dinosaur an ominous swaying gait as the cam and dowel open and close his deadly jaws. The upper arms are pinned tightly so they can be set in different positions, whereas the compound cuts on his tail give it a convincingly serpentine appearance.

The Body

Lay out the body (A) so the cam slot is parallel to the edge of the board. Drill the axle and peg holes. Using a few passes with dado blades or a wobble blade, cut out the slot for the cam. If your wobble blade won't cut the slot deep enough, use a handsaw and a chisel to cut it to the proper depth.

Cut out the outline of the body, except for the teeth. Leave a flat line along the top of the teeth; this will enable you to locate and drill the ½ in. diameter hole. Draw a line on the body corresponding to the center of the dowel. Use this line to set the body at the proper angle on the drill press to drill the ½ in. diameter hole. Clamp the body securely in this position. The hole is so deep that you'll have to use a very long ½ in. bit, or an extension for your spade bit. This hole

will take some time. You will have to back the bit all the way out to clean the hole and the bit as you go. Also, the hole is deeper than the throw of most drill presses.

When you've drilled the hole, cut the outline of the teeth and edge sand the entire outline with 80 grit sandpaper. Flat sand both sides with 80 grit and 120 grit, and rout the outline on both sides (except the teeth). Now transfer the top view of the tail onto the top of the tail and cut it out on the band saw. Now edge sand this newly sawn area with 80 grit and 120 grit, and edge sand the rest of the body with 120 grit.

With the body in a vise, round over the edges of the tail with a four-in-hand rasp and 80 grit sandpaper. Then hand sand all the routed and filed edges with 120 grit.

The Head

Cut out the head spacer (⅛ in. thicker than the body) and the two ⅜ in. head sides. Edge sand the lower back of the head spacer where the dowel will push it; this will keep the dowel

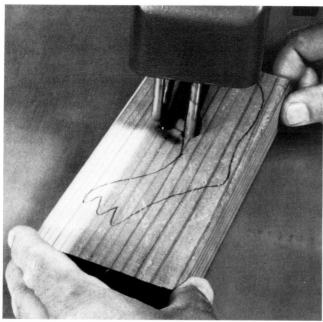

Figure 1. Cut the parts on a scroll saw. Work slowly and use a coarse saw blade. Wear eye protection.

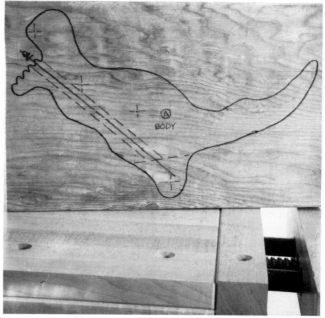

Figure 2. Lay out the body so the dowel hole is parallel to the length of the body. Use this line as a drilling guide.

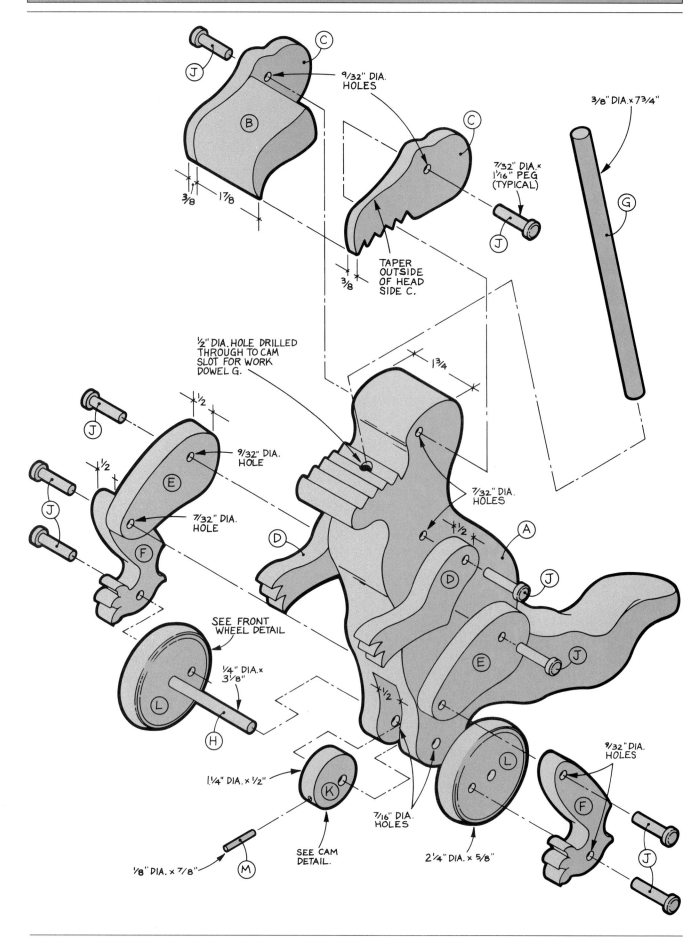

9/32" DIA. HOLES

3/8" DIA. x 7 3/4"

7/32" DIA. x 1 1/16" PEG (TYPICAL)

3/8

1 7/8

3/8

TAPER OUTSIDE OF HEAD SIDE C.

1/2" DIA. HOLE DRILLED THROUGH TO CAM SLOT FOR WORK DOWEL G.

1/2

1 3/4

9/32" DIA. HOLE

1/2

7/32" DIA. HOLES

7/32" DIA. HOLE

1/2

SEE FRONT WHEEL DETAIL

1/4" DIA. x 3 1/8"

1/2

1 1/4" DIA. x 1/2"

7/16" DIA. HOLES

9/32" DIA. HOLES

1/8" DIA. x 7/8"

SEE CAM DETAIL.

2 1/4" DIA. x 5/8"

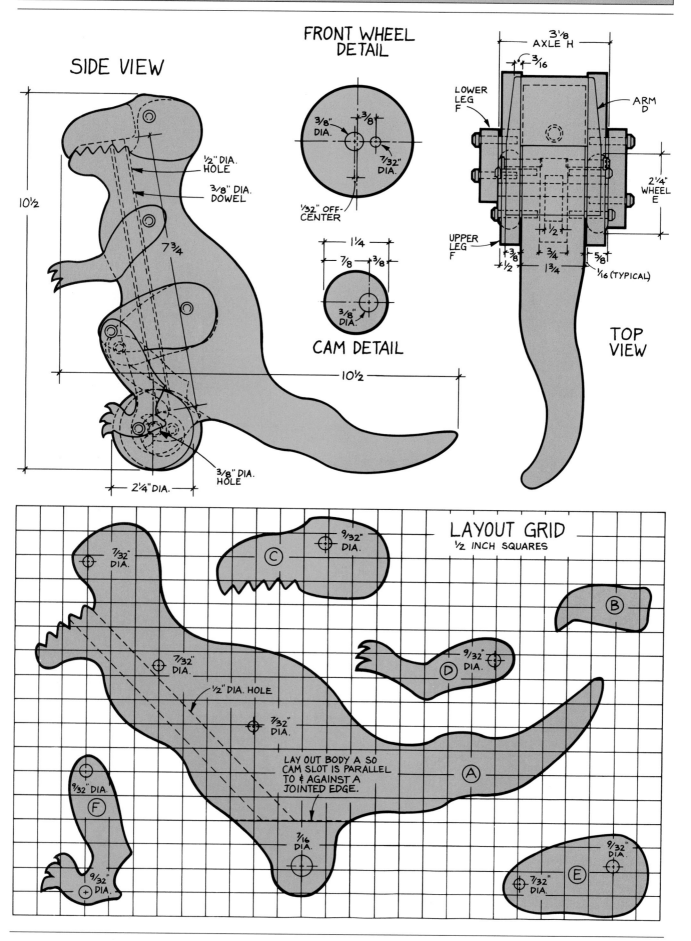

SIDE VIEW

FRONT WHEEL
DETAIL

3⅛
AXLE H

3/16

LOWER
LEG
F

ARM
D

½" DIA.
HOLE

3/8"
DIA.

3/8

½" DIA.
HOLE

3/8" DIA.
DOWEL

7/32"
DIA.

2¼"
WHEEL
E

10½

1/32" OFF-
CENTER

UPPER
LEG
F

7¾

1¼

½

7/8 3/8

3/8   5/8
½   ¾
1¾

1/16 (TYPICAL)

3/8"
DIA.

CAM DETAIL

10½

3/8" DIA.
HOLE

TOP
VIEW

2¼" DIA.

LAYOUT GRID
½ INCH SQUARES

7/32"
DIA.

9/32"
DIA.

Ⓒ

Ⓑ

7/32"
DIA.

½" DIA. HOLE

9/32"
DIA.

Ⓓ

7/32"
DIA.

9/32" DIA.

LAY OUT BODY A SO
CAM SLOT IS PARALLEL
TO & AGAINST A
JOINTED EDGE.

Ⓐ

Ⓕ

7/16
DIA.

9/32"
DIA.

9/32"
DIA.

Ⓔ

7/32"
DIA.

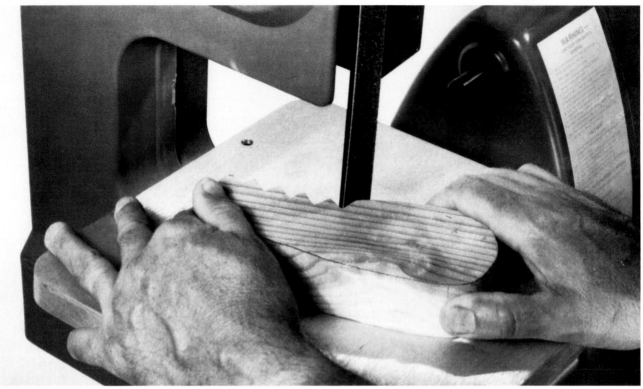

Figure 3. An abrasive strip sander with profile attachments is ideal for sanding the dinosaur's edges.

from catching. Flat sand both sides of the two ³⁄₈ in. head side pieces with 80 grit sandpaper. Carefully line up the pieces as you glue and clamp them.

When they are set up, locate and drill the eye peg hole. Edge sand the assembly with 80 grit and 120 grit sandpaper. Mark the taper on the top front of the jaw piece and cut off the two wedges. Then flat sand this sawn area with 80 grit, rocking it onto the flat side to make a smooth transition. Repeat with 120 grit. Rout the outline on both sides (except the teeth). Hand sand the routed edges, and round over the teeth a bit with 80 grit and then 120 grit.

The Arms and Legs

Lay out all six arm and leg pieces. Drill the peg holes (all ⁹⁄₃₂ in. except for the lower holes in the thigh pieces, which are ⁷⁄₃₂ inches). Cut out the pieces and flat sand with 80 grit and 120 grit sandpaper. Break the edges with 120 grit.

The Wheels and Cam

Drill the ⁷⁄₃₂ in. peg holes. Plug the axle hole and when the glue is dry, redrill the wheel axle holes (³⁄₈ in.) slightly off center. Make a cam (½ in. by 1¼ in.), plug the center hole and drill the off-center hole.

Assembly

Assemble the legs in opposite sets. Glue one front wheel to the axle. With the cam in place, slip the axle through and glue the other wheel on; make sure they are diagonally opposed, one wheel offset one way and the other wheel offset the other way. When the glue is dry, sand the axle hubs. Drill the ⅛ in. diameter hole through the cam and glue the ⅛ in. dowel in place. Glue and peg the thighs to the body.

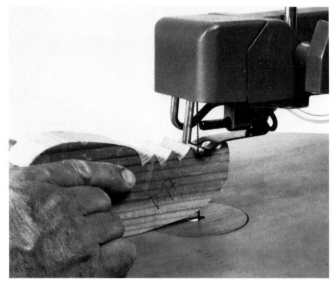

Figure 4. Make the head sides (C) from the same silhouette block. Then sand each surface to a taper on a disk sander. Finally, cut each side to thickness on the scroll saw.

Use the workbench to support the wheels, and glue and peg the feet to the wheels. Glue and peg the arms to the body. Drive the peg all the way in so the arms will stay where they are positioned. Glue and peg the head in place; use the clearance gauge if necessary. Cut the work dowel to length and round off the ends.

When all the glue is dry, oil the beast (and the dowel), slip the dowel in place and watch out! The unbeatable Tyrannosaurus is extinct no more! ☐

Designed and built by Dennis Watson

Mahogany Desk

If you need a desk but do not have a lot of space, this contemporary project should fit the bill.

At 16 in. deep, this desk requires only a small amount of floor space. The cover falls forward to reveal a spacious working surface and pigeonholes for stationery, envelopes and home office supplies. It's an attractive, functional desk with clean, simple lines. Honduras

mahogany with a darker padauk provides a subtle color contrast that accentuates the project.

Desk Unit Construction

The first order of business is to select stock. Honduras mahogany comes in fairly wide boards, but the 16 in. widths are hard to find, so you'll probably have to edge-glue two boards together. Rip the boards to be joined and then pass the edge through the jointer or hand plane to remove saw marks and true the edges. Glue and clamp the boards together with moderate pressure. Scrape the glue from the board surfaces before it hardens completely, and then sand and plane the boards smooth.

Rip the stock for the sides (A), top (B) and bottom (C) to width from 1$\frac{1}{16}$ in. mahogany; cut to length. Cut the angle on the two side pieces about $\frac{1}{16}$ in. oversize. You can trim them to the exact size using a jointer or hand plane. Round

over the front and top edges using a ½ in. round over router bit set to take a light cut, leaving a slightly curved edge.

Bore dowel holes to join the sides to the top and bottom using ⅜ in. by 2 in. dowels. Use five dowels at each top joint and eight at each bottom joint. Run a ½ in. by ¼ in. rabbet in the top, bottom and sides for the ¼ in. plywood back (D). Bevel the front edge of the top to match the angle of the sides. Dry-fit the cabinet together. When you are satisfied with the fit, glue the dowels and the joining pieces and clamp together. Make sure the cabinet is square before the glue sets. If necessary, shift the clamps slightly to bring it square.

Cut the door (E) slightly oversize, and then trim it to fit the opening with ¹⁄₁₆ in. clearance on each side. Glue and clamp the padauk trim (F) to the front edge of the door.

Pigeonhole Unit Construction

Cut the pieces to size for the pigeonhole unit. Rip the top and bottom (G), sides (H) and dividers (J) from ½ in. mahogany and cut to length. Cut the ¼ in. by ¼ in. stopped dadoes in the top, bottom and dividers for the ¼ in. partitions (K, L). Lightly pencil mark the locations for the dividers (J). Glue and assemble the unit with clamps. Check for squareness and then drill pilot holes. Secure the unit at all joints with No. 8 by 1¼ in. brass flathead screws. Countersink the heads flush.

Cut the partitions (K, L) to length. Make the circular cutouts in the front edges using a band saw or jigsaw. Dry-fit the parts together and apply a light bead of glue in the grooves; slide the partitions in place and clamp.

Rip ½ in. padauk for the pigeonhole drawer fronts (M) and mahogany for the drawer backs (N). Rip ¼ in. stock for the sides (P). Crosscut these pieces to length and run a ¼ in. by ¼ in. rabbet in each end of the front and back to accommodate the sides. Run a ¼ in. by ⅛ in. groove in the drawer fronts and sides for the ¼ in. plywood bottoms (Q). Make the

cutouts in the drawer fronts, following the grid supplied in the drawing, and assemble the drawers.

Cut the hinge mortises for the door. Lay the hinges in position and cut around the flaps with a sharp utility knife. Remove the waste and the notch for the hinge buckle using a sharp chisel.

Round over the door edges slightly and cut the finger pulls in the front edge using a ⅜ in. core box bit and router. Clamp scrap pieces of wood to the door edge to serve as router stops. Install the hinges after the door is properly fitted and trimmed.

Stand Construction

Having completed the cabinet portion of the project, you can now turn your attention to the stand. Rip the legs (S) 1¾ in. square from mahogany stock and cut to length. Cut ¼ in. by ¼ in. chamfers on the leg bottoms. Rip the side aprons (T), side rails (U), rear apron (V), front apron (W) and rear rails (X) from ¾ in. stock.

Mark and cut the arch on the bottom edge of the front apron ½ in. up from the center. Round over all four edges of the rails and the lower edges of the aprons, and drill the dowel holes as shown in the illustration. Dry-fit the stand together, and check to be sure that it is square and that all the joints pull up tight. Glue and clamp the stand and allow it to dry overnight. After it is dry, use a block plane and/or sandpaper to round over the corners of the legs.

The drawer supports (Y) are made from ¾ in. hard maple. Rip the drawer supports 2¼ in. wide and crosscut to length. Glue and screw the lower spacers (Z) to the back side of the aprons. Screw the lower drawer guides (AA) to the supports. Make the half lap cutouts on the front edge of all three supports; then lay them in place on the front apron. Mark the apron for the ¼ in. by 2¼ in. notches to accommodate the

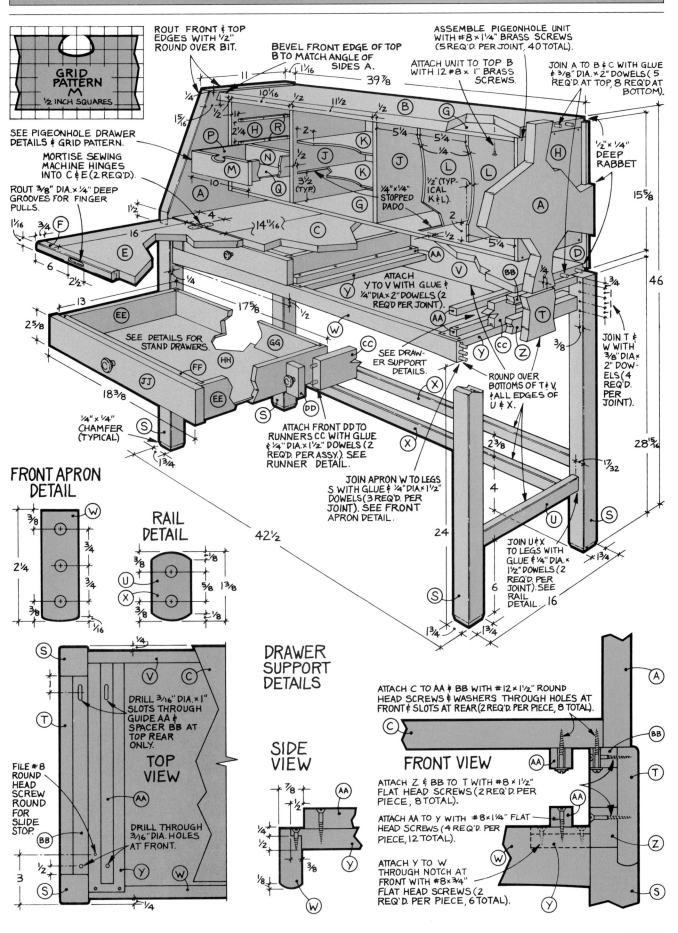

GRID PATTERN M
½ INCH SQUARES

ROUT FRONT & TOP EDGES WITH ½" ROUND OVER BIT.

BEVEL FRONT EDGE OF TOP B TO MATCH ANGLE OF SIDES A.

ASSEMBLE PIGEONHOLE UNIT WITH #8 × 1¼" BRASS SCREWS (5 REQ'D. PER JOINT, 40 TOTAL).

ATTACH UNIT TO TOP B WITH 12 #8 × 1" BRASS SCREWS.

JOIN A TO B & C WITH GLUE & ⅜" DIA. × 2" DOWELS (5 REQ'D. AT TOP, 8 REQ'D AT BOTTOM).

SEE PIGEONHOLE DRAWER DETAILS & GRID PATTERN.

MORTISE SEWING MACHINE HINGES INTO C & E (2 REQ'D.).

ROUT ⅜" DIA. × ¼" DEEP GROOVES FOR FINGER PULLS.

½" × ¼" DEEP RABBET

¼" × ¼" STOPPED DADO

½" (TYPICAL K & L)

ATTACH Y TO V WITH GLUE & ¼" DIA × 2" DOWELS (2 REQ'D PER JOINT).

SEE DETAILS FOR STAND DRAWERS.

SEE DRAWER SUPPORT DETAILS.

ROUND OVER BOTTOMS OF T & V, & ALL EDGES OF U & X.

JOIN T & W WITH ⅜" DIA × 2" DOWELS (4 REQ'D. PER JOINT).

¼" × ¼" CHAMFER (TYPICAL)

ATTACH FRONT DD TO RUNNERS CC WITH GLUE & ¼" DIA × 1½" DOWELS (2 REQ'D. PER ASSY.) SEE RUNNER DETAIL.

JOIN APRON W TO LEGS S WITH GLUE & ¼" DIA × 1½" DOWELS (3 REQ'D. PER JOINT). SEE FRONT APRON DETAIL.

JOIN U & X TO LEGS WITH GLUE & ¼" DIA. × 1½" DOWELS (2 REQ'D. PER JOINT). SEE RAIL DETAIL.

FRONT APRON DETAIL

RAIL DETAIL

DRAWER SUPPORT DETAILS

DRILL 3/16" DIA. × 1" SLOTS THROUGH GUIDE AA & SPACER BB AT TOP REAR ONLY.

TOP VIEW

FILE #8 ROUND HEAD SCREW ROUND FOR SLIDE STOP.

DRILL THROUGH 3/16" DIA. HOLES AT FRONT.

SIDE VIEW

FRONT VIEW

ATTACH C TO AA & BB WITH #12 × 1½" ROUND HEAD SCREWS & WASHERS THROUGH HOLES AT FRONT & SLOTS AT REAR (2 REQ'D. PER PIECE, 8 TOTAL).

ATTACH Z & BB TO T WITH #8 × 1½" FLAT HEAD SCREWS (2 REQ'D. PER PIECE, 8 TOTAL).

ATTACH AA TO Y WITH #8 × 1¼" FLAT HEAD SCREWS (4 REQ'D. PER PIECE, 12 TOTAL).

ATTACH Y TO W THROUGH NOTCH AT FRONT WITH #8 × ¾" FLAT HEAD SCREWS (2 REQ'D. PER PIECE, 6 TOTAL).

STAND DRAWER DETAILS

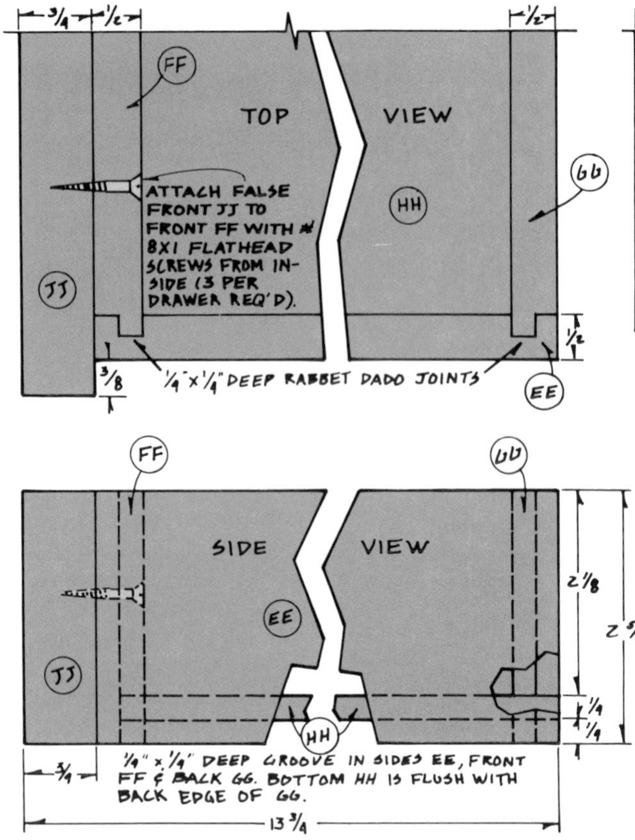
3/4
1/2
1/2
FF
TOP
VIEW
GG
HH
ATTACH FALSE FRONT JJ TO FRONT FF WITH #8X1 FLATHEAD SCREWS FROM INSIDE (3 PER DRAWER REQ'D).
JJ
1/2
3/8
1/4"X1/4" DEEP RABBET DADO JOINTS
EE
FF
GG
SIDE
VIEW
EE
JJ
HH
2 1/8
2 5/8
1/4
1/4
1/4" x 1/4" DEEP GROOVE IN SIDES EE, FRONT FF & BACK GG. BOTTOM HH IS FLUSH WITH BACK EDGE OF GG.
3/4
13 3/4

PIGEONHOLE DRAWER DETAILS

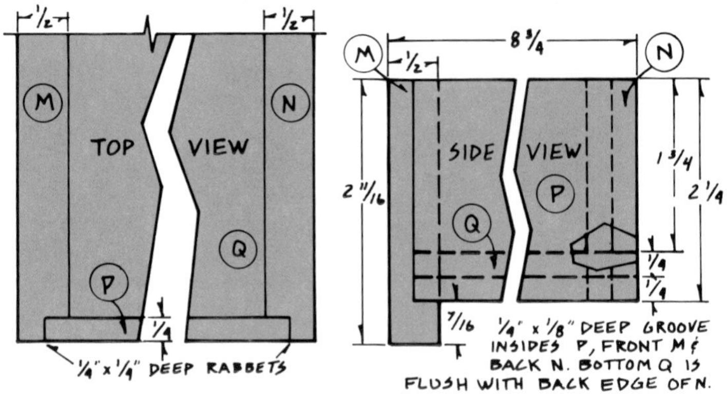
1/2
1/2
M
N
TOP
VIEW
Q
P
1/4
1/4"x1/4" DEEP RABBETS
8 3/4
M
1/2
N
SIDE
VIEW
P
Q
2 11/16
1 3/4
2 1/4
1/4
1/4
7/16
1/4" x 1/8" DEEP GROOVE INSIDES P, FRONT M & BACK N. BOTTOM Q IS FLUSH WITH BACK EDGE OF N.

RUNNER DETAIL

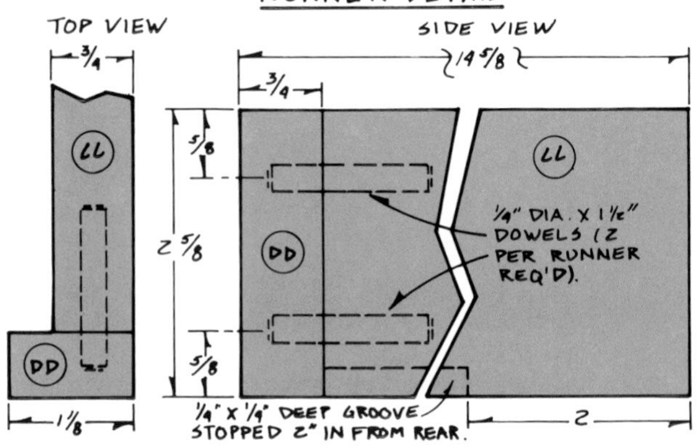
TOP VIEW
SIDE VIEW
3/4
LL
DD
1 1/8
14 5/8
3/4
5/8
2 5/8
5/8
LL
DD
1/4" DIA. X 1 1/2" DOWELS (2 PER RUNNER REQ'D).
1/4" X 1/4" DEEP GROOVE STOPPED 2" IN FROM REAR.
2

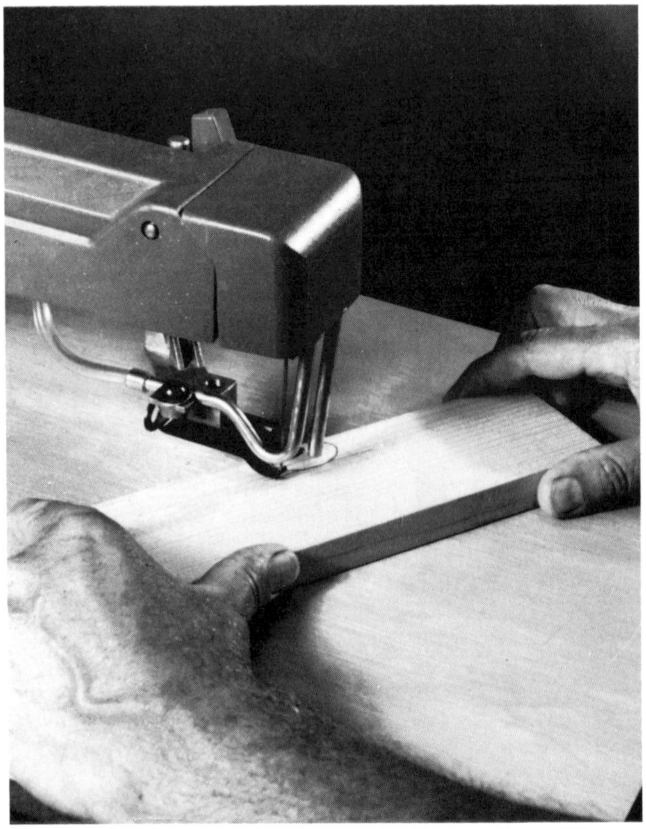

Figure 1. Cut the drawer face finger pull with a scroll saw. Wrap a 3/8 in. dowel with sandpaper to finish this hard to reach area.

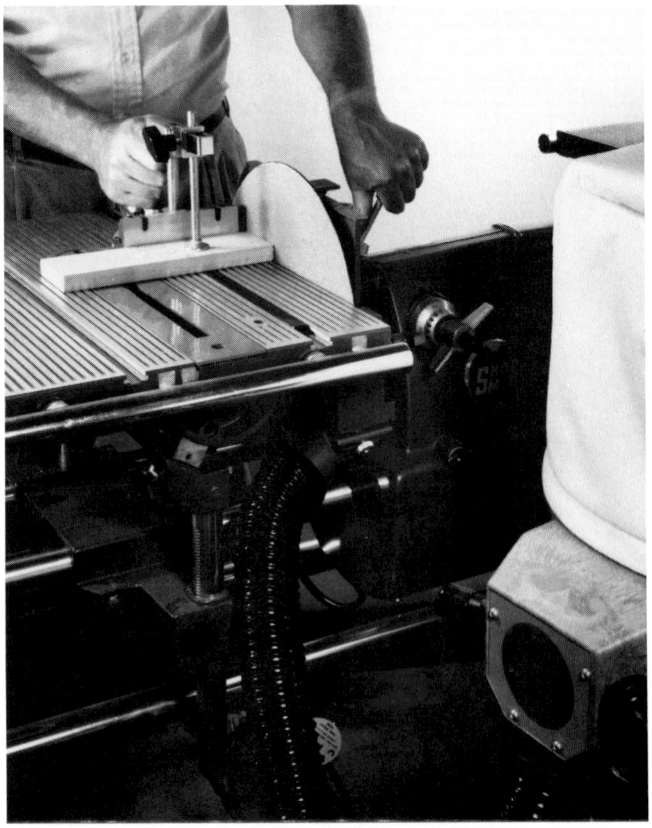

Figure 2. Use a stationary disk sander to sand the sides square. Apply light, even pressure and move the workpiece across the disk in one stroke.

BILL OF MATERIALS — Mahogany Desk

Finished Dimensions in Inches

A	Side	1¹/₁₆ xx 16 x 17¹/₁₆ mahogany	2
B	Top	1¹/₁₆ x 10 x 39⁷/₈ mahogany	1
C	Bottom	1¹/₁₆ x 14¹¹/₁₆ x 39⁷/₈ mahogany	1
D	Back	¼ x 15⅝ x 40⁷/₈ mahogany	1
E	Door	1¹/₁₆ x 16 x 39⁷/₈ mahogany	1
F	Trim	1¹/₁₆ x ¾ x 39⁷/₈ padauk	1
G	Top, Bottom	½ x 9 x 38¹³/₁₆ mahogany	2
H	Side	½ x 9 x 12 mahogany	2
J	Divider	½ x 9 x 11 mahogany	2
K	Partition	¼ x 8½ x 12 mahogany	2
L	Partition	¼ x 8½ x 11½ mahogany	2
M	Drawer Front	½ x 2¹¹/₁₆ x 10 padauk	4
N	Drawer Back	½ x 1¾ x 10 mahogany	4
P	Side	¼ x 2¼ x 8¼ mahogany	8
Q	Bottom	¼ x 8⅜ x 9¾ mahogany	4
R	Runner	½ x ¼ x 8 maple	8
S	Leg	1¾ x 1¾ x 28¹⁵/₁₆ mahogany	4
T	Side Apron	¾ x 4½ x 12½ mahogany	2
U	Side Rail	¾ x 1⅜ x 12½ mahogany	2
V	Rear Apron	¾ x 4½ x 39 mahogany	1
W	Front Apron	¾ x 2¼ x 39 mahogany	1
X	Rear Rail	¾ x 1⅜ x 39 mahogany	2
Y	Drawer Support	¾ x 2¼ x 14⅜ maple	3
Z	Lower Spacer	1 x 1½ x 12½ maple	2
AA	Drawer Guide	¾ x ¾ x 13⅞ maple	5
BB	Spacer	¾ x 1 x 12½ maple	2
CC	Runner	¾ x 2⅝ x 13⅞ maple	2
DD	False Front	¾ x 2⅝ x 1⅛ padauk	2
EE	Side	½ x 2⅝ x 13 oak	4
FF	Front	½ x 2⅝ x 17⅛ oak	2
GG	Back	½ x 2⅛ x 17⅛ oak	2
HH	Bottom	¼ x 12½ x 16⅝ mahogany plywood	2
JJ	False Front	¾ x 2⅝ x 18⅜ padauk	2

Figure 3. Drill the holes for the dowel joints with a stationary or portable drill guide. Set the drill depth carefully.

in the bottom; stop the groove 2 in. from the rear. Cut the false fronts (DD) for the runners from padauk and dowel the false fronts to the runners. Install the slide and then drive a retaining screw in place through the bottom of the drawer support. Remove the screw and file off the point and the threads, leaving about a ⅛ in. long by ⅛ in. diameter protrusion to fit into the slot in the runner bottom. Then insert the screw again.

Rip the stand drawer sides (EE), front (FF) and the back (GG) from ½ in. oak; then crosscut them to length. The sides are joined to the front and back using a rabbet and dado joint. Make a ¼ in. by ¼ in. dado cut in the sides and a ¼ in. by ¼ in. rabbet at each end of the front and back pieces. Run a ¼ in. by ¼ in. groove in the front and sides for the ¼ in. plywood bottom (HH). Glue and clamp the drawers together, making sure they are square.

Glue the grooves sparingly and slide the bottoms in place. Nail them to the drawer backs with small brads. Cut the false fronts (JJ) to size and screw them to the drawer fronts from inside the drawers. Break all the exposed edges of the false fronts slightly with sandpaper.

Sand all the surfaces of the desk and stand, first with 100 grit and then 120 grit sandpaper. Use Watco Natural Danish Oil to finish the desk. Apply three coats, rubbing in the first two coats with fine steel wool.

You might want to finish the inside of the desk with several coats of shellac cut about half and half with denatured alcohol. Oil-finished wood, when enclosed, has an unpleasant odor. However, you should finish the inside of the door with oil; if it is finished exactly the same on both sides, it will absorb moisture equally and not warp.

Finally, install small brass pulls on the drawers and runners and you are finished. □

supports. Cut the notches with a sharp chisel. Bore holes for the dowels that secure the back ends of the drawer supports to the rear apron (V). Glue and screw the supports in place. The upper spacers (BB) and upper guides (AA) are screwed to the bottom of the cabinet.

Since the bottom will expand and contract across the grain with changes in humidity, the rear screw holes in the upper spacers and guides should be slotted to allow for this movement. Secure the cabinet to the stand with screws driven through the slots in the rear and holes drilled near the front. Rip the runners (CC) to size and run a ¼ in. by ¼ in. groove

Project courtesy of *The Woodworker's Journal* magazine

Early American Dry Sink

With its country flavor and simple charm, this dry sink can be a kitchen's friendly catchall or a parlor's plant-filled island.

The design is simple. The dry sink is made in two sections, much the same as a hutch. Here, however, the stacking upper unit is replaced by three drawers and the open sink. The base is merely a box with facing boards screwed to the front and a door that fits flush with the face.

When making the dry sink, it is a good idea to construct the base and upper sections first, then make the drawers and door to fit the actual openings. However, you'll use the same setup to cut mortise-and-tenon joints in the base and in the door frame, so plan your operations carefully to save time.

Start by edge-joining boards for the wide panels. Unless you have access to very wide stock, you need to join boards for the sides (A) and bottom (B) of the base, the adjustable shelf (F) and the raised panel of the door (K). You also need to join boards for the bottom (N), sides (O) and back (R) of the upper section.

The grain runs vertically for the base sides, but horizontally for the upper section sides. When edge-gluing, remember to make the pieces a little bigger than needed and cut them to exact size after the glue dries. We don't use dowels because they weaken a long grain-to-long grain joint.

Next, cut the rest of the parts to size. Leave a little extra wood on the upper section parts that fit together for the 10 degree angle: the bottom (N), the side (O) and the front (S). That allows you some leeway in case the angles, which are cut later, aren't perfect.

Once the glued-up panels are dry and cut to size, plough the dadoes and rabbets in the base sides (A), upper section sides (O) and the shelves (P). You can use a dado head in your table or radial arm saw or rabbeting bits in a router.

Rout the sides (A) with a 3/8 in. deep by 1/4 in. wide rabbet for the back (G), make a 3/8 in. deep by 3/4 in. wide by 2 in. long notch for the stretcher (H) and, finally, a 1/4 in. deep by 3/4 in. wide dado for the bottom (B).

Groove the upper section sides (O) with 3/8 in. deep by 3/8 in. wide grooves for the bottom (N) and make 1/4 in. deep by 3/4 in. wide grooves for the shelves (P) and back (R).

Cut the upper section shelves (P) with a 1/4 in. deep by 3/4 in. wide dado for the drawer dividers (Q). Make a 3/8 in. long by 3/8 in. thick tongue for the bottom (N) that fits into the sides (O).

Cutting the various grooves, dadoes and rabbets goes fairly fast if you first make all the 1/4 in. wide cuts, then the

3/8 in. cuts, then the 3/4 in. cuts. However, you'll need to cut the notches for the stretcher (H) with a wood chisel.

Next, lay out and drill the 3/8 in. diameter holes for the 3/4 in. long adjustable-shelf pegs. Make the holes 3/8 in. deep. Then transfer the grid patterns to the stock and cut the profiles with a scroll saw or jigsaw. Clean up the cuts with a drum sander or wood files. It's best to hold off cleaning the profiles in the stiles (C) and bottom rail (E) until after you put the face frame subassembly together.

Now make the 10 degree slope on the front end of the upper section sides (O) with a table saw. Also use the table saw to cut the 10 degree slopes on parts N and S. We suggest dry-fitting upper section parts N and S after cutting the slopes in the sides (O). That way, if your first angle is slightly off, you can cut the others to match. We also suggest planing the angle on the top edge of the front (S) after assembly, a procedure that insures it will match the curve of the side.

Next, cut the mortises in the base stiles (C) and the tenons in the rails (D and E).

Note that the mortises and tenons for the base and the door frame are pretty much the same, so you may want to cut the base joints, assemble the carcass and use the same setup for the door joints. That way you'll make the door to the actual opening and not waste setup time.

To cut the 1/4 in. wide by 3/8 in. deep grooves in the door rails and stiles to accept the raised panel, use a 1/4 in. straight cutter in the router table. Set the fence 1/4 in. from the cutter. However, don't make the 3/8 in. deep cut in one pass. You'll get a smoother cut, with less strain on the motor, if it's done in three passes, with each pass removing 1/8 in. of material.

Cut the 1/4 in. wide mortises in the door and base stiles a shade over 1 1/8 in. deep. You can use the router setup to establish the dimensions and then deepen them with a chisel. Or you can cut them entirely with a mallet and chisel. Use a marking gauge when laying them out to insure uniformity.

When laying out and cutting the mortises and tenons, remember to decide beforehand which sides are faces and mark them as such. Then keep the same side out for all the marking and cutting. If you flip the pieces face-for-face, any small variations in wood thickness will be doubled and show up as sloppy joints. Here the mortise and both shoulders are 1/4 inches. Don't let the seeming symmetry trick you into turning the pieces over and ruining a joint. For the tenons use the table saw with a tenoning jig. First establish the shoulders, cutting carefully with a stop block on the miter gauge as shown in Fig. 1. Remove the rest of the shoulder with a tenoning jig, as shown in Fig. 2. Remember to keep the same face against the fence for all cuts and to make a trial tenon and try it in the actual mortises.

Assemble the face parts of the base (C, D and E). Sand the curved profile.

Next, lay out the locations for the 3/8 in. pegs in the door joints. Make the holes in stiles (I) 1/32 in. farther from the shoulder than the holes in the tenon of the rails (J). That will help snug up the joint when you put it together.

Then cut the door panel (K) using an extension on your fence, as shown in Fig. 3. Set the table saw blade to 1 1/2 in. high and tilt it 16 degrees. The fence should be 3/16 in. from the blade and the blade must angle away from the fence. Make some test cuts in scrap to get the panel just right. Because of

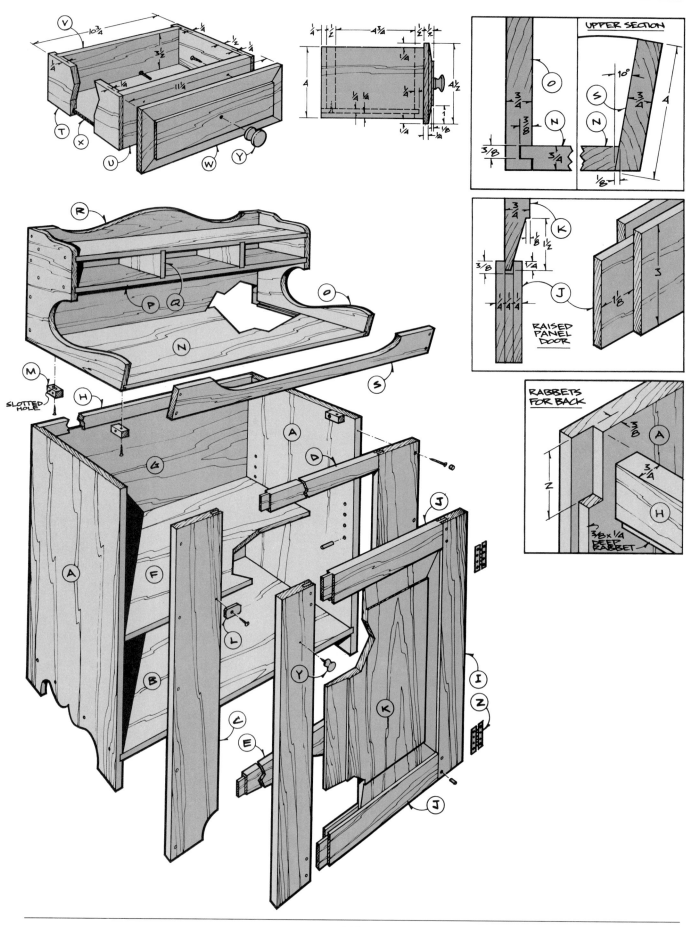

UPPER SECTION

RAISED PANEL DOOR

RABBETS FOR BACK

SLOTTED HOLE

3/8 x 1/4 DEEP RABBET

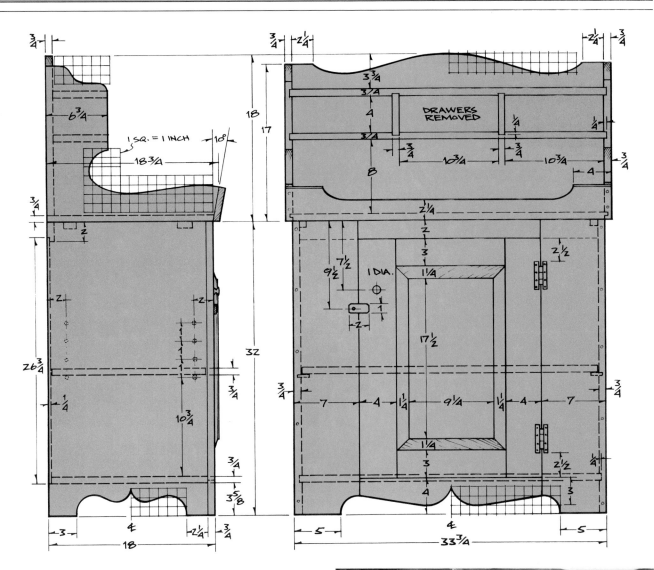

variations in wood thickness, as well as table saw accuracy, the degree of tilt should only be used as a guide. It's best to lay the panel dimensions out on a piece of scrap and set the saw to match.

When cutting the workpiece, clamp a feather board to the table so it hits the panel above the cut, as shown in Fig. 3. Cut across the grain first and then with the grain. That should minimize chip-out.

Cut the raised panel in the drawer faces (W) with the blade 1 in. high and inclined 19 degrees. Set the fence ¼ in. from the cut. Again, make a test cut on scrap before risking your workpiece.

The raised panels stand ⅛ in. proud on both the door and drawers. The saw leaves an angled cut at the shoulder, so you'll have to square the cuts with a sanding block. Remember that the raised panel of the door floats in the frame so it is free to expand and contract with changes in humidity. Next, dry-fit the door assembly, parts I, J and K. The panel shouldn't fit too snugly and shouldn't extend to the bottom of the grooves, because it needs room to expand. Add a dab of glue in the center at the top and bottom of the panel to equalize wood movement. After gluing, let the pins protrude slightly and sand them flush later.

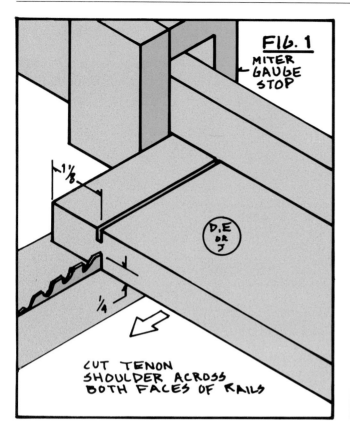

FIG. 1
MITER GAUGE STOP

1⅛

D,E OR J

¼

CUT TENON SHOULDER ACROSS BOTH FACES OF RAILS

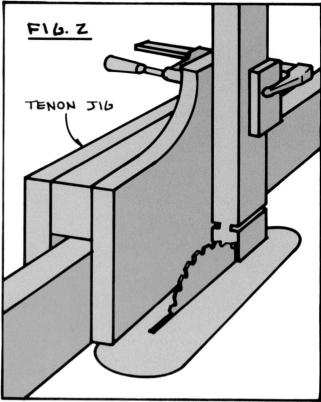

FIG. 2

TENON JIG

When gluing the parts, apply a little paste wax to the wood surface near the joints. Any glue squeeze-out won't penetrate the wood and you can clean off the wax with acetone or lacquer thinner.

Glue and screw the drawer faces to simple drawer boxes as shown. Make the boxes to the actual openings, glue and nail them together.

When assembling the dry sink, first glue up the base, then the upper section. Use screws to join all the pieces, even the drawer dividers. Counterbore the screws and fill with ⅜ in. diameter birch dowels or pine plugs. Let them stand proud

and trim them flush after the glue dries. Glue and screw the facing stile (C) and rail (D) assembly after setting the back (G) into its rabbet. The back helps square the piece.

Note that you must insert the adjustable shelf (F) before closing in the front and back. The shelf won't fit through the finished opening. If, however, you want to retain the option of removing the adjustable shelf (F), then screw — but don't glue — the back (G) in place.

When gluing the upper section, only apply glue to the front 2 in. of the bottom (N). Join the base and upper section with the four cleats screwed and glued to the sides (A). Use

BILL OF MATERIALS — Early American Dry Sink

Finished Dimensions in Inches

	Base		
A	Side	¾ x 17¼ x 32	2
B	Bottom	¾ x 17 x 32¾	1
C	Stile	¾ x 7 x 32	2
D	Top Rail	¾ x 2 x 32*	1
E	Bottom Rail	¾ x 3 x 22*	1
F	Adjustable Shelf	¾ x 16¾ x 32	1
G	Back	¼ x 26¾ x 33	1
H	Stretcher	¾ x 2 x 33	1
I	Door Stile	¾ x 4 x 26	2
J	Door Rail	¾ x 3 x 14*	2
K	Door Panel	¾ x 12¼ x 20½	1
L	Door Latch	¼ x 1 x 2	1
M	Cleat	¾ x 1 x 2	4
	Upper Section		
N	Bottom	¾ x 18⅛ x 34½	1

O	Side	¾ x 17 x 18¾	2
P	Shelf	¾ x 6 x 34¼	2
Q	Divider	¾ x 6 x 4½	2
R	Back	¾ x 17¼ x 34¼	1
S	Front	¾ x 4 x 35¼	1
	Drawers		
T	Side	½ x 4 x 6	6
U	Front	½ x 4 x 10¼	3
V	Back	½ x 3½ x 10¼	3
W	Face	½ x 4½ x 11¼	3
X	Bottom	¼ x 5¾ x 10¼	3
	Hardware		
Y	Ceramic Knob	1 in. dia.	4
Z	Hinge	1½ x 3	2
*Length includes tenons.			

slotted holes with ovalhead screws in the two rear cleats (M) so the bottom (N) can expand and contract. This assembly allows for wood movement, but directs any expansion toward the rear.

Sand and stain with Minwax Colonial Maple and finish with two coats of penetrating oil. Finally, hang the door, mount the wooden door latch (L) with a ¾ in. by No. 6 screw and add the ceramic knobs (Y) to the drawers and door. □

Figure 5. Aligning a board for dadoing on a table saw is easy when you mark the blade width on tape. First lay a piece of masking tape at the feed end, far enough away so you can make alignments and not lean over the saw blade. Then make a partial test cut and return the test piece so you can mark the dado width on the tape. Position the mark where you can comfortably see it.

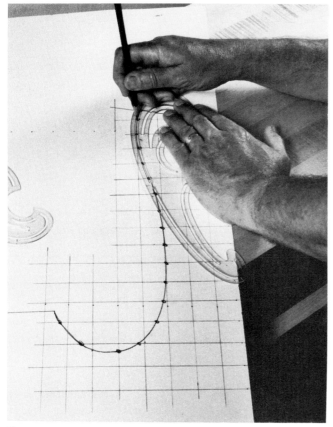

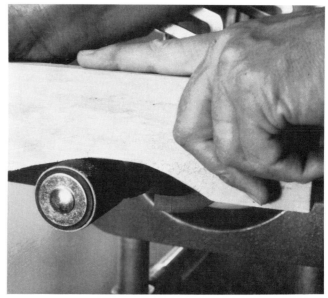

Figure 4. Lay out the side (O) pattern on cardboard with the aid of a drawing board and French curves. First mark the grid points where the pattern intersects the grid. Then connect the points with the French curve shown.

Figure 6. Use a drum sander to smooth the contoured workpieces. Install a 2 in. drum sander in a drill press, portable drill guide or lathe. Work quickly and the sanding drum's rotation should move into the grain.

Project designed and built by George Campbell

Game Table/Chair Combination

Modeled after the Shaker's chair table, our updated version has a touch of Scandinavia.

	BILL OF MATERIALS — Game Table/Chair Combination		
	Finished Dimensions in Inches		
A	Tabletop Board	¾ x 6 x 52 oak	3
B	Tabletop Board	¾ x 6 x 48 oak	2
C	Tabletop Board	¾ x 6 x 42 oak	2
D	Tabletop Board	¾ x 6 x 29 oak	2
E	Stile	¾ x 3 x 29 oak	4
F	Rail	¾ x 3 x 12 oak	4
G	Hinge Board	¾ x 3 x 22½ oak	1
H	Lid Board	¾ x 7 x 22⅜ oak	2
J	Front and Back	¾ x 6½ x 22½ oak	4
K	Side	¾ x 6½ x 15½ oak	4
L	Bottom	¾ x 7¾ x 21 oak	2
M	Cleat	¾ x 3 x 36 oak	4
N	Dowel	1 in. dia. x 2½ hardwood dowel	2

This beautiful oak project features a storage area for games and a pivot top that tilts back to form a chair. It is ideal for a family room where space is at a premium.

Before constructing the project materials, make sure you have or can purchase appropriate chairs. Then select straight, suitable lumber to complement the chairs.

The project requires a substantial number of dowels for joining. It is a good idea to practice joining on scrap pieces of lumber before you dowel the actual project. Board misalignment causes major finishing problems and blemishes the project.

Construction

Cut the components as shown in the bill of materials and begin by building the table top. On a flat surface, arrange the parts (A, B, C, D) to achieve an attractive alternate grain pattern. Also, alternate the grain direction to minimize warping.

Carefully mark the dowel locations; drill the mating dowel holes using the doweling jig.

Assemble the table top, using yellow carpenter's glue. Apply glue to the dowel holes with a small glue brush. Then clamp the assembly securely with clamps. Clamp from both sides to prevent bowing.

Tip ◆ Clamp large edge-glued boards on a flat surface anytime the panel is left overnight. Either too much or too little moisture can cause the panel to warp. Never lay a panel flat on concrete, where moisture is prevalent. Once the workpiece is assembled and supported, finish the project in a timely manner to avoid warping.

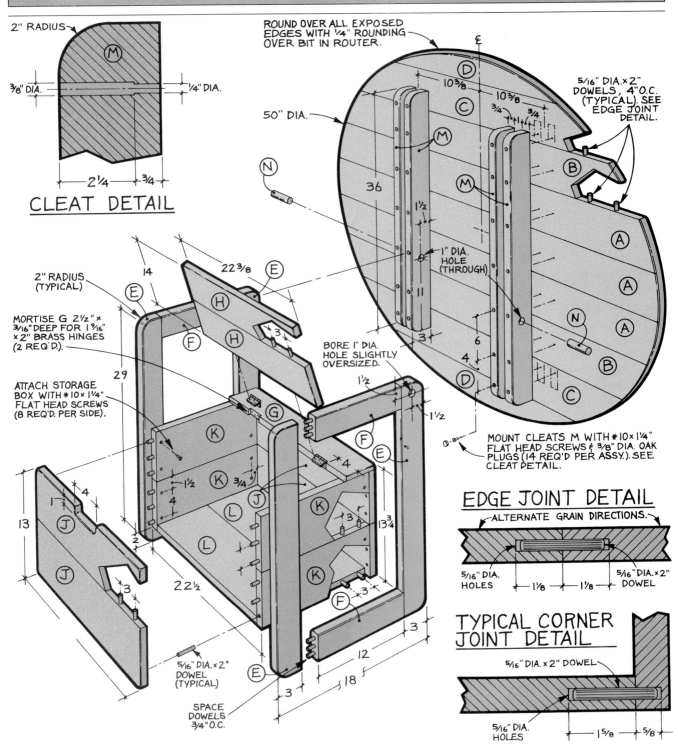

CLEAT DETAIL

2" RADIUS
3/8" DIA.
1/4" DIA.
2 1/4
3/4
M

ROUND OVER ALL EXPOSED EDGES WITH 1/4" ROUNDING OVER BIT IN ROUTER.

50" DIA.

5/16" DIA. x 2" DOWELS, 4" O.C. (TYPICAL). SEE EDGE JOINT DETAIL.

10 3/8   10 3/8
3/4   3/4

36

1 1/2

1" DIA. HOLE (THROUGH)

11

3

6

4

BORE 1" DIA. HOLE SLIGHTLY OVERSIZED.

MOUNT CLEATS M WITH #10 x 1 1/4" FLAT HEAD SCREWS & 3/8" DIA. OAK PLUGS (14 REQ'D PER ASSY.). SEE CLEAT DETAIL.

2" RADIUS (TYPICAL)

MORTISE G 2 1/2" x 3/16" DEEP FOR 1 9/16" x 2" BRASS HINGES (2 REQ'D).

ATTACH STORAGE BOX WITH #10 x 1 1/4" FLAT HEAD SCREWS (8 REQ'D. PER SIDE).

14   22 3/8   E
E
H
H
F
G
29
K
K   3/4
J
L
L
K
K
1 1/2
F
E
4
F   3
E
13 3/4
12
18
3

13
1   4
J
2
J
3
5/16" DIA. x 2" DOWEL (TYPICAL)

SPACE DOWELS 3/4" O.C.

3   22 1/2

EDGE JOINT DETAIL

ALTERNATE GRAIN DIRECTIONS.

5/16" DIA. HOLES
1 1/8   1 1/8
5/16" DIA. x 2" DOWEL

TYPICAL CORNER JOINT DETAIL

5/16" DIA. x 2" DOWEL

5/16" DIA. HOLES
1 5/8   5/8

Join the halves of the box panels (H, J, K, L) as shown in the diagram. Use the same doweling techniques as before.

Next, assemble the side frames (E, F) with dowels and glue, and clamp securely.

Once all assemblies have dried, lay out the profile of the top with a bar compass. Lay the bottom side up, and cut the circular pattern with a saber saw. Similarly, lay out and cut the rounded corners on the frame sides (E) and the cleats (M).

Sand all the components, starting with a coarse 80 grit belt in your belt sander. Work down to a fine 220 grit garnet paper on a straight line sander.

Next, use a doweling guide to drill holes for dowel pins in the ends of parts K and L of the storage box. Transfer the locations of these holes to their mating components with dowel center markers. Use a drill press or drill guide to form the 5/8 in. deep holes in J and K.

Glue and assemble the sides (K) to the bottom (L) and add the front and rear panels (J). Clamp the entire assembly and allow it to dry.

Use a dado blade to form the hinge mortises in the hinge board (G). Drill dowel holes as you did before. Then attach the box lid (H), applying the hinges first to the hinge board.

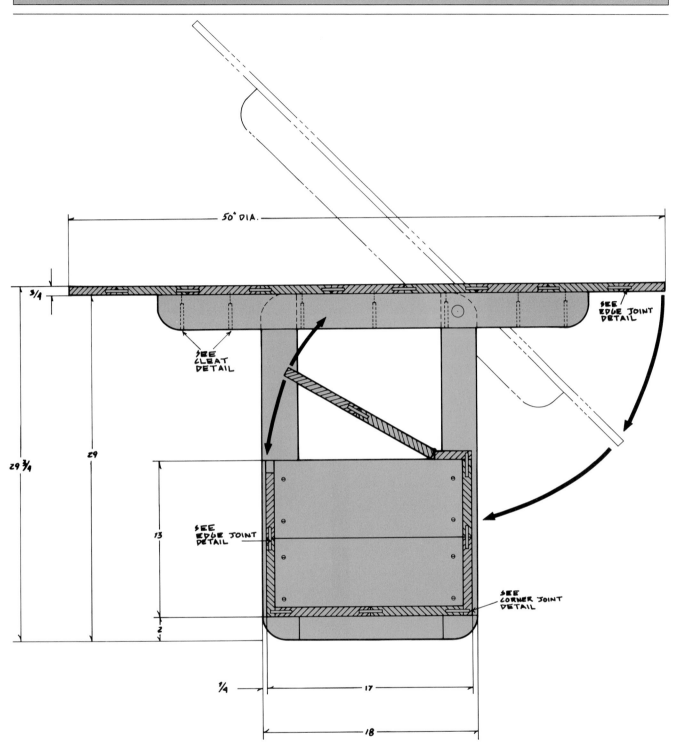

Use a drill press or drilling guide to bore and counterbore the pilot holes in the cleats (M) as shown in the diagram. Use a depth stop on the bit. Next, round over the edges as indicated in the diagram. Use a ¼ in. radius round over bit with pilot in your router.

Attach the side frames to the storage box. Set the box back ¼ in. from the front of the side frames and mark the positions of the pilot holes.

Lay out the locations of the cleats (M) on the underside of the table top. Attach the cleats to the top, fastening them temporarily with just two screws.

Set the top on the completed base, and check for the proper ⅛ in. clearances on each side of the side frames. Attach the cleats permanently with screws and glue; plug the holes with oak plugs. Replace the top on the base; center it accurately. Then bore the 1 in. diameter pivot holes. Enlarge the holes in the frames slightly with a drill-mounted rasp. Glue the oak pivot dowels (N) to the cleats.

Give the completed table its final sanding and apply a coat of stain. Follow this with at least three coats of a satin finish lacquer, such as Deft, sanding between coats with 600 grit emery paper. □

Project designed and built by Dennis Watson

Redwood Potting Bench

Potting chores are easier if you have a convenient place to work. This potting bench is designed to fill that need.

Aside from a large work space, this project also offers an upper shelf for completed jobs, drawers for storing supplies and a bin for wet potting soil.

Built of redwood for moisture and rot resistance, the bench is attractive and will last for years.

Start building the bench by cutting all of the components to the lengths shown in the diagram. Edge-glue the top boards with resorcinol glue, and clamp the assembly with pipe-type clamps, using two on each side of the panel.

Next, use a wobble-type dado blade on your table or radial arm saw to form the grooves and rabbets as shown in the diagram. When several components require the same operation, as is the case with the legs, clamp a stop block to the saw's fence to speed up the job.

Begin assembly by attaching the top and bottom rails to the legs with resorcinol glue and screws. Bore pilot holes with a screw pilot bit. Where screw heads will be exposed, counterbore with a ½ in. bit and glue screw hole plugs in place. Check the assemblies for squareness as you go.

Once both pairs of legs are assembled, add the side rails as shown in the diagram. Once again, counterbore exposed screw holes for wood plugs and glue the joints.

Add the outer drawer slides and supports to the base assembly after screwing the L-shaped slides to the supports. Next, assemble the center drawer slide components and install that assembly at the center of the bench. Measure carefully for smooth drawer action.

Use a ³⁄₁₆ in. straight bit in your router to make slots in the upper ledgers. These slots allow alignment of the bench top. Form the slots in a wide board, then rip the ledgers off the board. Clamp a short guide to the router's base to center the slots on the edge of the board.

Build the drawers next. If you haven't already made the grooves and rabbets in the shelf components, form them now with a dado blade. Notice the notches in the backs of the drawers. These allow the drawer to slide over the L-shaped slides. Assemble the drawers with glue and 6d finishing nails.

Screw and glue the lower ledgers to the inside of the lower rails, then add the bottom shelf boards, spacing them ¼ in. apart. Drive No. 8 by 1¼ in. flathead wood screws into the shelves from below.

Assemble the upper shelf unit with screws and glue, concealing the screw heads with wood plugs as you did before. Check squareness as you go.

BILL OF MATERIALS — Redwood Potting Bench

Finished Dimensions in Inches

A	Leg	3½ x 3½ x 36 redwood	4
B	Front & Rear Rail	2 x 4 x 60 redwood	2
C	Top Side Rail	2 x 4 x 26 redwood	2
D	Lower Front & Rear Rail	2 x 4 x 56 redwood	2
E	Lower Side Rail	2 x 4 x 20 redwood	2
F	Lower Rail Edger	¾ x ¾ x 56 redwood	2
G	Bottom Shelf	¾ x 5½ x 18½ redwood	10
H	Top	¾ x 25¼ x 58½ redwood	1
		(Edge Glue 1 x 8s)	
J	Top Ledger	¾ x 1 x 23 redwood	3
K	Drawer Support	2 x 4 x 23 fir plywood	3
L	Shelf Side	¾ x 11 x 18 redwood	2
M	Top Shelf	¾ x 10 x 56½ redwood	1
N	Back	¾ x 5½ x 56 redwood	1
P	Drawer Front & Back	¾ x 4 x 26 redwood	4
Q	Drawer Side	¾ x 4 x 23¼ redwood	4
R	Drawer Bottom	¼ x 22¾ x 25 fir plywood	2
S	Inside Drawer Guide	¾ x 1½ x 22¼ redwood	2
T	Outside Drawer Guide	¾ x ¾ x 22¼ redwood	2

By now the glue on the bench top will be dry. Scrape off excess glue with a wood chisel, then level the top with a plane. Finish up with a fine belt on your belt sander. Work carefully, since the soft redwood is easily marred.

Attach the top shelf assembly to the bench top with screws, driving them from the bottom of the bench top. Now, align the bench top on the base and attach it from below. Do not glue the top to the base; you may want to replace it later.

Trace around the plastic dishpan after locating it on the bench top, then cut the opening with a saber saw. If the dishpan's sides are tapered, trace around the top, then cut ³⁄₈ in. inside the line to allow the lip to overhang.

Sand the completed bench thoroughly. Start with 80 grit garnet paper and work to 150 grit, using hand and power sanders.

Once the bench is smooth, apply two coats of a clear wood sealer, such as Thompson's Water Seal, to protect the wood. Allow 24 hours between coats. □

Figure 1. The easiest method of cutting the drawer guides S and T is with the aid of a table saw. Cut the deep slot first using a feather board and push stick. Work from a wider and longer board. Then set a ¼ in. depth of cut to finish the workpiece.

Figure 2. Use a dado blade to cut the rabbets in each leg. Then smooth the cut with a wide wood chisel.

Figure 3. Proper sanding techniques are important because redwood gouges so easily. Begin sanding with a fine grit belt and work your way forward and backward, with the wood grain. Keep the belt sander moving, and keep both hands on the tool to maintain control.

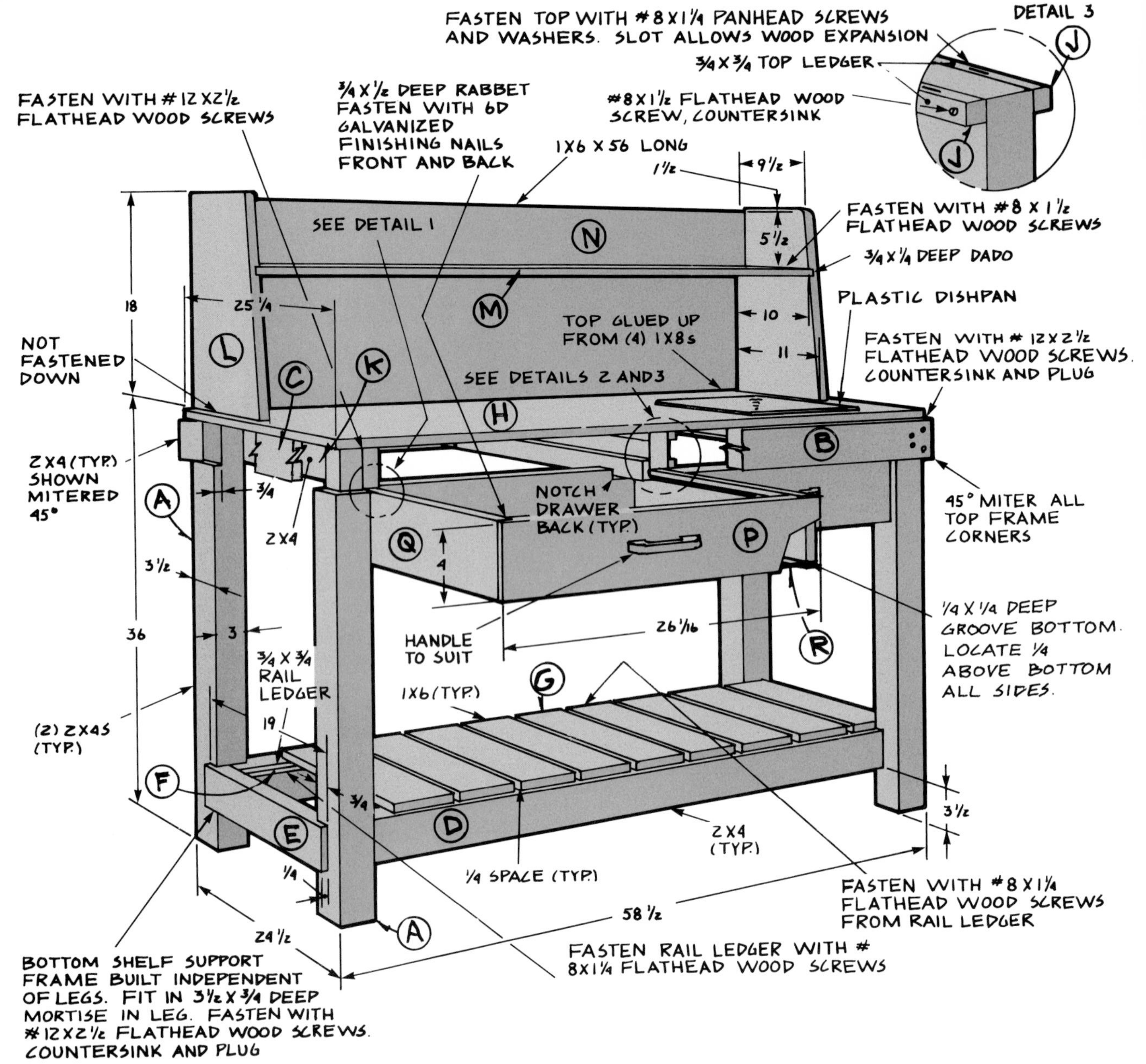
FASTEN TOP WITH #8 X 1¼ PANHEAD SCREWS AND WASHERS. SLOT ALLOWS WOOD EXPANSION
DETAIL 3
J
¾ X ¾ TOP LEDGER
#8 X 1½ FLATHEAD WOOD SCREW, COUNTERSINK
FASTEN WITH #12 X 2½ FLATHEAD WOOD SCREWS
¾ X ½ DEEP RABBET FASTEN WITH 6D GALVANIZED FINISHING NAILS FRONT AND BACK
1 X 6 X 56 LONG
1½
9½
5½
FASTEN WITH #8 X 1½ FLATHEAD WOOD SCREWS
¾ X ¼ DEEP DADO
SEE DETAIL 1
N
M
18
25¼
PLASTIC DISHPAN
TOP GLUED UP FROM (4) 1 X 8s
10
11
FASTEN WITH #12 X 2½ FLATHEAD WOOD SCREWS. COUNTERSINK AND PLUG
NOT FASTENED DOWN
L
C
K
SEE DETAILS 2 AND 3
H
B
2 X 4 (TYP.) SHOWN MITERED 45°
¾
A
2 X 4
NOTCH DRAWER BACK (TYP.)
Q
P
45° MITER ALL TOP FRAME CORNERS
3½
4
36
3
26 1/16
HANDLE TO SUIT
R
¼ X ¼ DEEP GROOVE BOTTOM. LOCATE ¼ ABOVE BOTTOM ALL SIDES.
¾ X ¾ RAIL LEDGER
G
1 X 6 (TYP.)
(2) 2 X 4S (TYP.)
19
F
¾
E
D
2 X 4 (TYP.)
3½
¼ SPACE (TYP.)
¼
58½
24½
A
FASTEN WITH #8 X 1¼ FLATHEAD WOOD SCREWS FROM RAIL LEDGER
FASTEN RAIL LEDGER WITH #8 X 1¼ FLATHEAD WOOD SCREWS
BOTTOM SHELF SUPPORT FRAME BUILT INDEPENDENT OF LEGS. FIT IN 3½ X ¾ DEEP MORTISE IN LEG. FASTEN WITH #12 X 2½ FLATHEAD WOOD SCREWS. COUNTERSINK AND PLUG

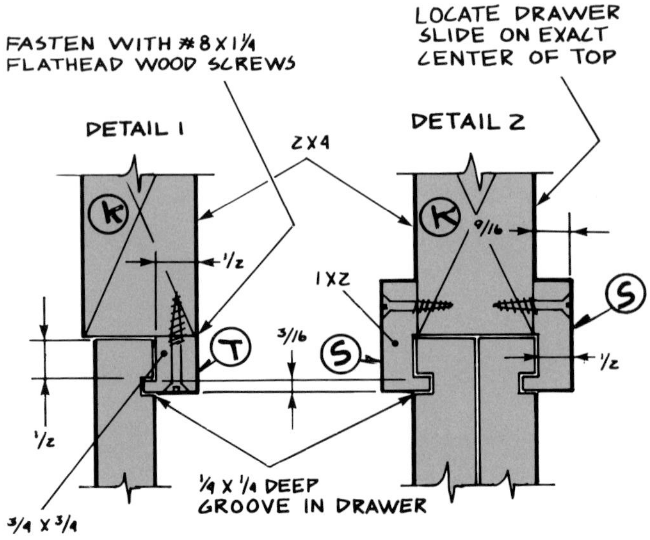
FASTEN WITH #8 X 1¼ FLATHEAD WOOD SCREWS
LOCATE DRAWER SLIDE ON EXACT CENTER OF TOP
DETAIL 1
DETAIL 2
2 X 4
K
K
½
9/16
1 X 2
S
S
T
3/16
½
½
¼ X ¼ DEEP GROOVE IN DRAWER
¾ X ¾

Project designed and built by Graham Blackburn

Walnut Dining Table

This table, although a relatively simple design at first glance, is also extremely elegant and suitable for the most luxurious settings.

The elegance of this table is achieved largely by the shapes and proportions of the three main elements that comprise it — the top (A) and the two end supporting pieces (B). The interesting techniques required in its construction, such as the beading of the side rails, the beveling and stringing of the top, and the compass planing of the sides, are understated elements that only become apparent as you try to analyze exactly why the table has such a sophisticated air. The very simplicity of the table's overall design makes it suitable for use with a wide range of chair styles and similarly enables it to seem at home in a wide range of decors and different styles of interior decoration.

Basic Construction

Since almost all the joinery for this table is exposed, it must be executed as neatly as possible. Any carelessness will be glaringly obvious. However, since we are basically only talking about edge-joining a number of boards, the techniques required should be easily within reach of most woodworkers. More important and more interesting is *what* boards you are joining. The basic simplicity of the design makes the use of highly figured wood, such as walnut, eminently suitable. Use the grain patterns to advantage when arranging the boards to form the top and ends. Choose with some idea of a particular effect in mind — such as alternating light and dark or emphasizing any vertical flame patterns for the ends.

After choosing your boards, mill them flat and straight, and join them with the method of your choice. For instance use simple rubbed glue joints, dowels or splines. Whatever your method, you should end up with three large slabs: the top, measuring a little more than 6 ft., 6 in. long by 36 in. wide; and two ends, each measuring a little more than 28 in. high by 30 in. wide. The *little more* allows you to cut the ends of all three pieces perfectly square. It is easiest to cut the ends with a circular saw running against a fence clamped to the work. A precaution worth taking when using a circular saw like this is to apply a strip of masking tape to the top surface of the cut to help prevent any splintering.

The next step is to plane or surface the faces of the three parts as flat and as smooth as possible. Use a hand or power plane, or work your way through a series of increasingly fine abrasive papers using a belt sander.

Stringing

Now for some fun. The stringing, which in this case is ⅛ in. ebonized inlay strips available in 3 ft. lengths from various suppliers (such as Constantine, 2050 Eastchester Road, Bronx, NY 10461), is most easily laid in grooves the same width as itself but just a tad shallower. Make the grooves with special veining cutters, simple scratch stocks or even wooden plough planes. The simplest method is to use a moto-tool with a small router attachment. This tool has an adjustable fence, and it's a simple matter to set the fence and the depth gauge so that the groove is cut approximately 2½ in. in from the edge and just a little shallower than the thickness of the stringing. Square up and clean out the corners with a wood chisel, and then squeeze a bead of white or yellow glue into the groove. Cut the strips of the inlay to length using square butt joints where lengths meet along the straight and mitered joints at the corners. Press them in with a hard rubber or wooden roller. Wipe away any excess glue that may have been squeezed out, and allow it to dry thoroughly before planing or sanding flat. Sand carefully; if impatience gets the better of you, the inlay may end up below the surface of the table when the glue does dry because evaporating moisture shrinks the inlay.

Bearing this caveat in mind, it's a good idea to lay the top aside at this point and focus on the end pieces. These should be similarly surfaced or planed as flat and smooth as possible and then marked out for the curvature of the sides. The curve is actually quite shallow — being no more than 2 in. deep at its deepest point — but in order for the ends to give a feeling of lift to the top and balance at the bottom, this deepest point is located only 9 in. from the top. Using clamps or a helpful friend, position a thin strip of lath (or something else consistently pliable) so that you can draw a line connecting the top and bottom of the sides with a mark 2 in. in from the side and 9 in. down from the top. Band saw as closely to this line as possible (use a bowsaw if you don't have a band saw) and then position the piece in the bench vise so that you can plane the sawn edge.

Smooth the radiused edges with a compass or circular plane. If one is not available to you, install a large drum sander in a portable drill guide and sand the edges, taking long strokes. Make sure you run the drum into the wood and not with it.

Once you have planed or sanded all four curves (two on each end piece), the end pieces are almost complete except for a length of stopped stringing that runs across the bottom outside face of each end about 2½ in. up from the floor. The stringing is *stopped* because it finishes 2 in. in from each side. The point where it stops may be left round. Shape the end of the inlay to fit the rounded end of the groove or square it with a small chisel. Make sure the chisel is sharp.

BILL OF MATERIALS — Walnut Dining Table

Finished Dimensions in Inches

A	Top	1½ x 36 x 78	1
B	End	1½ x 27½ x 30	2
C	Undercarriage Side	1½ x 3 x 46½	2
D	Undercarriage End	1½ x 3 x 27¼	2
E	Stringing	⅛ x ⅛ x 216	1

There remains one final operation that you would only notice if it were left undone, which is to put a shallow arch in the bottom of each end piece so that they touch the ground only at their outside corners. Plane just enough to form a shallow curve (not noticeable to the casual eye) and to insure a non-rocking table base should the floor be less than perfectly flat.

Beveling

With a pencil gauge, mark a line 1½ in. in from the edge on the top surface. Secure the top to your bench top using handscrews or other clamps. Plane the bevel, starting with the ends. It helps considerably if you also make a pencil line around the edge of the top to indicate the depth of the bevel. For a top that is 1¼ in. thick, a bevel that is ¼ in. deep is very effective and leaves a vertical edge that is both substantial and in proportion.

The Ends First

Although the top should be flat, clamping it to the bench with a few shavings under the center of the end forces a slight crown sufficient to allow you to plane right to the pencil line. If the top cupped even slightly, you would not be able to do this, and the resulting bevel would have a curved edge. It looks best if the bevel is very crisp and all in one plane. The surface of the finished bevel should not consist of a series of facets, so each pass of the plane should be as complete as possible. To prevent the ends from chipping, plane inwards from the sides. At the same time, hold the plane in a severely skewed position. Use the longest plane in your armory to get maximum sole on the work and yet maintain a skewed approach sufficient to produce a smooth cut.

Then the Sides

After beveling both ends of the top (and not before), plane the bevels on the sides of the top. There should be no difficulty in planing to both lines or even in dealing with contrary grain (simply plane in the other direction), but what you *must* pay attention to now is the arris at the corners. An arris is the junction of two surfaces in different planes, in this case the side and end bevels. As you plane, watch that the outside end of the arris stops exactly at the corner of the table top and that the inside end finishes right where the two pencil lines on the top intersect. Furthermore, make sure that the arris is a *straight* line. It is all too easy to end up with a curved arris that wanders off the edge of the table, completely missing the corner. Go slowly, and make each pass of the plane count. If you should overplane the mark, you will have to take more off the ends again. In this case, plane in from the edges.

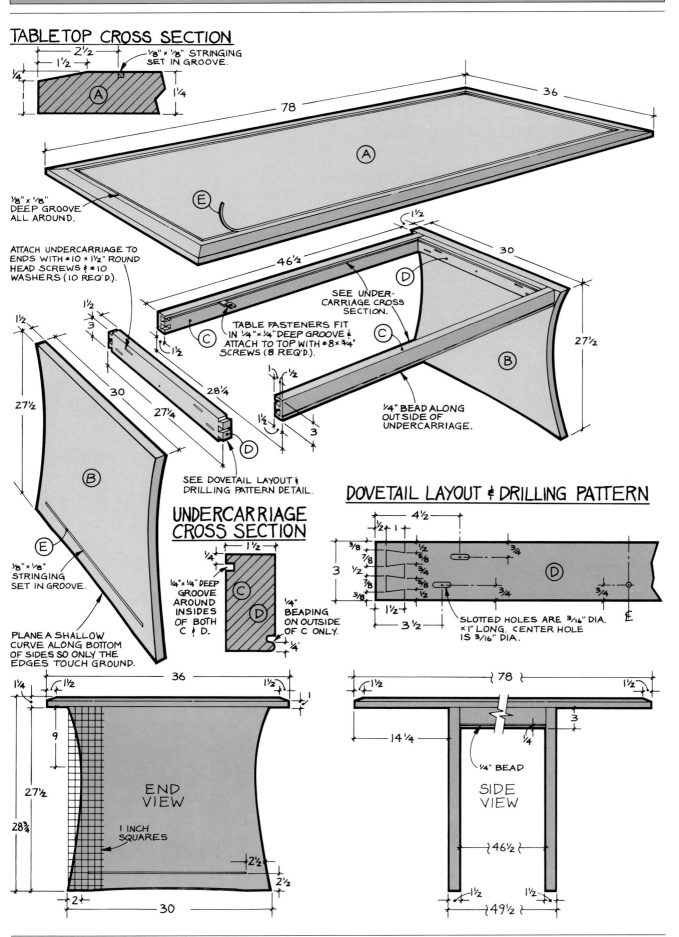

TABLETOP CROSS SECTION

2½
1½
¼
⅛" × ⅛" STRINGING SET IN GROOVE.
Ⓐ
1¼

78
36
Ⓐ
Ⓔ

⅛" × ⅛" DEEP GROOVE ALL AROUND.

ATTACH UNDERCARRIAGE TO ENDS WITH #10 × 1½" ROUND HEAD SCREWS & #10 WASHERS (10 REQ'D.).

46½
30
1½
Ⓓ
SEE UNDER-CARRIAGE CROSS SECTION.
27½

1½
1½
3
Ⓒ
1½
TABLE FASTENERS FIT IN ¼" × ¼" DEEP GROOVE & ATTACH TO TOP WITH #8 × ¾" SCREWS (8 REQ'D.).
Ⓒ
Ⓑ

1½
1½
27½
30
27¼
Ⓑ
28¼
Ⓓ
1
½
1½
3
¼" BEAD ALONG OUTSIDE OF UNDERCARRIAGE.

Ⓔ
⅛" × ⅛" STRINGING SET IN GROOVE.

SEE DOVETAIL LAYOUT & DRILLING PATTERN DETAIL.

PLANE A SHALLOW CURVE ALONG BOTTOM OF SIDES SO ONLY THE EDGES TOUCH GROUND.

UNDERCARRIAGE CROSS SECTION

1½
¼
¼" × ¼" DEEP GROOVE AROUND INSIDES OF BOTH C & D.
Ⓒ
Ⓓ
¼" BEADING ON OUTSIDE OF C ONLY.
¼

DOVETAIL LAYOUT & DRILLING PATTERN

4½
½
1
⅜
7/8
½
7/8
⅜
3
½
5/8
¾
¾
5/8
½
¾
¾
Ⓓ
¾
¾
E
1½
3½
SLOTTED HOLES ARE 3/16" DIA. × 1" LONG. CENTER HOLE IS 3/16" DIA.

END VIEW

1¼
1½
36
1½
1
9
27½
28¾
1 INCH SQUARES
2½
2½
2
30

SIDE VIEW

1½
78
1½
3
14¼
¼
¼" BEAD
46½
1½
1½
49½

Figure 1. Carefully mark the guide lines for the table's bevels with a marking gauge. Then take long, shallow passes with a bench plane. Cut to the guide lines, cutting the cross grain edges first.

Finally the Top

When you have planed the bevels to your satisfaction, turn your attention to leveling the stringing. You can sand this flat if you want to, but there is an added advantage in planing: it helps to define the top edge of the bevel. At this point you are ready for the final preparation of the top before applying the finish. Planing may be sufficient, or you may want to polish with extremely fine abrasive. Gently round all the edges, perhaps with just a wipe of some 400 grit garnet paper.

Finish the stringing and edges of the end pieces similarly to the top, and then stack all three pieces safely out of the way.

Holding it all Together

The undercarriage is the structural heart of this table and yet is the least significant element in the design. All that is visible when the table is complete are the two relatively narrow rails.

Start by getting out four pieces of 3 in. wide by at least 1½ in. thick boards. Any wider and people might have difficulty getting their legs under the table, and any narrower or thinner and the support strength might be compromised.

Plane the undercarriage sides (C) and ends (D) true and square, and lay out lap dovetails so that the ends are dovetailed into the sides, showing none of the joint on the sides. Even though none of this tricky joinery will show, do not get sloppy, because the original purpose of dovetails is not to be flashy but to provide maximum strength. Just because no one will ever see these lapped masterpieces is no reason to think you can get away with a few loose pins — you need all the strength a well cut joint has to offer. The undercarriage serves as support and a place to affix the top, while also providing lateral stabilization (like a stretcher). These are fairly hefty pins and tails, so use your favorite technique to minimize the labor (drill much of the waste away where possible, for example). Cut a ¼ in. groove located ¼ in. from the top edge on the inside face of the undercarriage for the table fasteners. Lay out the dovetails in such a way that this groove runs into a pin cavity and not a tail.

Figure 2. Mark the dovetails for the undercarriage and remove waste area with a Forstner bit. Then define the dovetails with sharp wood chisels.

Figure 3. An alternative to making the bead that runs on the table top is to attach a router with an edge-guide and run it along the edge. Make sure to mark the stop points. When finished, square the bead with a small wood chisel.

Beading

The ¼ in. bead that runs along the outside bottom edge of the undercarriage sides has a dual purpose. First, it softens the edge, making it more comfortable to a leg pressed up to it and preventing an otherwise sharp corner from being damaged; and second, it provides an interesting line of shadow on an otherwise plain piece. It is not immediately noticeable, but is always enjoyable when finally discovered. It is also fun to make. The best method is to use a wooden beading plane of the right size. A universal or combination plane also does an excellent job, especially if you are lucky enough to possess the auxiliary beading shoe originally supplied with the complete tool. Lacking either of these tools or any other type of beading plane, you can use a router with a small veining bit and a fence set at ¼ inch. As a last resort, you can always improvise a scratch stock — just a piece of scraper steel filed to the shape of the quirk that defines the bead and set in a wooden handle.

Putting it all Together

Before finally gluing the pieces of the undercarriage together, make provision for the slot-screwing that fastens the undercarriage ends (D) to the end pieces (B). Five screws per end are enough, and the middle one does not need to be slotted. Use the biggest screws compatible with the thickness of the material; the threads should engage only the end pieces and the shanks should slide in the slots of the undercarriage ends. When you do assemble the undercarriage, make sure that its ends (D) sit in flush (inside the side pieces), or else the ends of the side pieces (C) will not butt up tightly to the table ends.

With the undercarriage assembled, clamp the end pieces to the ends of the undercarriage and install the screws through the slots. Here the important thing is to keep the tops of the ends flush with the top of the undercarriage so that the table top sits perfectly flat.

Making sure that the top is evenly centered on the assembled base is a matter of trial and error. First set the top on by eye; then gently tap the top until the overhangs at each end and both sides are matched. Clamp the top to the undercarriage at this point, and use the metal table fasteners to hold it down.

If you mark the ends and the top with a number or letter punch, reassembly in the same order can be guaranteed and transportation becomes less of a hassle.

Finishing

The success of the finishing depends largely on the care exercised in the preparation, but do not overlook the necessity of finishing *all* surfaces equally, especially the underside of the top. This minimizes any tendency to warp, for any moisture content variation is the same on both surfaces. One of the best treatments for a dining table is repeated thin applications of a penetrating oil like Watco. Let each coat dry thoroughly before applying the next. Eventually a very durable gloss builds up that withstands much water and alcohol. Should disaster strike, repairing this kind of finish is not too difficult. □

Project designed and built by George Campbell

Oak Bookcase

Build this cabinet and you can show off your woodworking skills *and* your book collection.

Frame and panel sides, combined with simple glass panel doors, give this project a light, airy feeling while a hand-rubbed finish shows off the oak grain. You will be able to accommodate almost any size book with the project's adjustable shelves.

Begin by ripping ¾ in. oak stock ⅛ in. wider than the dimensions shown in the bill of materials. Joint the edges to bring the materials to their correct widths and then cut the components to length.

Build the cabinet's sides first. Clamp the stiles (C) and rails (D) together temporarily. Then use a ¼ in. radius round over bit with pilot in your router to form the inside profiles.

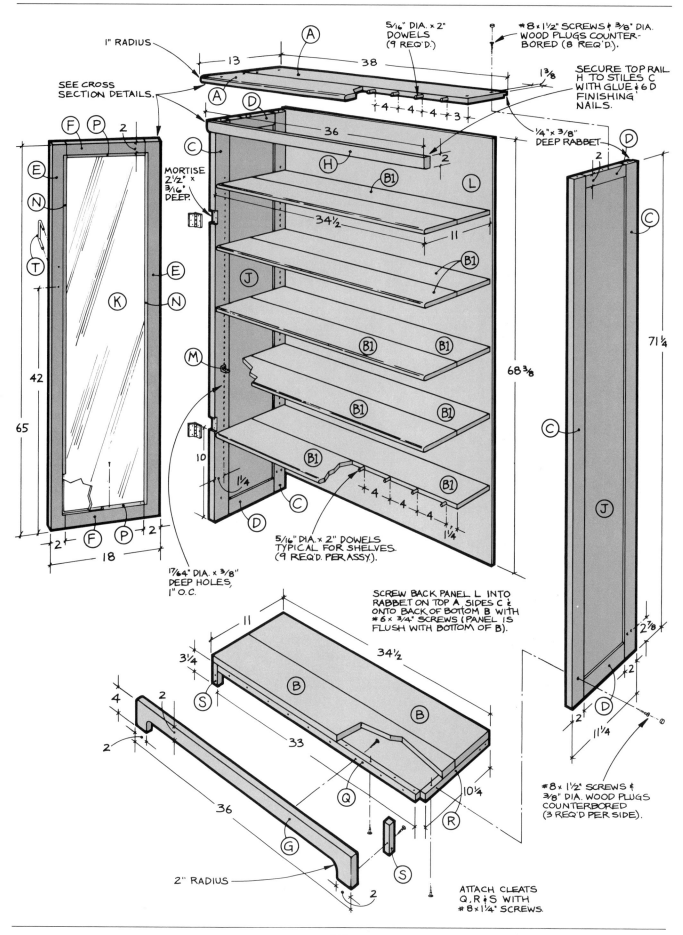

1" RADIUS

SEE CROSS SECTION DETAILS.

13

38

5/16" DIA. x 2" DOWELS (9 REQ'D.)

#8 x 1½" SCREWS & ⅜" DIA. WOOD PLUGS COUNTERBORED (8 REQ'D.).

SECURE TOP RAIL H TO STILES C WITH GLUE & 6D FINISHING NAILS.

1⅜

¼" x ⅜" DEEP RABBET

2

MORTISE 2½" x 3/16" DEEP.

36

2

4 · 4 · 4 · 3

34½

11

68⅜

71¼

42

65

2

18

2

17/64" DIA. x ⅜" DEEP HOLES, 1" O.C.

10

1¼

5/16" DIA. x 2" DOWELS TYPICAL FOR SHELVES. (9 REQ'D. PER ASSY.).

4 · 4 · 4

1¼

SCREW BACK PANEL L INTO RABBET ON TOP A SIDES C & ONTO BACK OF BOTTOM B WITH #6 x ¾" SCREWS (PANEL IS FLUSH WITH BOTTOM OF B).

2⅞

2

11

3¼

34½

4

2

2

33

10¼

2

36

2" RADIUS

11¼

2

#8 x 1½" SCREWS & ⅜" DIA. WOOD PLUGS COUNTERBORED (3 REQ'D PER SIDE).

ATTACH CLEATS Q, R & S WITH #8 x 1¼" SCREWS.

2

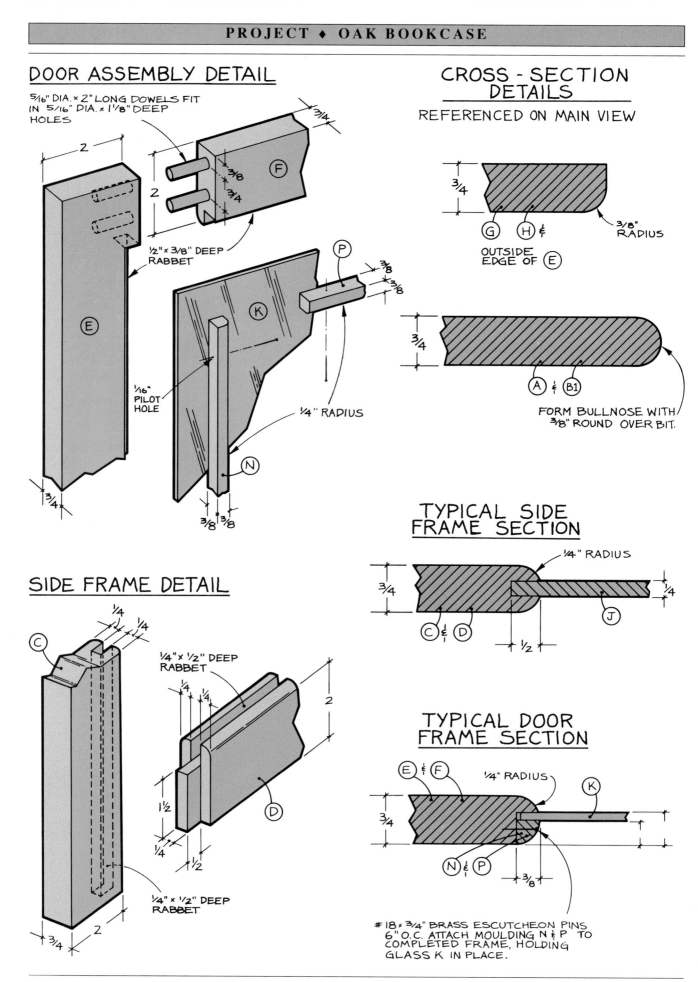

DOOR ASSEMBLY DETAIL

5/16" DIA. × 2" LONG DOWELS FIT
IN 5/16" DIA. × 1 1/8" DEEP
HOLES

2

3/4

2

3/8

3/4

(F)

1/2" × 3/8" DEEP
RABBET

(P)

3/8

3/8

(E)

(K)

1/16"
PILOT
HOLE

1/4" RADIUS

(N)

3/4

3/8 3/8

CROSS - SECTION DETAILS

REFERENCED ON MAIN VIEW

3/4

(G)   (H) ¢

3/8"
RADIUS

OUTSIDE
EDGE OF (E)

3/4

(A) ¢ (B1)

FORM BULLNOSE WITH
3/8" ROUND OVER BIT.

SIDE FRAME DETAIL

(C)

1/4   1/4

1/4" × 1/2" DEEP
RABBET

1/4   1/4

2

1 1/2

1/4

1/2

(D)

1/4" × 1/2" DEEP
RABBET

2

3/4

TYPICAL SIDE FRAME SECTION

1/4" RADIUS

3/4

1/4

(C) ¢ (D)

1/2

(J)

TYPICAL DOOR FRAME SECTION

(E) ¢ (F)

1/4" RADIUS

(K)

3/4

(N) ¢ (P)

3/8

#18 × 3/4" BRASS ESCUTCHEON PINS
6" O.C. ATTACH MOULDING N & P TO
COMPLETED FRAME, HOLDING
GLASS K IN PLACE.

BILL OF MATERIALS — Oak Bookcase

Finished Dimensions in Inches

A	Top	¾ x 6½ x 38 oak	2
B	Bottom Shelf	¾ x 5½ x 34½ oak	2
B1	Shelf	¾ x 5½ x 34¼ oak	10
C	Side Stile	¾ x 2 x 71¼ oak	4
D	Side Rail	¾ x 2 x 8¼ oak	4
E	Door Stile	¾ x 2 x 65 oak	4
F	Door Rail	¾ x 2 x 13¹⁵⁄₁₆ oak	4
G	Kick Rail	¾ x 4 x 36 oak	1
H	Top Rail	¾ x 2 x 36 oak	1
J	Panel	¼ x 8 x 68 oak plywood	2
K	Glass panel	14⁹⁄₁₆ x 61⅝ single strength window glass	2
L	Back	¼ x 35⅛ x 68⅜ oak plywood	1
M	Brass shelf clips		20
N	Moulding	⅜ x ⅜ x 61¾ oak	4
P	Moulding	⅜ x ⅜ x 13¹⁵⁄₁₆ oak	4
Q	Cleat	¾ x ¾ x 33 oak	1
R	Cleat	¾ x ¾ x 10¼ oak	2
S	Cleat	¾ x ¾ x 3¼ oak	2
T	Brass Wire Door Pull	3 in.	2

Figure 1. Use a ¼ in. by ½ in. slotting bit to form the panel grooves after milling the edge profiles.

Figure 2. After milling the rabbets into the assembled door frame, square the corners with a wood chisel.

Next, mill the ¼ in. by ½ in. slots in the separate components. Use a slotting bit with pilot in a table-mounted router.

Form the ½ in. long tenons on the rails (D) with a dado blade on your saw. Adjust the depth of cut carefully. Use the dado blade, too, to cut the mortises for the hinges in the front stiles.

Assemble the sides, gluing the frame joints only. Check for squareness and clamp securely. Once the glue has dried, drill the holes for the shelf hangers; sand the assemblies.

Next, lay out the door components, and mark them to indicate faces and outside edges. Round over the outer edges of the outside stiles (E) with a ⅜ in. radius round over bit with pilot.

Drill mating holes for the dowel pins in the rails and stiles (E, F); then assemble the door frames. Check squareness carefully.

While the frames are drying, make the retaining mouldings (P, N). Round over one edge of a length of ⅜ in. thick stock with the ¼ in. radius round over bit.

Rabbet the door frames to accommodate the glass and moulding. Then sand the door and the mouldings and lay the glass panels in the rabbets. Install the mouldings with brass escutcheon pins after drilling ¹⁄₁₆ in. pilot holes through the mouldings.

Assemble the halves of the shelves (B, B1) and the top (A). Use a doweling jig to help drill accurate holes for the dowel pins. Glue and clamp securely.

Sand the components well; then form the bull-nosed edges with two passes of the ⅜ in. radius round over bit.

Lay out and cut the profile of the cabinet's kick rail (G); then round over the contour and the ends with the same ⅜ in. bit. Do the same for the top rail (H).

Begin final assembly by building the base assembly as shown in the diagram. Drill pilot holes in the cleats (Q, R, S), and attach them to the bottom shelf (B) and the kick rail (G) with screws and glue.

On level sawhorses, clamp the sides to the base assembly. Align the components and mark the correct positions and the location of screw holes. Disassemble and apply glue to the edges of the base and the cleats. Add the sides, clamp securely and install the screws.

Glue the top rail (H) in position and clamp. Measure the diagonals of the cabinet to check its squareness. Install the cabinet top (A) after drilling counterbored pilot holes; then glue in the wood hole plugs.

Now, turn the case over and form the rabbets for the back panel with the rabbeting bit you used before. Square the corners by hand, and install the back panel (L).

Turn the case over once more and carefully hang the doors. Clamp center supports in place while marking the hinge positions on the door frames.

Once the doors are hung, drill holes for the pulls and install the bullet catches. The striker plates fit in shallow mortises chiseled into the rails.

Remove the doors for finishing, then give all components a final sanding. Apply a coat of stain (we used Tungseal's Light Oak) followed by three coats of Formby's Low Gloss Tung Oil Finish. Sand lightly between coats with 600 grit emery paper.

Once the finish has dried, install the shelves, re-hang the doors and install the door pulls. □

Project courtesy of Jonathan Press

Cutting Board

Transform scrap materials into beautiful cutting boards.

Cutting boards are not only useful for cutting vegetables, fruits, meats and the like but they also make handsome serving trays for cheese and crackers, cut fruits and a variety of other combinations.

You can use virtually any wood but choose close grain woods like maple for cutting. Most other woods should work well for serving trays.

The wood used to form the cutting board is cut into pairs. Thus you start with one center piece for the handle and glue each matching pair on both sides of the center piece. This results in a symmetrical pattern that balances the cutting board visually.

Use the faced wood surface as the area to edge-glue. This forms a straight glue joint. Cut the strips to ¾ in. heights (cutting board thickness) so the edges can be surfaced after edge-gluing. If you cut the strips to thickness, these surfaces

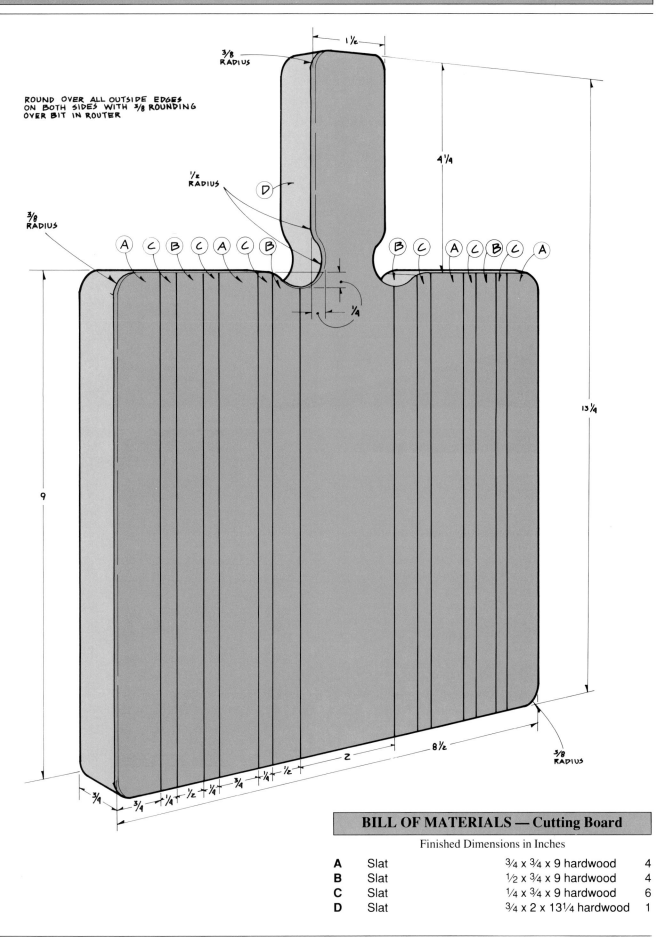

ROUND OVER ALL OUTSIDE EDGES
ON BOTH SIDES WITH 3/8 ROUNDING
OVER BIT IN ROUTER

3/8 RADIUS

1/2 RADIUS

3/8 RADIUS

1 1/2

4 1/4

13 1/4

9

3/8 RADIUS

1/4

2

8 1/2

3/4

3/4

1/4

1/2

1/4

3/4

1/4

1/2

BILL OF MATERIALS — Cutting Board

Finished Dimensions in Inches

A	Slat	3/4 x 3/4 x 9 hardwood	4
B	Slat	1/2 x 3/4 x 9 hardwood	4
C	Slat	1/4 x 3/4 x 9 hardwood	6
D	Slat	3/4 x 2 x 13 1/4 hardwood	1

Figure 1. After laminating the board, run it through a thickness planer. Remove a maximum of 1/16 in. on a pass to prevent wood tear out. Remove an equal amount of material from both surfaces.

Figure 2. Drill 1 in. diameter holes near the base of the handle with a Forstner bit. Use a backer board to prevent wood tear out.

will be difficult to finish because they are so small — unless you have a thickness planer.

Make an overall cutting board pattern out of paper or cardboard and lay and arrange the cut strips onto the pattern. When the arrangement suits you, prepare the workpieces for gluing.

Place wax paper on a flat surface where you are to glue the cutting board. Carefully keep all workpieces in their correct order. Then brush on a *thin* coat of carpenter's glue to one mating surface. Join and rub each workpiece firmly as you proceed through the gluing process. Secure the assembly with bar clamps and with one cross beam placed across the assembly's middle. Place wax paper under the cross beam. Clamp this beam to prevent the strips from sliding up as you apply side clamping pressure. Do not apply too much clamping pressure. Make sure the strips sit flat on the work surface. Then allow the assembly to dry for 24 hours.

Once the glue has cured remove the glue that has squeezed up with an old wood chisel. This makes it easier to finish the wood surfaces. Ideally, run the blank through a thickness planer to dress both surface areas. If you do not have a thickness planer use bench planes or a belt sander. Then transfer the pattern's design to the assembly. Drill the two radii at the handle's base with a Forstner bit, positioned in a drill press or drill guide.

Next, cut the board's perimeter with a band saw, using a 1/4 in. or 3/8 in. blade. Carefully round the corner radii and sand all edges with an abrasive sander. Finally, rout the edges with a round over bit with bearing guide. Work the router counterclockwise.

Fine sand the cutting board and apply several coats of vegetable oil or some of the cutting board oils available at fine cutlery shops. □

Figure 3. Use an abrasive strip sander to round and dress the project's edges. Use a fine grit sanding belt.

TECHNIQUES

Reprinted from *The Popular Science Router Book* by Doug Geller

Selecting Router Bits

Make sure you choose the right router bits for your projects.

Some router bits can be grouped according to function, while others do not fit neatly into a given category. Let's take a look at some of the more common groupings.

Straight Bits

The most extensively used of all router bits, straight bits are used to make grooves, rabbets, dadoes, mortises and tenons. Straight bits are also used in a multitude of other operations, including edge-to-edge jointing, hinge mortising, circle cutting, and so on. A straight bit, when viewed from above, is circular, which explains the rounded end it leaves on a stopped groove. Different manufacturers offer the bits in different widths. The smallest size available is 1/16 in. (1.5 mm). Other common sizes available include 1/8 in., 1/4 in., 5/16 in., 3/8 in., 1/2 in, 5/8 in., 3/4 in., 13/16 in., 7/8 in. and 1 in. (3, 6, 7.9, 9, 12, 15, 19, 20.6, 22 and 25 mm). Lengths will vary also. The length of the cutting edge on a 1/4 in. (6 mm) bit, for example, can vary from 5/16 in. to 1 1/8 in. (7.9 to 27 mm). Some bits with 1/2 in. (12 mm) shanks can be purchased in lengths of up to 2 in. (50.8).

Edge-Forming Bits

Of all the router bits, the decorative edge-forming bits raise the most eyebrows, since they can transform the plain edge of a board into a classic shape with craftsmanlike precision in just a few moments. It is extraordinary to see what a difference a stopped chamfer can make on a post of a trestle table, or how a Roman ogee edge can add elegance to the top of a nightstand. Edge-forming bits are also used to make mouldings.

The Roman Ogee. A truly classic shape, the Roman ogee edge can be incorporated into many styles of furniture. Some router bit manufacturers also offer a simple ogee bit.

Figure 1. From left to right, a 3/4 in. (19 mm) carbide bit with 1/2 in. (12 mm) shank; a 3/8 in. (9 mm) carbide bit with 1/4 in. (6 mm) shank; a 3/16 in. (4.7 mm) carbide bit with 1/4 in. (6 mm) shank; a 1/16 in. (1.5 mm) high speed steel bit with 1/4 in. (6 mm) shank.

The Chamfer Bit. The chamfer bit is too often overlooked by the amateur woodworker, who often opts for a more dramatic-looking profile. Originally used to take the sharpness off the corners of boards (beveling), the chamfer produces a delicate touch on even the most rustic of furniture.

The Rounding Over Bit. Sometimes referred to as a "quarter round," this bit produces a beautiful rounded edge. The cutter can be used at different depths to produce varying results. When it is dropped a little past maximum radius, a thumbnail moulding is produced. When used with a matched cove cutter, a rule joint can be made. The rule joint is a choice method for connecting a dropleaf to a table. Use a smaller pilot, and the rounding over bit becomes a beading bit.

The Beading Bit. The beading bit produces a fine detail for period furniture. The rounded edge formed by a beading bit is similar to the radius produced by a rounding over bit, except that the beading is punctuated by two shoulders. For example, this beading is commonly used as a decorative detail on door and cabinet frames, table tops and aprons.

Figure 2. A Roman ogee was used to make this elegant detail for a baseboard moulding.

Figure 3. The Roman ogee bit is used to cut a decorative shape for a table top.

Figure 4. Here we have a stopped chamfer on a trestle post.

Figure 5. A rounding over bit is used to produce a soft edge on this banister rail.

Figure 6. The bottom moulding on this Shaker reproduction was made with a rounding over bit dropped just past the maximum radius. Called a "thumbnail" moulding, this detail is echoed on the reproduction's drawer front.

Figure 7. The beading bit produces delicate mouldings such as these.

Figure 8. The cove bit was used here to make a delicate edge on this zebrawood box.

The Cove Bit. The cove bit is used for a wide variety of tasks. It may be used to make moulding, rule joints and finger-grip handles for doors and drawers.

The Rabbeting Bit. The rabbeting bit is essentially a straight-cutting bit with a pilot added. The distance from the pilot to the outer edge of the cutter determines the amount to be rabbeted, or cut away. The depth of the rabbet is determined by the position of the router base. Rabbeting bits can form rabbets from ¼ in. to ¾ in. (6 to 9 mm), but rabbets of any size can also be made by using a straight cutting bit in conjunction with an edge-guide.

Groove-Forming Bits.

Groove-forming bits are similar to decorative edge bits, except that they are designed to cut within the body of wood rather than along its edge. As such, they do not have pilots, so you will need another system for guiding the router.

Figure 9. The finger grip for the back of this door was made with a cove bit.

Figure 10. This shows a ⅜ in. (9 mm) rabbeting bit. The ⅜ in. (9 mm) indicates how far the bit cuts in, not down.

Groove-forming bits are often used on doors and drawer faces to simulate the effect of frame and panel construction.

The V-Groove Bit. The V-groove bit is an interior decorative bit that is often used to simulate the effect of a carver's parting tool. It can also be used in lettering, where letter templates are used, and to simulate V-groove paneling.

The Core-Box Bit. The core-box bit, which produces a semicircular groove, is typically available in widths from ¼ in. to ¾ in. (6 to 19 mm). It is especially effective in fluting flat surfaces. The core-box bit is also used for making drainboard fluting on carving boards and for making finger grips for drawers and doors.

The Veining Bit. The veining bit and its close cousin, the round-nose bit, are used for general decorative line work and fluting.

The Slotting Cutter. The slotting cutter is a general grooving bit, particularly useful for making spline grooves. It is available in kerfs of ¹⁄₁₆ in. (1.5 mm) to ¼ in. (6 mm).

Laminate-Trimming Bits

Laminate-trimming bits are most often used to trim plastic laminates (such as Formica) flush with the wood to which

Figure 11. A typical groove-forming bit, designed to cut within the body of a piece of wood.

they have been glued. One type of laminate-trimming bit, the flush-trimming bit, has a ball bearing pilot and carbide tipped edges. Other trimming bits will not only flush the overhanging laminate, but will also finish it with a beveled edge, the angle varying from 7 to 22 degrees. The flush-trimming bit is actually one of the most useful bits in the woodworker's arsenal. You will use it to flush contiguous pieces of wood and in repetitive pattern cutting.

Figure 12. The V-groove bit is used to create the effect of V-groove paneling on this door.

Other Common Bits.

The Hinge-Mortising Bit. This bit is designed for cutting mortises for hinges because it cuts fast and is capable of plunging. (Plunging is the lowering of a bit into a piece of wood.) Straight cutting bits, however, can also plunge and are often substituted for hinge-mortising bits. Since the amateur or occasional woodworker would probably use the multi-purpose straight cutting bit for these tasks rather than purchase both bits, the hinge-mortising bit is usually reserved for professional woodworkers.

The Dovetail Bit. When used in combination with dovetail templates, this bit can produce the dovetail joint, which many feel is one of the finest joints in cabinetry. It can also be used to make slotted dovetails.

Custom Bits

Sometimes the solution to a woodworking problem is arrived at with a specifically designed router bit. Many independent bit manufacturers will customize bits, and they can make just about anything you can imagine. Put your idea into a sketch. Let them tell you if the design is feasible and what it will cost. An excellent example of how a custom bit is used to solve a problem is found in Fig. 16.

Recommended Basic Kit of Router Bits

When reading through a list of cutters, such as the one presented on the preceding pages, it is very easy to fall into the basic buyer's trap: "Oh, I will need this one, and I will definitely need that one," and so on. It is not necessary to own

Figure 13. The core-box bit.

Figure 14. The slotting cutter.

Figure 15. The dovetail bit, often used with dovetail jigs.

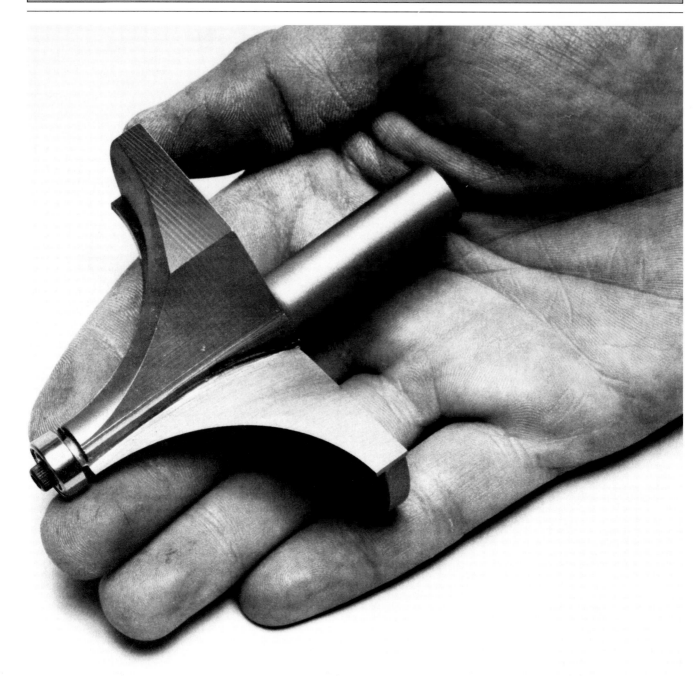

Figure 16. This is a large, custom made rounding over bit with a 1⅛ in. (27 mm) radius, made by the Fred M. Velepec Co.

every cutter; indeed, it would cost a small fortune. Many cutters can perform multiple roles. The ¾ in. (19 mm) straight cutting bit, for example, can be used not only to make ¾ in. (19 mm) and wider dadoes, but it can also make rabbets of any size. The same cutter can also cut a hinge mortise and can even be used to make circles.

If you want to make dovetails you will need a dovetail bit. Generally speaking, however, purchase your router bits as you need them.

Below is a list of what is considered to be a good basic kit. Buy all carbide tipped bits if your budget permits.

♦ ¼ in. (6 mm) straight cutting bit (carbide)

♦ ½ in. (12 mm) straight cutting bit, with ½ in. (12 mm) shank and the longest cutting edge available (carbide)
♦ ¾ in. (19 mm) straight cutting bit (carbide)
♦ Roman ogee edge (high speed steel or carbide)
♦ ½ in. (12 mm) rounding over bit (high speed steel or carbide)
♦ Chamfer bit (carbide or high speed steel)
♦ ⅜ in. (9 mm) rabbeting bit (carbide with ball bearing pilot)
♦ Flush-trimming bit — 1 in. (25 mm) in length (carbide only)

Project courtesy of *The Woodworker's Journal* magazine

Making Tambour Doors

With a little know-how you too can make attractive tambour doors.

The tambour is one of those special elements that make woodworking so fascinating. Rare indeed is the little boy or girl who does not wonder at the way the tambour of grandpa's rolltop desk works and where it disap-

pears. Indeed, watching a well fitted tambour top or front snake effortlessly along the hidden grooves is intriguing, even for adults.

The key words, of course, are *well fitted*. Trying to deal with a tambour that is too tight, too loose, or warped and that consequently catches, sticks, drags, jams sideways, gets frozen in place or pops out of its grooves is frustrating. Although the tambour has been widely used in many different types of furniture since its origin in 17th century France, it is every bit as fickle now as it was then. Getting the tambour door right requires careful planning and attention to detail.

Design

There are two specific types of tambour construction: that which is joined by wires and the fabric backed variety. Although the wired style allows the back of the tambour to be exposed, the fabric backed tambour is better suited to home workshop construction. Therefore, we concentrate on this latter style in this techniques story.

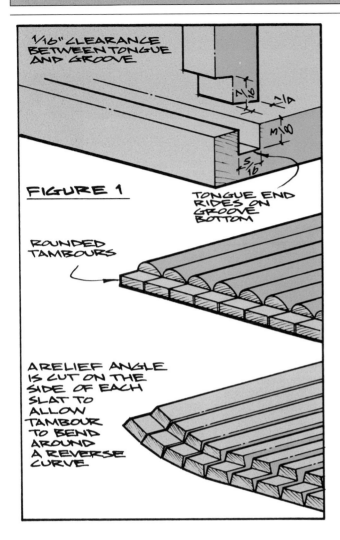

1/16" CLEARANCE BETWEEN TONGUE AND GROOVE

FIGURE 1

TONGUE END RIDES ON GROOVE BOTTOM

ROUNDED TAMBOURS

A RELIEF ANGLE IS CUT ON THE SIDE OF EACH SLAT TO ALLOW TAMBOUR TO BEND AROUND A REVERSE CURVE

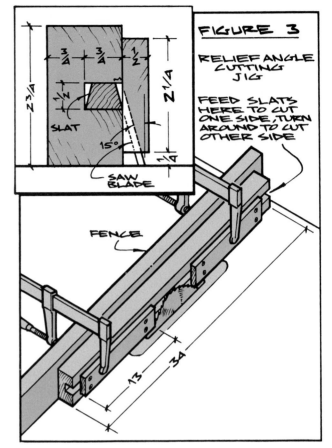

FIGURE 3

RELIEF ANGLE CUTTING JIG

FEED SLATS HERE TO CUT ONE SIDE, TURN AROUND TO CUT OTHER SIDE

SLAT

SAW BLADE

15°

FENCE

13   34

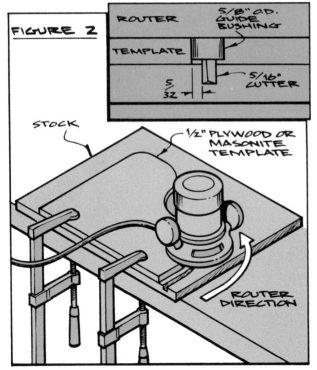

FIGURE 2

ROUTER

5/8" O.D. GUIDE BUSHING

TEMPLATE

5/16" CUTTER

5/32

STOCK

1/2" PLYWOOD OR MASONITE TEMPLATE

ROUTER DIRECTION

The illustrations that accompany this article show the tambour top of the Desk With Tambour Top project.

The design of the piece of furniture; the size and shape of the individual tambours; and the size, depth, profile and curve or radius of the tracking groove are all critical elements whose interdependent nature requires that each be precisely worked out and developed with respect to the other.

The Carcass

A strong, stable, well constructed carcass is important because the parts into which the tambour grooves are cut must be absolutely rigid and parallel. Remember that you may have to design a false back (or sides for a vertical tambour) both to isolate the tambour from the contents of the case and to conceal the fabric side from view when the tambour is open.

The Tracking Grooves

The tracking grooves must be laid out with respect to the radius that the tambour can make without binding. The groove must also be laid out so that the length of the tambour when closed fills the required space and yet retracts as needed when opened. Note that the tambour groove in the desk is laid out so that, when open, the tambour stops one tambour slat shy of the handle.

When laying out the groove you must also consider the weight of the tambour. The groove should at least partially balance the tambour weight between opening and closing, so the tambour does not fall back down when fully opened or require too great an effort to control while opening or closing.

As a general rule for size, tracking grooves should fall within a range from 3/16 in. to 3/8 in. wide, with the depth dimension usually slightly greater than the width. The groove for the desk is 3/8 in. deep by 5/16 in. wide.

The Tambours

Individual tambours come in a variety of shapes — from purely rectangular to half round. The shape of the tambours are dictated by the general design of the piece and by factors such as whether or not a reverse curve is incorporated into the tracking groove. If such is the case, the tambours must have a relief cut on either side sufficient to accommodate whatever the reverse curve may be. Nearly all tambours are made with a shoulder on the exposed side, which serves to conceal the tracking groove. The tambour tongue is typically rectangular or slightly wider than it is thick. Fig. 1 shows various tambours and a detail of a tracking groove.

The final tambour length is just slightly less than the actual groove-to-groove dimen-

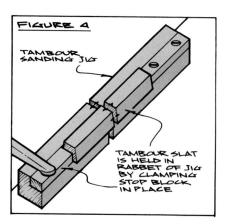

FIGURE 4

TAMBOUR SANDING JIG

TAMBOUR SLAT IS HELD IN RABBET OF JIG BY CLAMPING STOP BLOCK IN PLACE

sion. Although on the desk we show a 33¾ in. total tambour length, the actual length is about 1/32 in. less to provide clearance. The tambour shoulders are 7/16 in., providing 1/16 in. clearance on either side so the shoulders do not scuff the inside of the case sides. The tambour tongue thickness of 1/4 in. allows the tambour to pass freely through the various curves in the 5/16 in. wide tracking groove.

Although many simple tambours can be worked out on paper, we strongly recommend making test mock-ups of any unusual or tightly radiused designs. The mock-up need only be of a small section, but it will insure that the design is feasible. After the carcass is built, it is too late for a design flaw discovery. We used a mock-up to first test the tambours in the desk.

Routing the Tracking Grooves

After laying out your design, construct a template as a guide in making the tracking groove. Size the template to accommodate a specific guide bushing and the router bit. As shown in Fig. 2, size the 1/2 in. thick plywood template 5/32 in. smaller than the inside groove profile and use with a 5/8 in. outside diameter guide bushing and the 5/16 in. diameter straight cutter. As noted in Fig. 2, move the router *counterclockwise* around the perimeter of the template. Naturally, for the opposite or left side groove, start the counterclockwise router motion at the *back end* of the tracking groove. Also note that we rout the tracking groove *before* cutting the carcass sides to shape. This way the final profile of the sides is cut exactly parallel to the tracking grooves. Wear eye protection when routing.

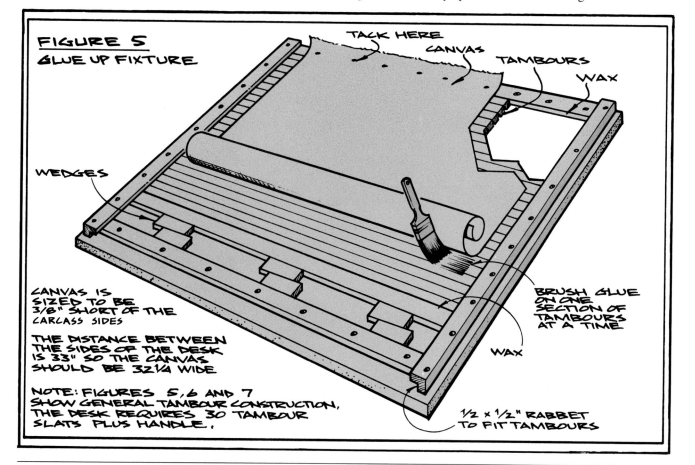

FIGURE 5
GLUE UP FIXTURE

TACK HERE

CANVAS

TAMBOURS

WAX

WEDGES

CANVAS IS SIZED TO BE 3/8" SHORT OF THE CARCASS SIDES

THE DISTANCE BETWEEN THE SIDES OF THE DESK IS 33" SO THE CANVAS SHOULD BE 32¼ WIDE

NOTE: FIGURES 5, 6 AND 7 SHOW GENERAL TAMBOUR CONSTRUCTION, THE DESK REQUIRES 30 TAMBOUR SLATS PLUS HANDLE.

BRUSH GLUE ON ONE SECTION OF TAMBOURS AT A TIME

WAX

½ × ½" RABBET TO FIT TAMBOURS

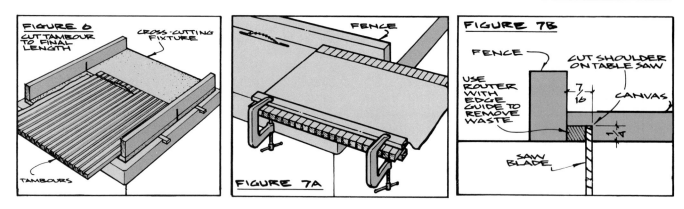

FIGURE 6
CUT TAMBOUR TO FINAL LENGTH

CROSS-CUTTING FIXTURE

TAMBOURS

FENCE

FIGURE 7A

FIGURE 7B

FENCE

USE ROUTER WITH EDGE GUIDE TO REMOVE WASTE

CUT SHOULDER ON TABLE SAW

7/16

CANVAS

SAW BLADE

Remember, make your plywood or Masonite template very carefully, since the tracking grooves ultimately reflect every little hump or inconsistency in the template. You must accurately locate and clamp the template to the sides so that both tracking grooves are exact mirror images of each other and precisely parallel to one and other. Since it is best that the actual router cuts be as smooth as possible, do not hog out too much stock or labor the router. We used four depth settings to achieve our final ⅜ in. tracking groove depth.

Once the routing is complete, use a dowel wrapped with sandpaper to clean out and smooth the grooves. Prefinish the inside surfaces, wax the grooves with paraffin, and assemble the case *before* making the individual tambours, being careful that *no* glue gets into the grooves.

Making the Tambours

Start with the tambours somewhat longer and wider than the intended final size. We recommend cutting about 30 percent more tambours than required, since some will inevitably have to be discarded due to warping.

After flattening and milling stock to achieve final tambour thickness, allow the boards from which you will rip the individual tambours to acclimate. Then rip the tambours to final width, sticker and allow to dry for at least 24 hours. Discard any pieces that have warped, twisted or are otherwise no longer straight.

Because our tracking groove incorporates a reverse curve, the tambours must have a relief angle cut into their sides. Although a router or shaper can be used for this, we chose the table saw. Fig. 3 shows a table saw jig for cutting this relief angle.

Note that the saw blade must be set at a 15 degree angle, the jig clamped to the saw table and the blade then raised up slightly into the jig. Slide the tambour through to cut the first side, then reverse it and pass through to cut the opposite side. Make a second jig (Fig. 4) to hold each tambour for final sanding. Sand only the sides, since the face is sanded after tambour glue-up.

Now make a gluing fixture to hold the tambours in place while the fabric or canvas backing is applied to their back side. Our jig (Fig. 5) is made on a particleboard base. The rabbeted side boards must be positioned to hold the tambours tightly. Cut three end pieces the same thickness as the tambours to fit under the rabbet and also cut a number of wedges as shown. If your handle is to be glued up on the canvas, make provisions for it. Our handle is applied after, thereby simplifying the glue-up process.

Wax the end pieces as indicated, wedge the tambours up tight and screw the rabbeted side pieces down securely to hold them flush.

Next, apply the fabric back. We used 10 oz. art canvas sold at most art supply stores. The canvas is sized to come up at least ⅜ in. short of either carcass side and should overhang several inches on either end. The extra canvas at the front is needed to apply the handle section. We used melt-type hide glue, since it thickens quickly. Start at one end, positioning and lining up the canvas and tacking it to the end piece. Now brush the hot glue over the first section of three or four tambours, making certain coverage is complete. Press the canvas in place using a block of wood to work out from the center, smoothing the canvas parallel to the tambours. Peel the canvas back slightly to expose the glue line, then brush glue onto the next three or four tambours, overlapping the glue to insure total coverage. Continue this process until all the tambours are canvased over. *Do not* stretch the canvas perpendicular to the tambours. Also, do not brush glue on or work the canvas smooth perpendicular to the tambours, as this will tend to force the glue between the individual tambours. Allow the tambour to dry overnight in the glue-up fixture before removing it.

When completely dry, measure the groove-to-groove distance (narrowest point) and cut the tambour to final length on the table saw using the crosscutting fixture shown in Fig. 6. Next, clamp the tambour end that overhangs the table saw (Fig. 7A), set the blade depth and establish the tongue shoulders as illustrated in Fig. 7B. Clean the waste out using the router, a straight bit and the edge-guide. Use a sanding block to final sand and smooth the tambour tongue.

Test fit and adjust the tambour as necessary. Remember, the tambour shoulder should not rub on the case.

Last of all, make the handle. A variety of handle designs are acceptable. Some are applied while others feature a shaped or extended end tambour serving as a pull. Our handle is the applied type and utilizes a rabbet to conceal the canvas and accept a backing strip. The backing strip actually sandwiches the canvas in the handle rabbet. Location dowels in either end of the handle ride in the tracking grooves to keep it on line. Details of the handle appear in the Desk With Tambour Top project.

Using paraffin, wax both the tambour tongues and the tracking grooves before final assembly.

Apply the final finish before installing the tambour. It is best to leave the canvas unfinished for maximum life and flexibility. □

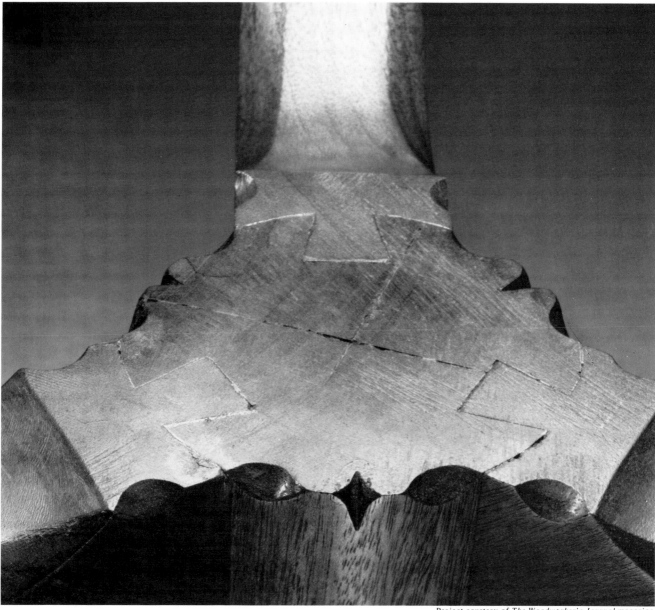

Project courtesy of *The Woodworker's Journal* magazine

Making Tripod Legs

Slotted dovetails are used to join legs to the pedestal.

One of the more fascinating elements of traditional furniture design is the use of dovetails to join shaped table legs to a turned central pedestal. The result is a joint that, when carefully cut and fit, is exceptionally strong.

Paula Garbarino, who built the 18th century Philadelphia Tilt-Top Table featured in this book, tells us that when breakage does occur, it is typically a splitting of the bottom end of the pedestal and not a failure of the dovetail joint. For this reason it is important to make the pedestal as wide in diameter as design limits permit. On large tables, you should also increase the depth and width of the dovetails.

This special technique applies specifically to the Tilt-Top Table project, as do the dimensions and angles shown in the following steps. However, the basic technique can be used anywhere you need to join legs to a central pedestal. Except for the use of the band saw and table saw, which speed the work and provide better accuracy, little in the technique has changed from the time when the original version of this tilt-top table was built about 200 years ago.

To begin, rough cut the three 2 in. thick by 6 in. wide by 16 in. long blanks for the legs. If you have never tried this

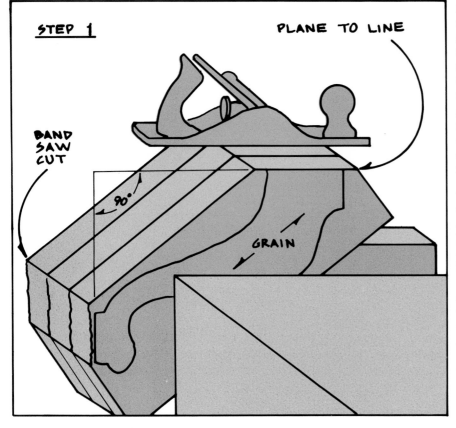

STEP 1

PLANE TO LINE

BAND SAW CUT

90°

GRAIN

technique before, we recommend making a practice leg first to test all the setups. Now lay out the side profile of the leg on each of the three blanks. Use a full-size cardboard or plywood template to lay out the profiles so all three legs are consistent. Also note the grain orientation, which is important for maximum strength. Use the band saw to cut the corners at the sole of the foot and dovetail joint close to — but not touching — the line. Next, as shown in Step 1, clamp the three legs together in the bench vise, and hand plane to the line. The joint and sole surfaces that you are planing must be perpendicular to each other. The template should have provided an accurate pattern, but check with a framing square to be sure.

Next, remove the leg blanks from the vise and cut the side profiles on the band saw, keeping outside of the pencil line (Step 2). Then re-clamp the legs in the vise and use the rasp to fair all three legs to the same profile (Step 3). This helps to insure that the legs turn out looking the same.

Now, using a small block drilled to accept a pencil so the point of the pencil

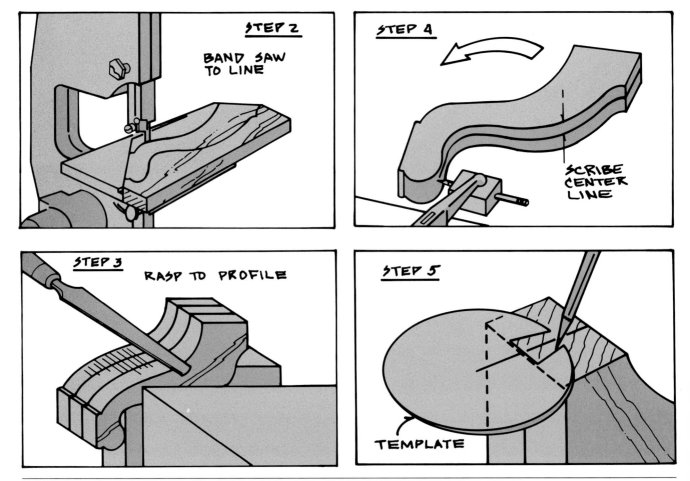

STEP 2

BAND SAW TO LINE

STEP 4

SCRIBE CENTER LINE

STEP 3

RASP TO PROFILE

STEP 5

TEMPLATE

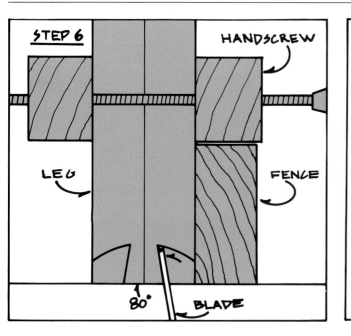

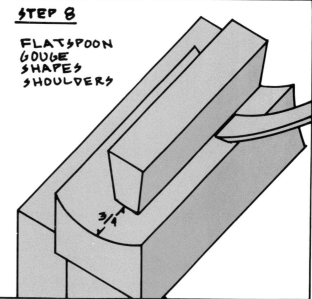

is 1 in. up from your bench surface, mark the center line all the way around each leg (Step 4). As shown, clamp the pencil block to the bench and rotate the leg past the pencil point. This line is needed for realignment of the leg with the pedestal and also serves as a guide when shaping the leg.

Now make a cardboard or plywood circle template the diameter of the leg end of the pedestal. Lay out the dovetail dimensions on the template. Then transfer a centered dovetail to each leg, top and bottom. Draw the curve of the cylinder at the base of the dovetail using the circle template (Step 5). With the foot in the air, first cut the sides of the dovetail on the table saw (Step 6). As the illustration shows, tilt the table saw blade 80 degrees. Set the fence so the cut leaves the pencil line. Clamp a hand screw to the leg, riding the top of the fence, to provide extra support and security. Next, with the leg flat on its side, cut the shoulders (Step 7). Tilt the blade to 70 degrees, and cut as close as possible to the curve drawn from the template but leave the line. Have scrap wood behind this second cut to push out the waste and avoid kickback of the cut-off.

In Step 8 clamp each leg in the bench vise, notch the top end of the dovetail back ¾ in. and then use a flat spoon gouge to cope the shoulders of the dovetail to fit the curve of the pedestal. You may want to undercut a bit to insure a flush fit, but the visible line where the leg meets the pedestal must remain straight. This straight edge is required if the leg is to

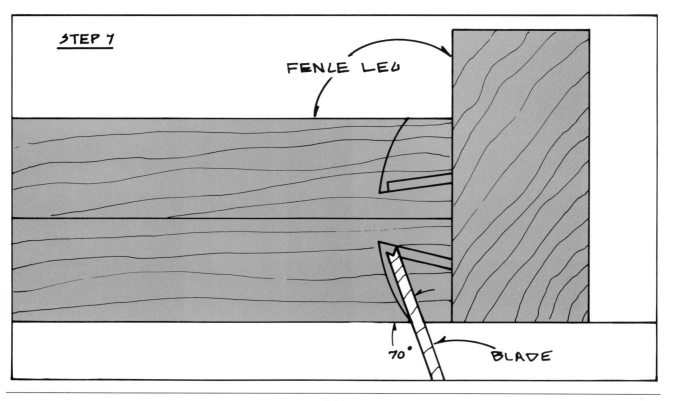

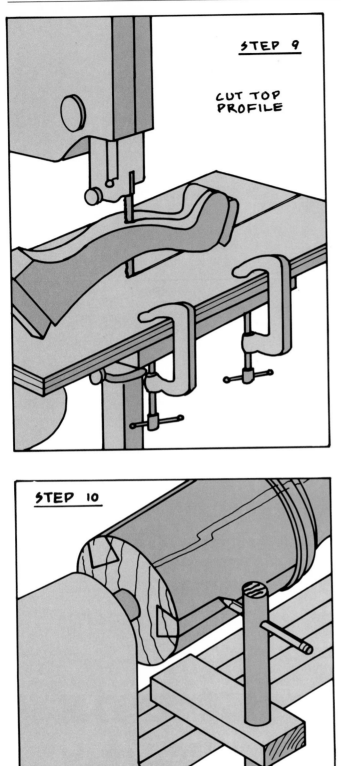

STEP 9

CUT TOP
PROFILE

STEP 10

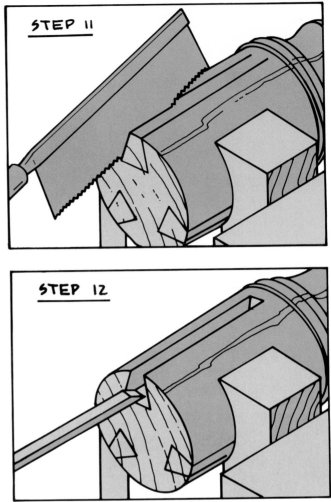

STEP 11

STEP 12

fit properly to the pedestal. The top of the leg where the dovetail is notched back must also be coped to match the curve of the pedestal.

Next, use the band saw to taper the sides of the leg. Make a paper template that is 2 in. at the dovetail, 1¼ in. at the ankle and returns quickly to 2 in. at the foot as a guide for tracing the top profile on the legs. Then, using an auxiliary plywood

table on the band saw as shown in Step 9, cut to the scribed line. Note that the leg rests on two points for this operation.

Now shape each leg, roughing in with the mallet and chisel or with a spokeshave. Use a rasp, files and cabinet scraper to smooth the legs to final form. Carve the ³⁄₁₆ in. high pad under the foot with a V-parting tool and small gouges.

Next, cut the dovetail mortises in the pedestal. First, lay out the center points of the three dovetails 120 degrees apart on the bottom end of the pedestal, and carry the lines to the edge. Then use the dovetail of each foot as the pattern for laying out each of the dovetail mortises. Number the legs and corresponding dovetails so that they won't be confused later. Return the pedestal to the lathe. Use a pencil holding jig to extend the scribed lines for each dovetail up the pedestal the length of the dovetail. As shown in Step 10, the jig rides off the bed of the lathe.

Now clamp the pedestal in the bench vise, using band-sawn blocks that match the pedestal curve, and saw up to the pencil lines with a dovetail saw (Step 11). Chisel out the waste, and pare the mortise walls and floor to fit the leg dovetail (Step 12). The fit of the leg should not be forced. If the fit is a little loose, the tail can be shimmed with a piece of veneer. The critical point is that the shoulder edge of the leg be tight against the cylinder. Legs should be glued on only when all other cutting and fitting is completed. □